# Grandmothers
## as
## Caregivers

# FAMILY CAREGIVER APPLICATIONS SERIES

## Series Editors
David E. Biegel, *Case Western Reserve University*
Richard Schulz, *University of Pittsburgh*

The **Family Caregiver Applications Series** is an interdisciplinary book series focusing on the application of knowledge about family caregiving, both within and across dependent populations, extending into the practice and policy arenas. The volumes are well-grounded theoretically and empirically, advance existing knowledge in the field, and are state-of-the-art works designed to fill existing gaps in the literature.

## Advisory Board Members

## Volumes in This Series:

Family Caregiver Applications Series
Volume 2

# Grandmothers
## as
## Caregivers

*Raising Children of the
Crack Cocaine Epidemic*

## Meredith Minkler
## Kathleen M. Roe

Published in cooperation with the
Center for Practice Innovations,
Mandel School of Applied Social Sciences
Case Western Reserve University

**SAGE** Publications
*International Educational and Professional Publisher*
Newbury Park   London   New Delhi

*For information address*:

SAGE Publications, Inc.
2455 Teller Road
Newbury Park, California 91320

SAGE Publications Ltd.
6 Bonhill Street
London EC2A 4PU
United Kingdom

SAGE Publications India Pvt. Ltd.
M-32 Market
Greater Kailash I
New Delhi 110 048 India

Printed in the United States of America

**Library of Congress Cataloging-in-Publication Data**

Minkler, Meredith.
    Grandmothers as caregivers: raising children of the crack cocaine
epidemic / Meredith Minkler, Kathleen M. Roe.
            p.   cm.   —(Family caregiver applications series; v. 2)
    Includes bibliographical references and index.
    ISBN 0-8039-4846-8.   —ISBN 0-8039-4847-6 (pbk.)
    1. Children of narcotic addicts—United States—Family relationships.
2. Children of narcotic addicts—United States—Family
relationships.   3. Grandparenting—United States.   4. Crack (Drug)—
United States.   5. Cocaine habit—United States.   I. Roe, Kathleen
M.  II. Title.  III. Series.
HV5825.M58    1993
362.29'83'0973—dc20                                      92-38077

93   94   95   96   10   9   8   7   6   5   4   3   2   1

Sage Production Editor:  Diane S. Foster

# Contents

# Series Editors' Foreword

This book represents a significant departure from the mainstream of caregiving literature. Meredith Minkler and Kathleen M. Roe have focused their attention on a group of caregivers that most of us rarely encounter and many of us don't know exist: a truly forgotten group of caregivers—grandparents who are raising their grandchildren and their great grandchildren. This book is based on a study of black women living in Oakland, California, who have become caregivers because of drug problems among their children. They are the surrogate parents for a generation of infants, preschoolers, and young children whose parents have become victims of the crack cocaine epidemic.

Both qualitative and quantitative methodologies are effectively used to tell the individual stories of these grandmothers, describe their commonalities, and relate them to broader social problems and policy issues. The authors enable the reader vividly to "hear the voices" of these grandmothers while at the same time presenting the social policies that shape their lives.

In discussing the trials and tribulations of these grandmother caregivers who are serving in roles they never anticipated, we learn of their joys as well as their sorrows, of their strengths and resources, and of their commitment to family. Nonetheless, the strains of their caregiving experience are all too apparent, as is the failure of public policy to understand, consider, and address their particular needs.

We are especially pleased to have this book as part of the *Family Caregiver Applications Series*. While it may represent a departure from the mainstream of caregiving research as it exists today, we feel it is a harbinger of future research in this area—a focus on special populations. Understanding grandparent caregivers, like many other subgroups of caregivers, requires that we focus intentionally on this group and that we exploit the full array of research methodologies available to us. The melding of qualitative and quantitative research methods is, in our view, the only way to tell effectively the story of these grandmothers while at the same time linking their concerns to the appropriate social policy context. The reader will be both fascinated and informed by the pages that follow.

Richard Schulz
David E. Biegel
*Series Editors*

# Preface

According to conventional wisdom, the nuclear family emerged as an economically rational response to the demands of industrialization. Factories sprang up where capital invested, and imposed the increasing requirements of geographical mobility. Ultimately, so the story goes, there was the progressive prejudicing of the work force against all family members except "dad-the-breadwinner." But local empirical reality is more complex than such wide and sweeping brush strokes can portray, and thus there is always room for "special circumstances" in family affairs. Richard Sennett's *Families Against the City* (1970) traces the emergence of the nuclear family in late 19th century Chicago, and provides evidence that extended family households in this period actually had an easier time adjusting to the changing economic and social environment than did the smaller nuclear units. Thus even when the nation was in the throes of its first great transformation from agriculture to industry, no single "ideal" was ideal in practice.

In the current period we hear similar popular folk wisdom about the nuclear family as the functional ideal. The nation in undergoing its second great transformation, this time from industrial to service sector domination. The reshaping of the work force and family life now occupies much of our national dialogue. Yet, despite an abundance of counterevidence, we continue to be suffused with the myth of the universal efficacy of dad-at-work while mom-stays-at-home-with-the-kids. This ideal reflects the reality of less than a quarter of all American family households. As with Sennett's portrait of the earlier period in our history, we get parallel images today of "special circumstance" economic successes of Cuban, Chinese, Dominican, and Korean extended families (Light & Bonacich, 1988; Portes & Rumbaut, 1990; Portes & Zhou, 1992).

At the other end of the familial pole, 40% of the households in our major cities have single parents as heads-of-household, bypassing the nuclear structure. By the mid-1980s, 70% of all black families in poverty were headed by women, with just over half of all black children living in these families (Simms, 1986). As the 1990 census makes clear, African American women heads-of-household increasingly include mid-life and older women who are raising their grandchildren and great grandchildren, often in impoverished circumstances. More than 12% of all black children live with grandparents who have a primary responsibility for caregiving. In contrast, less than 6% of Hispanic/Latino and only 3.6% of white children are reared in this "skip of the generations" (U.S. Bureau of the Census, 1991a). Black families have had one of the strongest traditions of having extended kin in the household. Stack (1974), Gutman (1976), and McAdoo (1990) have each provided landmark documentation on the important role of kin-scription at the very roots of African American life. Support networks have long had strong and wide-ranging roles in child rearing in both slavery and postslavery conditions.

Placing this book by Meredith Minkler and Kathleen M. Roe in this larger sociohistorical context is useful if we are to avoid the tendency to see its topic as a unique headline-grabbing story—grandmothers as caregivers for the grandchildren of their crack-using children. What appear to be "strange" cases can sharpen our awareness of the power and the richness of the social forces operating to meld together the relationships of our everyday social worlds. This is not just another account of the unique problems of troubled members of a black community struggling with "disorganization." This is not just one more snapshot, albeit from another angle, of children born into adversity among low-income, crack-using black families in communities suffering from economic hardship. Instead, Minkler and Roe have given their subject matter a strong policy context, and they have also given their human subjects voice. In turn, those voices tell their own story of an indomitable will and heroic resilience in African American grandmothers rising to the needs of grandchildren without effective caregivers.

This is a story of personal sacrifice, of obstacles and hardships, and not a gratuitous romanticizing of near subsistence living. The desire to offer care is also mixed with strong occasions of resentment. The extraordinary situation of these grandmother caregivers amplifies the pervasive and unequal burden of caregiving across generations that falls upon women and particularly upon black women. The median family income for African Americans within Alameda County, California, the site of the study, is little more than half that of white households. But with even less than half the financial and material resources, we find a community with 3 times as many grandparents functioning as care-givers. The authors point out that the State of California adds to the burden of these grandmother caregivers as a matter of policy. California, and indeed most states, make it difficult to impossible for these grand-mothers to qualify for foster home status by placing bureaucratic barriers in front of them, and then coupling these with indignities in the way minimalist support is provided through the conduit of the AFDC welfare program.

The social policy frame of this reality reflects a continuing pattern in U.S. drug and welfare policy. The authors' overview of this policy overlaps with my own, namely, that since the early part of the century the nation's drug and welfare strategy has tried to differentiate between the morally "deserving" and "undeserving." The drug policy has focused upon separating "good and bad" and even now invokes the language of "weed and seed," treating racial and ethnic groups differently in terms of the focus of apprehension, adjudication, and enforcement. Even though their patterns of consumption appear to be similar, blacks are 3 times as likely to be arrested for cocaine use as whites, and they are 7 times as likely to be incarcerated for drug-related crimes as their white counterparts (Duster, 1992).

Despite very limited financial resources these caregivers must manage care of crack exposed children requiring more medical and related health and support care. Obtaining this care is difficult, requiring long waits in medical serving institutions. Grandmothers who are employed frequently quit work or report having to reduce the hours of their employment in order to cope with the demands of being primary caregivers for their grand- and great-grandchildren.

This tension of doing more with less, under great financial burdens, highlights the inequities of social welfare policies that discriminate first against grandmothers of all races as primary caregivers, and additionally against African Americans and relatives of crack exposed children who are viewed as morally suspect or un-needy. In a nation with the highest incarceration rate of any country in the world—and with a drug war taking its primary toll through the incarceration of black youth—the plight of African American grandmother caregivers of children born in the social fabric of the crack world is exacerbated by an inability to find basic economic and health support for their grandchildren. Their circumstance highlights the misplaced priorities of a society that directs significant public funds to police work, prisons, and jails, but blocks attempts to maintain caregiving by grandmothers. That is, in spite of the Family Preservation legislation that supports, in principle, keeping needy children with family members, those who read this book will understand how grandmothers have difficulty receiving state sanction and authorization as "official" caregivers. They are thus unable to obtain financial support as "foster" parents or AFDC primary caregivers.

The discrimination faced by grandparent caregivers propels Minkler and Roe to detail the experiences and struggles of these women caregivers as they highlight the distancing bureaucratization of the welfare system. Their data and analysis become a megaphone for a little-understood and less appreciated social problem at the margins of the national consciousness. Many of the problems of indignity and difficulty in gaining financial support for these grandmothers would be addressed if policy were changed through enabling legislation to allow these grandmothers to receive foster care benefits in their names as caregivers of these children.

In Minkler and Roe's careful analysis, the tension between African Americans as economically vulnerable and drug-using in a society that serves to marginalize and incarcerate them is counterposed to the successful and daily strength and flexibility of the African American kin system. They capture and reveal the strength and agency of those grandmothers who conscript themselves as primary child-care givers to fend off child abandonment or placement of their grandchildren in foster homes. They also point to the ingenuity and power of community-based support groups where grandmothers report finding strength and community in sharing their situation with others in similar situations. This book should heighten our awareness of the need for basic policy reform in social services—for the grandmother caregivers offer another example where current general and child welfare policies undermine rather than support the special efforts of kin to take care of their own.

Troy Duster, Ph.D.
*Professor of Sociology*
*University of California, Berkeley*

# Acknowledgments

This book owes its existence to many people who generously and consistently gave of their time, support, and encouragement.

Our deepest thanks go to the 71 women whose stories, pain, and extraordinary strength form the heart and soul of this book. Because we promised them anonymity, we cannot thank them by name, nor do we use their real names in the book. But in sharing so openly their lives and their experiences, they made it possible for us to help bring attention to the needs and concerns of grandparent caregivers.

The Grandparent Caregiver Study, on which much of this book is based, benefited from the assistance of an outstanding team of graduate student researchers from the Schools of Public Health and Social Welfare at the University of California at Berkeley and the Department of Health Science at San Jose State University. Rama-Selassie Barnwell, Relda Beckley Robinson, Lisa Moore, and Marilyn Price shared with us a belief in the importance of this project, and a deep respect and concern for the women who participated. The caring and sensitivity of our team members greatly enriched both the process and the outcomes of the study.

Our work was immeasurably strengthened by the extensive participation of our friend and colleague Frances Saunders. From her initial work as the project's "cultural guide," to her very careful critique of the manuscript, Frankie's multiple roles in this project, and her unwavering support and enthusiasm, were unparalleled. We couldn't have done it without her.

We are deeply indebted to an outstanding Community Advisory Committee, whose members' faith in us and in the importance of this project was critical to its success. In particular, we wish to acknowledge our wonderful and energetic chair, Celestine Greene, and core group members Sadie Cobb, Marjorie Holloway, Supervisor Nathan Miley, Joyce

Owens-Smith, Dr. Lenora Poe, Gayle Quinn, Sister Pat Seer, Zakiya Somburu, and Caroline Street. Their help in every aspect of the study, from gaining entrée into the community to translating the findings into action, was beyond our greatest hopes and expectations.

We gratefully acknowledge the key role played by the San Francisco Foundation, and particularly program officer Ruth Tebbetts, for providing the funding for the Grandparent Caregiver Study. Because the Foundation does not normally fund research, its willingness to take a chance on this project because of its perceived policy relevance was especially appreciated. We are also grateful to San Jose State University for a series of minigrants from the College of Applied Sciences and Arts, and to the California State University (CSU) system for a grant from the CSU Funds for Research, Scholarship, and Creative Activity.

We extend our special gratitude to The Retirement Research Foundation for providing a grant to support the writing of this book.

Kaiser Permanente Medical Center, the Clorox Foundation, and several other organizations helped fund a special celebration for the grandparent caregivers who participated in the Grandparent Caregiver Study. We express our thanks to each of these contributors for helping us "give back" in small measure to the women who gave so much of themselves to this project.

Although much of the book draws on the life experiences and perceptions of the grandparent caregivers we interviewed, many other individuals contributed their insights, particularly as we developed the broader framework for our analysis. We gratefully acknowledge the work of Linda Burton, Patricia Collins, Jewelle Gibbs, and the many other women of color whose scholarship greatly enriched our thinking and writing in this area.

We thank, too, the individuals who helped us understand the intricacies of the legal and policy issues surrounding grandparent caregiving: Dion Aroner, Assemblyman Tom Bates, Ellen Barry, Leza Davis, Stacy Hughes, Supervisor Don Perata, Shirley Roberson, Marianne Takas, and Alan Watahara.

Although it is impossible to mention them all by name, numerous leaders of the growing grandparent caregiver movement around the country shared with us their knowledge and their enthusiasm, and this book is enriched by their help as well.

We are also indebted to several individuals and organizations whose own work has helped build on the findings of the Grandparent Caregiver Study and translate them into action. We express our thanks in particular to Janet Sainer, Danylle Rudin, and the Brookdale Foundation Group for their generous support of the Brookdale Grandparent Caregiver Information Project; to Lillian Rabinowitz and the members of the Coalition for Grandparents Parenting Grandchildren; to Bishop Will Herzfeld and the Congregations' Community Health Project of Bethlehem Lutheran Church for helping lay the groundwork for a grandparent respite program; to Alma Smith, Sandra Nathan, Zakiya Somburu, and the Oakland Office on Aging's project, "Families United Against Crack Cocaine," for their newsletter for grandparent caregivers; and to Celestine Greene, Ethyl Molo, Rosie Carter, and Hazel Mayfield for developing and operating the grandparent caregivers' warmline.

This book benefited greatly from the suggestions and recommendations of Series Editors David Biegel and Richard Schulz, and from the enthusiastic support and assistance of Christine Smedley at Sage Publications, Inc. We are also deeply grateful to Diane Driver, Bobbie LaNoue, and Lydia Ferrante for their assistance with manuscript preparation; to the reference library staff at the School of Public Health and to Mike Gray for their unstinting help in tracking obscure or missing references; to Gregg Thomson and Bob Freeland who gave so generously of their time and expertise on data entry and early quantitative analysis; and to the staff at Buttercup Bakery for allowing us to pour over printouts and manuscript pages long after the coffee and scones had disappeared.

Throughout the long process of conducting the Grandparent Caregiver Study and writing this book, we had the unfailing support of close friends, colleagues, and mentors who believed in us and in this project. We gratefully acknowledge the support of Ida Willis, Helen Ross, Lela Llorens, Lawrence Wallack, and Serena Stanford. We are indebted in particular to three individuals, Lillian Rabinowitz, Troy Duster, and Ruth Sidel, whose own activism and passionate scholarship and whose belief in and encouragement of our own work on this project meant more than we can say.

Finally, we express our deep thanks to our families, who supported, sustained, and encouraged us, and who were infinitely patient through the many long hours consumed by this project. Our parents have been continuing sources of love and inspiration. Our husbands, Jerry Peters and Jerry Smith, provided not only emotional support but help whenever we needed it (particularly with the computer and fax machine!). In countless ways, they expressed their unwavering belief that the issues addressed in this book are indeed issues with which our families must be involved. To our own young sons, Jason and Cameron, we would add that the women we came to know through this project have, through their courage and caring, given new meaning to "family values." Through their own examples, they have enriched our understanding of what it means to raise children, lovingly and with infinite care, in today's troubled world.

# 1

---

# Introduction

Every weekday at 5 o'clock, 49-year-old Betty Driscoll leaves her job as a legal assistant in a high-rise office building and hurries across town by bus to pick her grandchild up from day care. Three-year-old Sandra was born drug exposed, and both of her parents are involved with crack. When Betty gained legal custody of her granddaughter, she was finally able to quit worrying about whether the girl was being neglected, abused, or getting enough to eat. But her newfound peace of mind was not without cost: gone are Friday evenings spent socializing with friends, and the money needed for a car repair or a new dress. Betty looks wistful as she reflects on the ups and downs of her new life: "When I look at her in the morning, I think what a long way we'll come together. Then after work I'm tired, and I pick her up and wonder, how am I gonna manage?"

Across town in a crowded, East Oakland apartment, Mary Byrnes, 56, looks at the clock and thinks back to a time, not long ago, when she too was leaving work at the end of the day. Although she deeply loves her two live-in grandchildren, full-time caregiving for a 2-month-old and a 17-month-old meant leaving the part-time job that had given her dignity, along with income: "At least then I could pay my bills and buy me some shoes now and then. Now I don't feel right. I don't feel like a whole person anymore."

In her home in another part of the city, 62-year-old Naomi McFarland puts the finishing touches on a poem she has written that afternoon. In a few minutes, she will pick up her 4-year-old grandson Samuel from preschool and spend a quiet evening with him and her husband of 37 years. No TV is allowed after dinner when Mrs. McFarland works with Samuel on numbers, current events, and the countless stories they read together each evening. This child, left in the McFarland's care by his father, their son, when Samuel was just an infant, has become "the most precious thing in the world" to Mrs. McFarland. She worries about what will happen to her grandson if something happens to her. But she is certain that God gave her this "second chance" for a reason. And so she takes good care of Samuel, and of herself, so that "we can be together just as long as we possibly can."

In a partially boarded up house that was badly damaged in the 1989 Loma Prieta earthquake, 76-year-old Lena Johnson rocks the 9-month-old great grandson who sleeps in her lap. The child's mother, homeless and on crack, is unable to care for her baby, but resents her grandmother's stepping in. Mrs. Johnson sometimes fears for her physical safety when the baby's mother appears at the door, abusive and high. But her greatest fear is that the social workers will come and take the baby, either returning him to his mother or taking him away from the family altogether and placing him in foster care. "I can't function like I used to," Mrs. Johnson confesses, "but I give him love, and that's more than his Mama ever did."

Betty Driscoll, Mary Byrnes, Naomi McFarland, and Lena Johnson are just four of a growing number of grandparents nationwide for whom middle age and late life have become a time of "unplanned parenthood." Although all are African American women in Oakland, California, stories like theirs are increasingly common among grandparents of all ethnic groups and social classes in cities from Seattle to New York and from Tampa to St. Paul. The U.S. Bureau of the Census (1991a) estimates that 3.2 million children under 18 live with their grandparents or other relatives—a figure that represents an increase of close to 40% over the last decade. In about a third of these cases, neither parent is present, and the Betty Driscolls, the Mary Byrneses, the Naomi McFarlands, and the Lena Johnsons are playing a critical role as surrogate parent as well as grandparent.

Yet the census estimates are likely to underplay severely the real magnitude of grandparent caregiving, particularly in inner-city areas hard hit by the crack epidemic. In many such areas, grandparents living in senior housing facilities are quietly keeping the grandchildren or great grandchildren of their drug involved offspring. Since such housing does not permit children, grandparents may jeopardize their own living situation as they try to keep managers "in the dark" in order to provide a safe home for their grandchildren (Generations United, 1992).

More frequently, a grandmother may be raising grandchildren in her own home and yet not fighting for legal custody lest she draw the authorities' attention to a drug involved child, or make that child angry and resentful. The delicate legal tightrope walked by such grandparents further contributes to their invisibility as caregivers, and hence to our lack of information about the real extent of this phenomenon.

Whatever their true numbers, however, grandparent caregivers in the 1990s are playing a key role in "skipped generation" families—families where the parents are absent and grandparents are stepping in to raise their grandchildren. Yet unlike the substantial media coverage devoted to family members caring for the frail elderly, grandparent caregivers have only recently come to the attention of journalists and television talk show hosts, and the coverage received has been limited primarily to human interest stories (Creighton, 1991; Kennedy, 1991; Monson, 1990).

The grandparents who are raising their grandchildren and great grandchildren are indeed the nation's forgotten caregivers. It is toward the end of giving voice to their stories, and capturing the strengths, the courage, the pain, and the insights of these forgotten caregivers that this book is undertaken.

A second and equally important purpose of this book, however, is to move from "personal troubles" to "public issues" (Mills, 1959), connecting the experiences of grandmother caregivers with broader social problems and policy issues. As we shall attempt to demonstrate, the experience of grandmothers raising the children of the crack cocaine epidemic must be viewed within the context of high unemployment among black inner-city youth, and of deep cuts in social programs at the same time that the gap between rich and poor has reached record heights (Phillips, 1990).

The feelings and experiences of grandparent caregivers must be must viewed, too, within the context of a society that has historically drawn sharp distinctions between deserving and undeserving subgroups in the population. As we shall see in the chapters that follow, the vast majority of grandparent caregivers, like single mothers and low-income people, are treated via policies predicated on the notion of their "undeservingness" (Katz, 1989). In a society that assumes families have a "duty to care" for their own, they are penalized for being related to the children in their care, and denied the very supports and adequate financial aid that would assist them in fulfilling this often difficult and demanding new role. In short, it is our hope in this book to tell the stories of a special group of grandmothers raising their grandchildren, but to do so in a manner that recognizes and highlights the social and political contexts of their day-to-day realities. We tell their stories, not only because they are a testament to the often incredible courage and caring of the women involved, but also because these stories have urgent and important implications for policy, if we as a society will but listen.

## FOCUS ON THE
## AFRICAN AMERICAN GRANDMOTHER

The book focuses in particular on a special subset of grandparent caregivers—black women in Oakland, California, who are raising their infant and preschool aged grandchildren, great grandchildren, or grand-nieces and -nephews as a direct consequence of the crack involvement of their parents. We have chosen this focus for several reasons.

A focus on grandparent caregiving in the African American community first is warranted given the greater experience of black grandparents with this critical role. Approximately 12% of all black children in America today live with their grandparents, compared to 5.8% of Hispanic children and 3.6% of white children (U.S. Bureau of the Census, 1991a). In some predominately black inner-city areas, these rates may be considerably higher. A recent survey of the Head Start population in Oakland, California, for example, revealed that 20% of enrolled children were in the care of grandparents (Nathan, 1990). And in the city's Frick Junior High School, the principal and a school social worker estimated that more than half of their 750 students live with neither a mother nor a father (Gross, 1992). In parts of Detroit, New York, and other cities with large, low-income African American populations, some public school principals similarly are acknowledging that between 30% and 70% of the children in their classrooms are living with grandparents or other relatives (Gross, 1992; T. Lambert, personal communication, November 1991).

Although, as we shall see, grandfathers and male partners frequently play an important part in caregiving, high rates of widowhood, separation, and divorce among mid-life and older black women (Chatters & Taylor, 1990), and the tendency for men to play a supportive secondary, rather than a primary, caregiving role (Abel, 1991; Collins, 1990; Kivett, 1991), suggest the importance of looking first and foremost at the grandmother as caregiver.

Our focus on African American grandmothers also reflects the fact that although grandparent caregiving cuts across ethnic group lines, the historic kinkeeping role of the black grandmother gives the newer role special salience in the African American community. Writings on the historic role of the black grandmother are filled with references to the "unusual strengths" of older black women (Gibson, 1986), their wisdom and leadership (Jones, 1973), and the central role they have occupied as kinkeepers and "guardian of the generation" (Aschenbrenner, 1978; Frazier, 1966; Hill, 1971; McAdoo, 1978, 1980, 1986). As discussed in Chapter 2, historical accounts have traced the pivotal "stabilizing role" of elders in black family life to their roots in West African culture and tradition. These accounts further point up how this kinkeeper function served as an integral survival strategy through slavery and its bitter aftermath (Sudarkasa, 1981; Wilson, 1989).

Such explorations provide a unique sense of continuity in the family roles of older black women. Yet as Burton and Dilworth-Anderson (1991) suggest, the contemporary role of black grandmothers can only be understood in the context of the dramatically altered demographic and sociocultural conditions within which they now live. Thus, although it may be tempting to see the growing number of black grandmother caregivers as a rather simple and straightforward continuation of a prominent cultural role, the reasons for such caregiving today may make the contemporary experience quite different from its predecessors.

As Burton and Dilworth-Anderson (1991) point out, for example, grandmother caregivers who assume this role in the 1990s as a consequence of their daughter's teenage pregnancy or drug addiction may have very different reactions to their role than did grandmothers several decades ago who kept their grandchildren while the children's parents migrated north to seek a better life for their families.

Burton's (1985) study of grandparent caregiving in a small Southern town in the early 1980s indeed demonstrates the often considerable resentment and conflict that may be experienced by young grandmothers in their late twenties and early thirties, for whom a daughter's teenage pregnancy meant an often significant disruption of their own lives and an unwelcome early transition into grandparenthood.

In our own study, grandmothers' despair over the crack involvement of their sons and daughters often caused still deeper pain and anguish around the assumption of the caregiver role. Although the women we interviewed willingly and lovingly accepted full-time caregiving as an alternative to having their grandchildren neglected or removed from the family and placed in foster care, many expressed anger, resentment, and depression over the prospect of "second-time-around" parenthood under these circumstances.

## GRANDPARENT CAREGIVING
## AND THE CRACK COCAINE EPIDEMIC

The book's focus on women raising their grandchildren as a direct consequence of the crack involvement of the children's parents is also a purposeful one. Although numerous factors have contributed to the rise in grandparent caregiving over the last decade, few have had as dramatic an effect as the crack cocaine epidemic (Feig, 1990).

The cocaine epidemic, which began among the upper middle class in the mid-1970s, spread to low-income communities a decade later with the introduction of a Caribbean form of the drug costing a fraction of the powdered variety (Koppelman & Jones, 1989; Villarreal, McKinney, & Quackenbush, 1992). A smokable and extremely potent form of cocaine, crack (or rock) now ranks among the most addictive drugs known to medical science (Issacs, Martin, & Willoughby, 1987; Koppelman & Jones, 1989). The intense but short-lived nature of the "high" often leaves users severely depressed, paranoid, and desperate for a repeat of the sensation. As a consequence, crack addiction can occur within days or weeks of the first experience (Koppelman & Jones, 1989).

The remembered intensity of the euphoria produced by crack also makes the habit extremely difficult to break. Drug researchers thus report that although 60% of heroin addicts and 80%-85% of alcoholics can remain off those substances for up to 6 months in treatment programs, only about a quarter of crack abusers can stay drug free for this period of time (McLellan et al., 1992). And although some promising treatment breakthroughs are being made (U.S. General Accounting Office [USGAO], 1991), and a dramatic 30% drop in cocaine-related emergency room visits has been observed nationwide (Sobel, 1990), a quick end to the epidemic appears unlikely. As discussed in later chapters, both the continued supply of the drug and the high demand for it in inner-city neighborhoods, where poverty and high unemployment often encourage drug sale and use, suggest instead the continuation of a "crack problem" of significant proportions.

Crack is more popular among women than heroin and other hard drugs, with often devastating effects not only on women users themselves, but also on their children (Koppelman & Jones, 1989; USGAO,

1991). The intensity of the craving for crack makes it not uncommon for young mothers to sell diapers and baby clothes in order to pay for the next hit (see Chapter 4 this volume). Grandmothers who "inherit" their grandchildren under these circumstances often find themselves caring for youngsters whose short lives have been filled with abuse and neglect (Poe, 1992). When the children have been prenatally exposed to crack, this picture is often bleaker still. Such children may be penalized not only by the physiological and behavioral consequences of early drug exposure and/or abuse and neglect, but also by society's labeling and processing of what it regards as a "lost generation" of "crack babies" (Barth, 1991b; Goodman, 1992; S. Jackson, 1990).

Although accurate figures are difficult to come by, a frequently cited 1988 survey of 36 hospitals nationwide revealed that 11% of pregnant women used illicit drugs, with cocaine the most common (Chasnoff, 1988). The National Association for Perinatal Addiction Research and Education estimates that some 375,000 infants may be drug exposed annually, most often as a consequence of their mothers' cocaine use (U.S. General Accounting Office [USGAO], 1990). Although other researchers suggest a slightly lower figure, the drug exposure rate for infants born in large urban hospitals frequently hovers at 15%-20% (Lewis, Bennett, & Schmeder, 1989; Moody, 1990; Toufexis, 1991; Zuckerman et al., 1989). And the cost of hospital care for cocaine exposed newborns has been placed at more than $500 million annually (Phibbs, Bateman, & Schwartz, 1991).

Babies who were exposed to cocaine in the uterus are more likely to have low birth weights and to be premature or depressed at birth (Chouteau, Manerou, & Leppert, 1988; Coles & Finnegan, 1991; Petitti & Coleman, 1990). Frequent tremors and startles, irritability, poor muscle tone, and poor eating and sleeping patterns also have been reported (Chasnoff et al., 1989; Chychula & Okore, 1990; Howard, Rodning, & Kropenske, 1989).

As discussed in Chapter 10, however, the longer term consequences of prenatal cocaine exposure have increasingly been subject to debate. Although many observers have associated such exposure with problems such as hyperactivity and learning deficits, for example (Barth, 1991a; Lewis et al., 1989; Moody, 1990), Chasnoff, Griffith, Freier, and Murray's (1992) 2-year follow-up of cocaine exposed infants revealed their developmental functioning to be within the normal range.

When children who have been prenatally exposed to cocaine do suffer developmental problems, moreover, it is often impossible to determine whether these are the consequences of cocaine exposure per se, or of any of a host of other factors. Since cocaine users frequently also abuse alcohol and other drugs, for example, and since poor nutrition, lack of prenatal care, and sexually transmitted diseases including AIDS are common among pregnant women who are using cocaine, the prenatal contributors to an infant's subsequent developmental problems are difficult to sort out (Coles, 1991; Koren, Shear, Graham, & Einarson, 1989; USGAO, 1991).

Teasing apart the effects of prenatal drug exposure and of the abuse and neglect that often follows birth into a drug involved household may be equally problematic (Coles, 1991; Zuckerman, 1991).

Regardless of the specific causes, however, children of the crack cocaine epidemic may suffer a variety of physical and socio-behavioral problems (Howard et al., 1989). And the grandparents caring for such children often find themselves in unfamiliar and frightening new child-rearing territory.

The violence associated with the selling and using of crack cocaine in areas characterized by high unemployment rates and poverty also means that many grandmothers are not only raising their grandchildren but doing so in drug-created "war zones" (Burton, 1991b; Reed, 1988; Villarreal et al., 1992). Under such circumstances, grandmothers not only fear for the children who can't safely go outdoors to play, but also for themselves, the easy targets of both domestic and neighborhood violence (see Chapter 10 this volume).

Finally, in households where the crack pipe may be passed around among siblings in much the same way as a marijuana joint, and in poor neighborhoods where pressures to sell and/or use crack are frequently intense, grandmothers may find that not one but several of their children are involved with the drug. The grandmother who used to be able to depend on a son or daughter for assistance with child care and other tasks may, as a result of the epidemic, find that such support is no longer readily available.

Under all of these circumstances, the already demanding nature of grandparent caregiving takes on important new dimensions.

## THE RISKS OF TOPIC SELECTION

Having laid out our reasons for choosing to focus specifically on the experience of black grandmothers raising their grandchildren as a consequence of the crack cocaine epidemic, it is important to also make explicit our cautions and concerns—for in choosing this topic, we take several calculated risks.

In her classic book, *When and Where I Enter: The Impact of Black Women on Race and Sex in America,* Giddings (1984) noted the tendency for books on black women to focus on exceptional groups and individuals—women who are revered for making "contributions," despite the combined burdens of racism and sexism that they face. In the same manner, grandparent caregivers in general, and black grandmother caregivers in particular, have been characterized as "unsung heroines" and "silent saviors," who are quietly "bearing the burden" of the drug epidemic (Creighton, 1991; Kennedy, 1991). Through such characterizations, scholarly and popular writings in this area risk stereotyping the black grandmother as a nurturing and self-sacrificing matriarch without needs or wants of her own (Christian, 1985; see also Chapter 2 this volume).

Although our study clearly highlights the strengths and nurturing capacities that enabled many of the women we interviewed to fulfill the new caregiver role, our findings also detail the personal costs, the anger, and the frustration and despair that such caregiving often entailed. As noted earlier, by relying heavily on the words and the voices of the caregivers themselves, we attempt to capture the complexities and diversity of the women, and to present their views and experiences in as authentic a manner as possible.

Whether white women can or should even try to conduct research on the experiences of African American women has, of course, been subject to debate (Collins, 1990; Hooks, 1984, 1989). In part, such questions reflect broader skepticism about whether members of a dominant culture can ever accurately research and make sense of the life experiences of an oppressed group. As Stack (1974, p. ix) has asked, "Is it possible for an outsider who symbolizes the dominant culture to enter a black community, win the community's participation and approval, acquire reliable data, and judge its reliability?"

For others, the questions raised are primarily ethical in nature and reflect the difficulty researchers from a dominant social or ethnic group may have in getting beyond a subject/object dichotomy when studying oppressed populations. In Hooks's (1989, p. 43) words,

> Even if perceived "authorities" writing about a group to which they do not belong and/or over which they wield power, are progressive [and]

caring, . . . as long as their authority is constituted by either the absence of the voices of the individuals whose experiences they seek to address, or the dismissal of those voices as unimportant, the subject-object dichotomy is reinforced.

In the latter regard, several prominent black scholars and writers (Collins, 1990; Hooks, 1989; Walker, 1983) have expressed concern and sometimes anger over those white feminist writings that are seen as ignoring or downplaying the experiences and contributions of women of color. The legacy of such concerns has added another dimension to the skepticism surrounding white women who attempt to study black women's experience.

Finally, La Rue (1970) has argued that there is a fundamental difference between *suppression,* which has characterized white women's experience, and the *oppression* that is a daily fact of life for black women. Summarizing this perspective, Dilworth-Anderson, Johnson, and Burton (in press) point out that "oppression represents an almost total restriction from and access to the benefits, rights and privileges of a society," whereas suppression suggests "having restrictions and limitations to the system, but to a much lesser degree." By appearing to overstate the similarities between black and white women's life experiences, the work of many white feminists has been criticized as failing to comprehend this critical distinction (Collins, 1990; Hooks, 1989).

Yet as black feminist author Patricia H. Collins (1990) suggests, although the very real differences between black and white women's experiences must be acknowledged and appreciated, they should not be used as grounds for excluding the experiences of other ethnic groups from one's scholarship. Collins (1990, pp. 9-10) indeed has expressed her concern that "white women who possess great competence in researching a range of issues omit women of color from their work claiming that they are unqualified to understand the 'black woman's experience.' " Like the tendency of some white feminists to ignore the writings of women of color, such behavior, she suggests, reflects "a basic unwillingness by many white feminists to alter the paradigms that guide their work" (1990, p. 10).

In reality, as Stack (1974, p. xiv) has observed, "A researcher in the social sciences is practically always defined as an outsider in a study, even if he or she has close attachment and commitment to the community, and shares a similar cultural background." In undertaking the Grandparent Caregiver Study, we were indeed "outsiders," both culturally and by virtue of our roles as researchers. As outsiders, we couldn't begin to know the particular pain of watching the deterioration of an adult child on crack, or the intense and often conflicting emotions that may come into play when a woman "puts her life on hold" to become surrogate parent to her grandchildren. Nor certainly could we know the myriad of feelings and experiences that go with being an older African American woman at a time when the epidemics of drugs, violence, AIDS, and teenage pregnancy both reflect and compound the more endemic problems to which poverty and racism have historically given rise.

Yet as Duster (1987a, p. 8) has argued, "the most fundamental issue in a study of one group by another concerns which questions are raised," rather than the skin color of the researchers. As cultural outsiders exploring a topic of deep personal and professional interest, we began this study committed to "asking the right questions." And in some ways, our status as outsiders may have helped us with this task.

As outsiders familiar with the range of issues that have surfaced in the study of family caregiving across ethnic groups, for example, we could pose questions designed to help women think about their caregiving roles in some new ways. Ideally, in the process, we could enable them to see dimensions of themselves and of their lives that they hadn't previously thought about or explored in this depth. Similarly, our familiarity with the nature and substance of U.S. public policies for "undeserving" population groups (e.g., poor women and children and relative caregivers) enabled us to ask questions that could elicit the type of data needed by those working to effect change.

Our ability to "ask the right questions" was enhanced by an exceptional team of African American graduate students, and an active Community Advisory Group made up predominantly of women of color. As discussed in more detail in Chapter 3, their insights and dedication, and those of many other individuals connected with the Grandparent Caregiver Study, helped us to gain entrée and to present both the research and our interpretation of findings in a manner that attempted to be as culturally sensitive and authentic as possible.

As Chapter 3 will also suggest, our choice of research methods, and the manner in which this book is crafted, both were selected to enable us to draw on and present the lived experience of grandmother caregivers in their own words, to the greatest extent possible. Finally, we have drawn heavily on the works of such African American scholars as Linda M. Burton, Peggy Dilworth-Anderson, Joyce Ladner, Bell Hooks, Jewelle Gibbs, Rose Gibson, Hariette Pipes McAdoo, and

Patricia H. Collins, and our understanding of the complexities of our topic will hopefully reflect the insights gained from this rich literature.

A final note of caution involves our decision to focus on those African American grandmothers who are raising children specifically as a consequence of the crack cocaine epidemic. As noted earlier, the devastating impact of the sale and use of crack cocaine in many low-income black communities, and the changes it has brought about in the lives of grandparent caregivers, make this topic both timely and important. Yet in choosing this focus, we risk reinforcing images of the cocaine problem in America as a predominantly "black problem."

In reality, of course, the use of this drug continues to cut across class and ethnic group lines. A recent hospital-based study in Florida, for example, showed identical levels of the use of cocaine and other drugs among black and white pregnant women (Chasnoff, Landress, & Barett, 1990). Yet as this study also demonstrated, African American women were 10 times more likely to be reported to health authorities for substance abuse than were white women, and poor women were similarly more likely to be reported than were their wealthier counterparts. The far greater tendency for black users to be identified and reported is key among the reasons for the growing public perception of cocaine use as a "black problem" (Harris, 1991).

The emergence of the inexpensive crack form of cocaine, and the growing disparities between rich and poor that occurred in the 1980s (Phillips, 1990), did, of course, make low-income populations particularly vulnerable to involvement with this highly potent form of the drug (Villarreal et al., 1992). The economic realities of inner-city life, moreover, and the fact that crack dealing was easy and profitable for unemployed youths, resulted in the drug trade being confined primarily to low-income minority neighborhoods (Villarreal et al., 1992). For this reason, too, the drug problem has tended to be inaccurately identified as a problem of the African American community.

As noted earlier, we chose to focus on black grandmothers raising the children of crack involved parents because of the often profound ways in which the drug epidemic has changed the experience of grandparent caregiving. By examining the lives of one group of African American grandmothers as they cope with the consequences of the epidemic, we hope to illuminate their unique experiences and concerns. At the same time, however, we will endeavor to direct attention to the broader implications and issues raised as these effect a variety of diverse population groups.

## THE STUDY SETTING

The city of Oakland, California, provided an appropriate setting for our study of grandmother caregivers in the crack cocaine crisis in several important respects. The sixth largest city in California, with a population of 365,000, Oakland displays many of the strengths and many of the problems and challenges of the nation's large urban areas.

The city is highly diverse ethnically and socioeconomically. African Americans constitute the single largest ethnic group in the city (44%), with Caucasians making up approximately a quarter of the population and Hispanics and Asians representing 16% and 14%, respectively. With more than 50 languages spoken in the city's public schools, Oakland has been called "the most integrated city in the United States" (Ruben, 1991).

In addition to its diversity, however, Oakland is characterized by a high rate of poverty. Thirty percent of households receive public assistance, and in East and West Oakland, where most participants in our study resided, close to 40,000 children live in poverty (Ruben, 1991).

Like many cities across the country, Oakland has seen a significant increase in single parent families, largely in response to the long-term economic and social crises that have severely depleted the ranks of young black males (Gibbs, 1990; Gibbs et al., 1988; Snyder, 1992). Two thirds of Oakland's black families are now headed by single women (Snyder, 1992). And although such households often include strong extended families that provide a nurturing child-rearing environment (McAdoo, 1978; Stack, 1974), their substantially higher poverty rates are a harsh fact of life. Approximately 46% of the students in Oakland's elementary and junior high schools are in families receiving Aid to Families with Dependent Children (AFDC), for example, and in East and West Oakland high schools, this figure climbs significantly higher (Oakland Public Schools, 1991). Such figures are in keeping with the national data, which demonstrated that in 1989, 71% of children under 18 in central city areas were living in poverty (U.S. Bureau of the Census, 1990).

Oakland also shares with many large urban areas the fact of having been hard hit by the crack epidemic in the mid- to late 1980s. And although there are encouraging indications of a recent decline in casual crack use, hard-core addiction remains a significant problem (delVecchio, 1991).

As in other parts of the nation, grandparents in Oakland have been heavily effected by the epidemic. As noted earlier, an estimated 20% of the City's Head Start children are being cared for by their grandparents (Nathan, 1990). And a survey by Oakland's Office on Aging of the 500 client cases it manages revealed one in four to have crack problems in their homes (Nathan, 1990).

The number of cocaine exposed babies born in Oakland's large public hospital appears to have peaked in 1989, at 22% of high-risk infants tested, and had dropped to 10% by August of 1991 (J. Jackson, personal communication, March 1992). At the time of this study, such steep declines had not yet been witnessed in cities like Detroit and Boston (delVecchio, 1991). Yet for Oakland and its grandmother caregivers, the epidemic and its consequences are far from over.

Oakland has played a leadership role in response to the crack crisis on a variety of levels, and for this reason, too, the city provides an important context for our study. Calling crack "the number one problem in the African American community," the Oakland Crack Task Force, a coalition of some 200 groups and agencies, works actively on a variety of education and prevention approaches. Such efforts are beginning to pay off, with health and police officials citing crack education and prevention programs for pregnant women as playing a key role in decreasing the number of potential new users (D. Markam & J. Jackson, personal communications, March 4, 1992).

The concerns of grandparent caregivers and the children they are raising have also been vigorously addressed. Oakland's Office on Aging and the city's Intergenerational Task Force on Crack Cocaine together have undertaken an ambitious, federally funded program of training for grandparent and youth volunteers committed to attacking the problems faced by caregivers and their grandchildren (Brookdale Grandparent Caregiver Information Project [Brookdale], 1992a). Grandparents Day celebrations for caregivers, a grandparent "warm line" run out of a concerned city supervisor's office, and grandparent respite centers and support groups are among the other interventions developed to ease the burden of the grandparents who are raising an important and vulnerable part of the city's next generation (see Chapter 12 this volume).

In sum, both the magnitude of the crack problem faced by Oakland and the city's extensive and sometimes heroic efforts to confront that problem made Oakland a logical "home base" for our study.

## ORGANIZATION OF THE BOOK

The book draws heavily on hundreds of hours of interviews with 71 African American women in Oakland, each of whom was raising at least one grandchild, great grandchild, or grandniece or -nephew as a direct consequence of the crack cocaine epidemic. The women, who ranged in age from 41 to 79, shared their lives and their experiences to provide a rich and in-depth look at the nature, dynamics, and health and social consequences of this complex and challenging role. With their help, we attempt to illuminate grandparent caregiving "from the inside," on the assumption that there is much African American women can tell other grandparents and the general public, as well as scholars, policymakers, service providers, and researchers about this vital and often neglected experience.

Chapter 2 lays out the social and cultural contexts within which grandparent caregiving takes place. We consider first the invisibility of much of women's work as caregivers and the perspectives of feminist, and particularly black feminist, thinkers on the gendered division of labor that tends to "sentimentalize and devalue" family caregiving (Abel, 1991). We then turn to a more in-depth consideration of the cultural context of grandparent caregiving in African American communities, looking in particular at the traditional role of the black grandmother within the extended family. As we shall suggest, both the rich tradition of the black grandmother as kinkeeper and "guardian of the generation" (Frazier, 1966) and the newer, more tenuous grandparent role occupied and desired by many black women today (L. Burton & Bengtson, 1985) have important implications for the assumption of caregiving for one's grandchildren in the crack cocaine epidemic.

Chapter 3 describes the purposes and contexts of the Grandparent Caregiver Study, and the methods used to illuminate the lived experience of the 71 women who shared their lives and insights with us. The advantages of an approach to research that combines qualitative and quantitative methods are discussed, as are the Grandparent Caregiver Study's efforts to have participation in the research constitute a positive and empowering experience for the women involved.

In Chapter 4, we examine the preexisting roles and responsibilities of grandparent caregivers, and how the assumption of the new caregiver role often dramatically changed their lives and daily routines. The family dynamics and circumstances surrounding the assumption of full-time caregiving are explored in depth, as are the "trigger events" that led to the taking on of this demanding new role.

Chapter 5 describes the physical and emotional health status of grand-mother caregivers, with special attention to how the women perceive their health, and their health behaviors, as changing during the course of caregiving. The often dramatic differences between the women's self-reported health status and other, more qualitative indicators of their health and well-being will be highlighted. We will look, too, at how grandmother caregivers cope with physical limitations and other health problems, and at some of the subgroups of caregivers who appear par-ticularly vulnerable to deterioration in their health after becoming care-givers for their grandchildren.

The high costs of caregiving from an economic perspective are ex-plored in Chapter 6. The increased economic vulnerability of grandpar-ents who become parents is examined, with special attention to the dual standard in welfare policies and programs that often penalizes women financially for being related to the youngsters they raise. The "holes in the safety net" encountered by grandparent caregivers, and the often dramatic reductions in their own standard of living as a consequence of the new role, are among the themes explored in this chapter.

Grandparent caregiving in the crack cocaine epidemic is, in part, a story of the high costs and sacrifices borne by the women who take on this challenging and often difficult role. But it is also about the strengths of caregivers and the resources they call upon to help them cope with the demands of their new life. In Chapter 7 we turn to the social support networks and resources of grandparent caregivers, and to the additions to and disruptions of their networks as a consequence of caregiving. We examine the women's family and friendship networks and their partic-ipation in churches and other organizations and voluntary activities. We look, too, at the special role of grandparent support groups in helping a subset of the women cope with the stresses of their new life.

Despite the extensively documented importance of social support for health and well being (Cohen & Syme, 1985) and the many roles such support played in the lives of the women we interviewed, the latter did not tend to rely on their social networks as their primary sources of sup-port in coping with the new role. In Chapter 8, we therefore look beyond social support to several key coping strategies and approaches em-ployed by grandmother caregivers to help them get through the day and manage their multiple and often conflicting roles and responsibili-ties. Five coping strategies are identified and described, with the words of the women themselves used extensively to illustrate these coping approaches.

We turn in Chapter 9 to the special challenges experienced by grandmothers who continue to work outside the home while raising infant and preschool age grandchildren. The often radical restructuring of work required to accommodate caregiving demands will be explored, as will the costs of such restructuring. The chapter looks, too, at what happens when jobs are lost or promotions forgone because of caregiving and at the failure of policies in the private and public sectors to address adequately the needs of employed family caregivers.

Although a salient fact of life for women of all ethnic groups, the continuity of caregiving over the life course is particularly pronounced in the African American community (McAdoo, 1990; Stack, 1974). In Chapter 10, we explore the continuity of caregiving, beginning with a look at those women who were simultaneously caring for their grandchildren and their frail elderly parents or grandparents. We then examine several other caregiving role combinations, such us caring for disabled adult children along with the grandchildren, or raising grandchildren, only to find one's self, a generation later, raising great grandchildren as well.

For many of the women in our study who had spent part of their own childhoods living with their grandmothers, the current role as caregiver for one's grandchildren took on special meaning. We conclude Chapter 10 with a look at the study participants' recollections and reminiscences about their own grandmothers' roles as caregivers, and how these remembrances in turn may influence the women's attitudes toward raising their grandchildren.

The historic role of the black grandmother, and its deeply personal analogue in the form of the special relationship many of the women in our study had with their own caregiving grandmothers, provides a special legacy for the women who are raising their children's children as a consequence of the crack cocaine epidemic. Yet as noted earlier, the nature of that epidemic, and the historic circumstances that surround it, make grandparent caregiving in this situation a qualitatively different experience from any that preceded it. In Chapter 11, we explore the special problems and challenges involved in raising the children of the crack cocaine crisis.

The health and social problems that may be faced by drug exposed children, the effects of society's labeling and stereotyping of "crack kids," and the aftereffects of the early abuse and neglect experienced by many children of the crack epidemic, may combine for grandparent caregivers to make for a particularly difficult caregiving role. Conflicts with the drug involved parents of the children in one's care, and the safety concerns inherent in raising children in neighborhoods often scarred by drug wars, will be seen to exacerbate further the difficulties involved in raising the children of the crack cocaine epidemic.

For about 20% of the women in our study, participation in weekly or monthly grandparent support groups dramatically increased their perceived ability to cope and provided a real sense that "I'm not in this alone." By the study's conclusion, several other women had begun volunteering with the earlier mentioned grandparent warm line, and still others were receiving training as peer counselors. In Chapter 12, we describe these and other community intervention and service programs to support and assist grandparent caregivers both in Oakland and around the country. The emergence of a grandparent caregiver movement, and of a national effort to assess the state of the art of community interventions and other programs and services to support and assist grandparent caregivers, also will be discussed.

As helpful as such interventions may be, however, real and substantive improvements in the circumstances of grandparent caregivers and the children in their care will require changes on a far broader level. In the final chapter, we examine the significant policy changes necessary to address both the needs of grandparent caregivers, and the factors giving rise to the increased prevalence of such caregiving, particularly in inner-city communities.

We will consider a variety of policy problems and solutions that are being discussed, and sometimes tried, on the local, state, and national levels. But we will also listen to the voices of an overlooked group of experts—the grandparents for whom caregiving as a consequence of the crack epidemic is a daily reality. Some of the policy changes these women would like to see will sound harsh and even brutal. Yet to borrow the language of Harvard professor and former Oakland resident Ishmael Reed (1988), the women in this study are "living at ground zero." They are closest to the heat, and their attitudes and beliefs, therefore, are not abstract and philosophical but grounded in the daily realities of life at the center of a national tragedy.

By placing these experiences and insights in the context of such broader problems as poverty and unemployment, the growing gap between rich and poor, and the lack of a coherent U.S. family policy, we will demonstrate again the intimate interdependence of "personal troubles and public issues" (Mills, 1959) in the lives of women raising their grandchildren as a consequence of the crack cocaine epidemic.

# 2

---

# Social and Cultural Contexts
of Caregiving

Like other forms of women's caregiving, the phenomenon of grandmothers raising grandchildren can only be understood within a broad
social and cultural context. In this chapter, we will extend our concern
with two overlapping contextual frameworks, each of which provides
important insights into the assumption and management of the role of
grandmother caregiver.

We will examine first the gendered division of labor around caregiving, and the perspectives of feminist, and particularly of black feminist,
thinkers on caring as constituting predominantly a "women's issue."
Insights from the literature on motherhood and black motherhood will
be examined, along with perspectives from the literature on caregiving
for the elderly, for their relevance to our understanding of women's roles
as grandparent caregivers.

We move then to a more in-depth consideration of the cultural context
of grandparent caregiving in African American communities, examining the historic and contemporary role of the traditional black grandmother within the extended family. We will consider, too, the more tenuous grandparent role that is occupied (and desired) by many black
women today, in contrast to the more stereotypic traditional role
(Burton & Bengtson, 1985). As we shall see, the cultural context of both
the traditional role, embedded in strong extended family formations,
and the newer and less defined grandparent role, has an important bearing
on the experience of grandmothers raising the children of the crack
cocaine epidemic.

## CARING AS A WOMEN'S ISSUE

As Baines, Evans, and Neysmith have suggested (1991, p. 29), "the relative invisibility of women's caring, the implicit assumption that it is natural for women to care, the lack of attention paid to the complexities involved in caring, and the contradictions caring poses for women" all must be considered if we are truly to appreciate the lived experience of women as caregivers.

The often unseen and undervalued nature of women's work as caregivers reflects in part the fact that caregiving has traditionally been viewed not as work at all, but rather as a "natural" way in which women relate to others by virtue of their gender (Abel, 1991; Baines et al., 1991; Dressel & Clark, 1990).

White feminist scholars such as Chodorow (1978) and Gilligan (1982) have explored the embeddedness of such "natural" behaviors in socialization processes through which boys and girls learn different ways of being in the world. In her classic work on the reproduction of mothering, Chodorow (1978, p. 7) thus has pointed out that:

> The sexual and familial division of labor in which women mother and are more involved in interpersonal, affective relationships than men, produces in daughters and sons a division of psychological capacities which leads them to reproduce this sexual and familial division of labor.

Gilligan's (1982, p. 160) interviews with women further have demonstrated how feminine identity is "defined in a context of relationship and judged by a standard of responsibility and care."

As noted in Chapter 1, the relevance of white feminist scholarship for understanding the lives of African American women has been questioned, in part on the basis that black women and white feminists have different life experiences and different ways of thinking about and perceiving oppression (Dilworth-Anderson et al., in press; Giddings, 1984; Hooks, 1984; La Rue, 1970). The applicability of the theses developed by scholars like Gilligan and Chodorow to black women's experience similarly has been challenged, since their insights are based largely on their work with white middle-class samples (Collins, 1990).

The notion that women in general, and black women in particular, are often defined by others in terms of a "natural" propensity toward mothering and caregiving is developed in the writings of women who define themselves as black feminists. As Collins (1990, p. 116) has noted:

Black male scholars in particular glorify Black motherhood by refusing to acknowledge the issues faced by Black mothers. . . . By claiming that Black women are richly endowed with devotion, self sacrifice and unconditional love—the attributes associated with archetypal motherhood—Black men inadvertently foster a different controlling image for Black women, that of the "superstrong Black mother" (Staples, 1973; Dance, 1979).

Such images, indeed, may come dangerously close to that of the "mammy" or Aunt Jemima figure—the dominant image of black women found in early white southern literature (S. Brown, 1969). As Christian (1985, p. 2) has pointed out:

Mammy is black in color, fat, nurturing, religious, kind, above all strong, and . . . enduring. She relates to the world as an all embracing figure, and she herself needs or demands little, her identity derived mainly from a nurturing service.

In contrast to these stereotypic images, portrayals of black women in the literature of such contemporary African American women writers as Toni Morrison, Alice Walker, Paule Marshall, and Gloria Naylor are complex and multidimensional (see Christian, 1985, for an in-depth exploration of this theme). Yet in the real world, as in much literature, the tendency toward an idealization and sanctification of black motherhood continues (Christian, 1985). And in many African American communities, as Christian (1985, p. 234) has observed, "the idea that mothers should live lives of sacrifice has come to be seen as the norm."

Weems (1984) has argued that the image of the "superstrong Black mother" can be as false and detrimental as that of the "happy slave" of an earlier day, and needs to be similarly debunked. Instead, black motherhood must be viewed as an institution that is "both dynamic and dialectical" (Collins, 1990, p. 118). For although mothering under the oppressive circumstances faced by many black women can be empowering and a source of recognition and validation, it also has high costs. In Collins's (1990, p. 133) words:

Black motherhood is fundamentally a contradictory institution. African-American communities value motherhood, but Black mothers' ability to cope with race, class and gender oppression should not be confused with transcending those conditions. Black motherhood can be rewarding, but it can also extract high personal costs. The range of Black women's reactions to motherhood reflect motherhood's contradictory nature.

Coping with unwanted pregnancies, experiencing the pain of knowing what lies ahead for black children, and giving up some of one's own dreams for achieving full creative potential are among the costs of black motherhood that Collins describes. Such costs, moreover, are borne not only by biological mothers in African American communities, but by "othermothers" as well—the women who help a mother raise her children or, in the case of grandmother caregivers, who take full responsibility for raising young children when their biological mothers are unable or unwilling to perform this role (Troester, 1984).

The experience of grandparent caregiving, then, can be understood in part in relation to the contradictory nature of women's work as mothers and othermothers, which is often rendered invisible as a consequence of the combination of physical labor, affection, and "emotion work" (Hochschild, 1983) that it entails. As Baines et al. (1991, p. 29) point out:

> The provision of comfort and nurturing to children, an elderly mother, or a disabled member of the family is arduous work, but it is usually undertaken in a network of personal relationships in which emotions of affection are mixed with resentment, and norms of family responsibility and obligation are intertwined.

For grandmother caregivers, as we shall see, the conflicting emotions and attitudes engendered by the combination of labor and love involved in the new role makes for an extremely complex caregiving experience.

Examining grandmother caregiving within a broad social context of gender and caregiving also focuses our attention on the profound connection between women's roles in childbearing and child rearing and their disadvantaged place in the labor force (Abel, 1991). The heavy concentration of women in low-paying jobs without good benefits or opportunities for advancement places them at a considerable disadvantage, and one that is compounded by the frequent necessity either to combine work with caregiving, or to terminate employment prematurely in order to become full-time caregivers (Minkler & Stone, 1985).

The occupational segregation of women in low-paying jobs in the secondary or peripheral sector of the economy is particularly pronounced among women of color. As Sidel (1990) points out, although women as a whole make up more than 80% of all clerical workers, for example, almost a quarter of all employed black women can be found in just 6 of the 48 clerical positions listed by the Department of Labor. Among service workers, black women similarly are crowded into a few low-status, low-paying jobs such as chambermaid, cleaner, and nurse's aide.

The irony confronted by African American women who leave their own children or grandchildren at home to go and clean other people's houses and care for other people's children or elderly relatives has not been lost on black feminist writers. June Jordan (1985, p. 105) describes her anger and shame at watching "one black woman after another" trudge to the bus stop after a day of cleaning or caregiving in an affluent white neighborhood, only to return home to "the frequently thankless chores of their own loneliness, their own families." As will be discussed in Chapter 9, the stresses involved in combining jobs with caregiving may be particularly pronounced for women in these and related occupations, whose paid work often closely resembles their caregiving responsibilities at home.

The higher labor force participation rates of African American women (U.S. Bureau of Labor Statistics, 1990) combine with their more extensive caregiving responsibilities at home to make for a difficult "double shift" existence. For low-income women living in inner-city neighborhoods with poor access to support services, these difficulties are often further compounded.

Finally, as we shall see, although the extended family can sometimes be relied upon to provide help with baby-sitting or eldercare while low-income black women are at work, the latter remain highly vulnerable to having to leave the work force in order to become full-time caregivers. Such women are far more likely than middle- and upper income women to be direct care *givers,* as opposed to care *managers* (Archbold, 1983; Cantor & Little, 1985), and are similarly more likely to have inflexible work schedules and few, if any, employee benefits that would enable them better to combine their responsibilities at work and at home. In our own study, fully a third of grandparent caregivers had had to leave work because of their new child-care roles at home (see Chapter 9 this volume). For almost all of these women, an already problematic financial future appeared bleaker still in face of their unexpected loss of income and job security.

The relative absence of accommodations at work that would aid caregivers in meeting their responsibilities at home reflects yet another aspect of the social context of caring as a "women's issue." As Abramovitz (1988) has noted, our profound societal commitment to the notion of women as caregivers has found expression in a pervasive "family ethic" that governs the sexual division of labor and is reinforced by our social welfare policies.

Premised on the notion that women have a primary responsibility for the care of family members, such policies neither address inherent issues of choice and of gender, race, and class justice in caregiving, nor provide caregivers with the support they need to carry out these roles adequately (Abel, 1987, 1991; England, Keigher, Miller, & Linsk, 1991).

The lack of adequate family leave policies for the workplace, and the dearth of publicly funded day care and long-term care services in this country, often place family caregivers, most of whom are women, in difficult straits (Abel, 1991; England et al., 1991). For grandparent caregivers, such problems are further compounded. As will be discussed in Chapters 6 and 13, for example, state legislation typically renders grandparent caregivers "second-class citizens," providing them with lower rates of child support, through a more stigmatizing source, than it does foster care parents who are unrelated to the children they are raising (Barry, 1991). The family ethic, which suggests that grandmothers have a duty to care for their grandchildren, thus interferes with the provision of the very resources that would enable grandparents to better carry out their newfound responsibilities.

In short, like mothers with young children and caregivers for the elderly, grandparent caregivers are penalized by a society in which caregivers are, at one and the same time, sentimentalized and devalued (Abel, 1991).

The phenomenon of grandparent caregiving occupies, in many ways, a complex and fascinating "middle ground" between mothering one's own children and caring for elderly parents or other relatives. Although grandmothers in youthful lineages may be as young as their late twenties, most are middle-aged or older women themselves, and occupy a place in the life cycle more akin to that of eldercare providers than of most mothers to young children. Like caregivers for the old, they typically have either completed their own child rearing or have only older teenage children remaining at home when their new caregiving responsibilities are assumed.

The lack of choice that leaves mothers and adult caregiving daughters without adequate supports as they strive to care for their young children or their elderly parents similarly penalizes grandparent caregivers. The fact that the latter are more likely to be low income, and/or women of color, moreover, often places them in an even more disadvantageous position in this regard.

Like both mothers and caregivers for the old, grandparent caregivers typically experience a myriad of conflicting emotions—relief and happiness that they are able to help their grandchildren, and anger and despair that they have been placed in this position. Among some of the women we interviewed, these already contradictory emotions were complicated still further by a sense of guilt. The notions that "somehow this could have been prevented if I'd raised my own children better," or "I have a second chance to raise a child up right," did indeed surface in a number of interviews, once again distinguishing the experience of grandparent caregiving from both that of mothering and of providing care for one's own elderly mother.

As noted above, the conflicting cultural attitudes that simultaneously sentimentalize and devalue mothers and caregivers for the old (Abel, 1987, 1991), similarly may be seen to operate with respect to grandmothers raising young children. Lauded in the press and by concerned politicians as "unsung heroines," grandmother caregivers—and particularly those raising drug exposed youngsters—are credited not only with saving a "lost generation" of children, but also with saving an already overburdened foster care system (Jost, 1991). Yet concurrently with these laudatory assessments, efforts in a number of states to provide grandparent caregivers with the same assistance received by foster care parents are routinely defeated (see Chapter 13 this volume). The earlier noted "family ethic" mentality (grandparents have a duty to care) combined with a certain queasiness over grandparents who are seen as perhaps being indirectly to blame (why did their own kids turn out so badly?) are among the factors contributing to society's contradictory emotions and attitudes toward its most recently discovered group of caregivers.

In sum, perspectives on caregiving as a women's issue, which highlight societal ambivalence around caregiving, severe constraints on women's choices and opportunities, and deeply conflicting personal feelings evoked by the combination of affection and labor comprising the caretaking role, provide a useful theoretical framework within which to examine the lived experience of grandmother caregivers. Within African American communities, a rich legacy of grandmother caregiving, the role of such caring within the black extended family, and recent sociodemographic changes impacting on the grandparental role, deepen and extend our understanding of contemporary grandparent caregiving and provide a useful and often interconnected conceptual framework for analysis. It is to the latter perspectives that we now turn.

## THE CULTURAL CONTEXT
## OF GRANDPARENT CAREGIVING
## IN AFRICAN AMERICAN COMMUNITIES

Grandparenthood has been described as a "contingent process" (Troll, 1985, p. 135), whose playing out is influenced by a host of variables including ethnicity and social class (Cherlin & Furstenberg, 1986; Jackson, 1986; Kivett, 1991), geographic proximity to and ages and gender of one's grandchildren (Shanas, 1979; Tinsley & Parke, 1984, 1987), and the "on" versus "off" timing of entry into the grandparental role (Burton & Bengtson, 1985; Troll, 1985). Yet as nurturers, grandparents are "the second line of defense," serving as a safety net for children whose parents are unable or unwilling to provide care (Kornhaber, 1985, p. 162).

As Burton and Dilworth-Anderson (1991) have pointed out, although research on grandparenthood has proliferated in the last decade (see Bengtson & Robertson, 1985; Hagestad & Burton, 1986), grandparenthood among African Americans has remained a relatively unexplored research domain. Despite the dearth of empirical work in this area, however, one facet of grandparenthood in African American extended families—the role of the black grandmother as surrogate parent—has long been appreciated. Conceptualizations of the black extended family, and of the historic and contemporary role of the grandmother within that family structure, provide, therefore, an important framework for this book.

A number of conceptual and ideological classification schemes have been proposed for understanding and analyzing scholarship on the African American family (Allen, 1978; Gibbs, 1990; Martin & Martin, 1978; Wilson, 1986). As Gibbs (1990) and Allen (1978) suggest, these schemes tend to be similar, and to have overlapping categories.

One of the most popular of these typologies (Martin & Martin, 1978) divides portrayals of the black extended family into two general categories: a "pathology-disorganization" perspective, which views the black family as inherently unstable, deviant, and maladaptive (Frazier, 1966; Moynihan, 1965; Myrdal, 1944; Rainwater, 1966), and a "strength-resiliency" perspective, which emphasizes the ability of black families to adapt and thrive despite adverse external forces (Billingsley, 1968; Hill, 1971; Stack, 1974).

Writing in the former tradition in the mid-1960s, for example, Moynihan (1965) described the black family as characterized by a "tangle of pathologies" and concluded that the black family was "at the heart of the deterioration of Negro society."

In sharp contrast, Stack's (1974) ethnographic study, *All Our Kin,* conducted during this same time period, led her to argue that within the low-income black community she studied, co-residence, three-generation households, and shared parenting and child-care arrangements constituted key "survival strategies." In her words (1974, p. 124):

> These highly adaptive structural features of urban black families comprise a resilient response to the socio-economic conditions of poverty, the inexorable unemployment of black women and men, and the access to scarce resources of a mother and her children as AFDC recipients. . . . The black urban family, embedded in a cooperative domestic exchange, proves to be an organized, tenacious, lifelong network.

More recent analysts have stressed the existence of a third perspective on African American family life, reflected in the work of Nobles (1974, 1978, 1988), Farley and Allen (1987), and others, for example, Billingsley (1968) and Stack (1974), who earlier were identified with the strength-resiliency perspective. Termed the cultural or "cultural variant" approach, this perspective views the African American family as "a distinctive cultural form that has evolved in America from a fusion of elements from African culture and adaptations to slavery, segregation, rural southern culture, and urban northern ghetto life" (Gibbs, 1990, p. 328).

The stabilizing role of black elders and the kinkeeping function of older black women is traced by cultural variant proponents to their roots in West African culture and tradition. The forced disruption of African families and kinship patterns as a consequence of slave trading similarly is seen as having led to both the creation of symbolic kin networks and to strong conceptions of family and kin obligations among multiple generations and families (Cohen, 1984; Genovese, 1976; Sudarkasa, 1981; Wilson, 1989). By the early 19th century, plantations typically contained large extended families, within which grandmothers held a revered status (Jones, 1973; Wilson, 1989).

Critical reviews of the literature in the pathology-disorganization, strength-resiliency, and cultural variant traditions are available elsewhere (Dodson, 1988; Gibbs, 1990; Martin & Martin, 1978; Taylor, Chatter, Tucker, & Lewis, 1990; Wilson, 1986) and are beyond the scope of this book. Of relevance here, however, is the fact that a number of analysts representing each of these diverse perspectives appear to share an appreciation—and indeed sometimes an idealization—of the critical role of the grandmother in African American family life.

Writing in the strength-resiliency tradition, for example, Jones's (1973) portrayal of black grandmothers from the early 1800s through the Civil Rights era of the mid-1960s suggests a continuation of their "lofty role," stressing the grandmother's extensive contributions to neighbors as well as kin and her frequent role as caregiver across generational and family lines.

A similarly positive portrayal of the black grandmother may be found in the work of such pathology-disorganization perspective analysts as E. Franklin Frazier. Despite the critical tone of much of his writing (Dodson, 1988; Martin & Martin, 1978), Frazier's (1966) accounts of the black grandmother rival those of the most positive strength-resiliency and cultural variant analysts. His depiction of the extended family "matriarch" is of a warm and compassionate yet determined individual whose many roles included those of teacher, mother, nurse and midwife, disciplinarian, spiritual guide, and "transmitter of the family heritage" (Frazier, 1966; Hill & Shackleford, 1975).

The often idealized portrayals of grandmothers in much of the social science literature on black family life, regardless of the perspective or tradition represented, are, indeed, themselves a phenomenon worthy of further study.

Although a rich tradition in African American fiction has explored and illuminated the role of the black grandmother (Christian, 1985; Holloway & Demetrakopoulos, 1986), relatively few empirical studies have focused specifically on this role. As Burton and Bengtson (1985) suggest, moreover, the research that has been conducted in this area has looked, with few exceptions, at the "traditional" role of the black grandmother as surrogate parent or "family matriarch," ignoring the occupancy, by many, of a more tenuous and ill-defined grandparent role.

Finally, our own review of this literature suggests that studies of the traditional role of black grandmothers are themselves limited in their tendency to focus on the grandparent's caregiving functions when the adult daughter remains present and a member of the household. Research on the caring functions of grandmothers in low-income families, for example, documents the heavy involvement of grandmothers in both child-care and household tasks, in part as a means of freeing the young mother to finish school, get a job, or in other ways engage in "self-improvement" activities (Brooks-Gunn & Chase Lansdale, 1991; Flaherty,

1988; Furstenberg & Crawford, 1978; Field, Widmayer, Stringer, & Ignatoff, 1980; Hogan, Hao, & Parish, 1990; Presser, 1989; Wilson, 1989). Although the multiple functions of grandparents and other extended family members are effectively illuminated through these explorations, the emphasis is on the extended family *unit,* including, importantly, the young mother and/or father, in negotiating and fulfilling a variety of family and work roles.

In the "skipped generation" families examined in our research, the general absence of the young children's parents due to their crack cocaine involvement, and the consequent full-time and often permanent nature of the caregiving role of grandmothers, made for a substantively different surrogate parenting experience than that described in most accounts of the traditional black grandmother. As noted in Chapter 1, moreover, the circumstances surrounding the assumption of caregiving in the crack epidemic also appeared to make for a qualitatively different experience of this role than that previously described.

In short, although historical and contemporary accounts of the black extended family, and of the traditional role of the grandmother within that family, provide an important anchor for the current research, they remain an incomplete framework for analysis. This incompleteness lies, in part, in the relative lack of attention paid to newer manifestations of the traditional grandmother role in skipped generation families, where the extended family is composed of grandparents and the young children in their care.

Finally, as noted earlier, the prevalence of newer, more tenuous manifestations of the grandmother role in African American families represents a further and largely unexplored aspect of the cultural context of caregiving (Burton & Bengtson, 1985). Burton's (1985) earlier mentioned study of grandparental role behavior revealed that for many of the younger grandmothers interviewed, competing role demands in multigenerational families, and discomfort with the association of grandparenthood with "being an elder" led to significant tensions in the new role. Such tensions, as Burton and Bengtson (1985, p. 77) have pointed out, "are not reported in portrayals of the 'traditional' black grandmother's role." For these younger grandmothers, and indeed, for perhaps even the majority of today's mid-life and older women, "the dominant grandparental role type may well be tenuous" (Burton & Bengtson, 1985, p. 67).

The popularity and likely prevalence of a more vague and ill-defined grandparent role in the black community provides important insights into our understanding of grandparent caregiving. For as we shall see, the assumption of a more traditional grandparent/surrogate parent role by the women in our study did not imply for the majority a belief in either the appropriateness or the desirability of this role.

For the most part, the women we interviewed had expected and looked forward to baby-sitting and helping out with the grandchildren, but in a peripheral rather than a central caregiving capacity. As one great grandmother put it:

> I'd just like to be on the sidelines and if needed, to be able to help out not because I *have* to but because I *want* to. There's a difference between doing things because you want to and doing things because you have to. When you do things because you want to, you can appreciate them more. But when you're doing things because you have to, you get some pretty bad thoughts sometimes.

As will be discussed in Chapter 10, fully three quarters of the women in our study had spent periods ranging from several months to many years as children living with their own grandparents, and the notion of a strong grandmother caregiver was thus often deeply ingrained. Many of the women had also helped raise nieces, nephews, and other children, in addition to their own offspring, prior to their assumption of caregiving in the crack cocaine epidemic.

Yet for many of these same women, intense conflict was seen to exist between the traditional role of the black grandmother and the desired, tenuous role—being "on the sidelines"—and helping out with the grandchildren "because I want to," and not because one is their sole or primary caregiver.

The cultural context of grandparent caregiving in African American communities is, in short, a complex one. It is shaped and conditioned not only by extended family norms and the traditional role of the black grandmother, but also by changing sociocultural and demographic conditions and the newer roles and family formations to which they have given rise.

Caring for one's grandchildren as a consequence of the current drug epidemic is, in many ways, a new and unique experience. Yet it is also an experience that cannot be understood in isolation from the broader gender and cultural contexts within which it is embedded.

As feminist writings on gender make clear, family caregiving is at once unseen and undervalued, both in relation to the public world of paid work and in public policies predicated on a "family ethic" stressing women's duty to care (Abel, 1991; Abramowitz, 1988). Occupants of the role are indeed "women in the middle," (Brody, 1981), caught between competing role demands and generations, and caught, too, between the myriad of conflicting emotions that make this—like other forms of family caring—an activity fraught with ambivalence and ambiguity.

The literature on African American family and community life deepens and extends our understanding of gender and caregiving within this ethnic group. The role of the black grandmother caregiver thus appears rich in a tradition emphasizing extended family norms and shared child care as key adaptive strategies. Yet the circumstances surrounding such caregiving in many black families and communities in the 1980s and 1990s make for a far more complex and challenging experience, emotionally, economically, and socially, than may previously have been the case.

In the chapters that follow we will explore many dimensions of grandparent caregiving, drawing most heavily on the experiences, feelings, and insights of black grandmothers whose assumption of the caregiving role was a direct consequence of the crack cocaine epidemic. Utilizing the combined conceptual frameworks presented above, we will attempt to explore the diversity and richness of grandparent caregiving under these unique historical circumstances. And we will consider, too, how our public policies treat, and often badly mistreat, the increasing numbers of women who have put their own lives "on hold" in order to become caregivers to their grandchildren.

# 3

## Hearing the Voices, Telling the Stories: The Grandparent Caregiver Study

Beginning a project like the Grandparent Caregiver Study was a little like starting on a journey—lots of high hopes and expectations coexisting with significant trepidation about all of the unknowns ahead.

There were things we were unsure of when we started. We didn't know whether we could do this on the ambitious timetable or limited budget we had constructed. We didn't know if we knew enough about the intricacies of crack addiction, child welfare regulations, or African American experience to ask the right questions or explore all of the relevant areas. We didn't know if black women would trust white women with details of their life experience, or if we as younger, white women would understand what was offered to us (see Burton & Bengtson, 1982, for a good discussion of some of these issues).

But there were other things we were very sure of. We were sure of the urgency and importance of the grandmothers' story being told. Their perspective would add depth to the historical record and provide a richer context for the needed policy changes and community interventions. We also had a profound confidence in people's ability to understand and express the circumstances and dynamics of their own lives. We felt that we had tools to help bring that understanding forward. We had an appreciation for and familiarity with Oakland after more than 20 years of community participation. And we had our own friendship of many years and excitement about doing this project together.

Aware of our limitations as "outsiders," we were convinced that being outsiders offered some important advantages (Duster, 1987a). We felt that our perspective might add a complementary depth and comparison to what the grandmothers told us. As outsiders, we might take less for granted. Indeed, our awareness of our outsider role forged our commitment to a particular approach to the project. As described by Lofland (1974, p. 4):

> The commitment to get close, to be factual, descriptive, and quotive constitutes a significant commitment to represent the participants in their own terms. This does not mean that one becomes an apologist for them, but rather that one faithfully depicts what goes on in their lives and what life is like for them . . . so that one's audience is at least partially able to project themselves into the point of view of the people depicted.

That became our goal. We knew that we could not give the definitive account of our respondents' experience, but we hoped that we could bring forward, and even shine new light on, the complex, sentient, and everyday experience of grandmother caregivers.

## METHODOLOGY

Bringing forward private, everyday experience and transforming it into data relevant to practitioners and policymakers required a study methodology that was at once flexible and systematic. We were committed to an approach that would honor the integrity of women's experience (Devault, 1990; Klein, 1983), that would expect and accommodate differences among respondents (Spender, 1983), and that could be flexible enough to embrace unexpected events that might occur during, or because of, the research process (Woodhouse & Livingood, 1991). We needed a framework that would allow the integration of different kinds of data (Denzin, 1970). And we needed a methodology that was able to utilize respondents' words as data, to make visible that which is seldom shared and frequently discounted, and to bring it all forward in the authentic voice of those who would tell us the stories (Devault, 1990; Du Bois, 1983; Marshall & Rossman, 1989).

We decided on an overall design that was exploratory, descriptive, and grounded in the principles of interactive, community-based research. Called "passionate scholarship" by Barbara Du Bois (1983), this approach

> demands rigor, precision, and responsibility [as] it makes possible a common endeavor of science-making that can actually engage the conjunctions

among values, purposes, methods and modes of knowing that can begin to integrate subjective with objectivity, substance with process, passion with responsibility, and the knower with the known. (p. 112)

Our design was participatory, emphasizing the building of partnerships, in which community members worked with the researchers in all stages of the research process, from initial conceptualization through utilization of results (Hall, 1975). This commitment influenced all of our decisions and required walking the often fine line between retaining scientific merit as a research project and fostering a sense of local ownership and responsibility (Carlaw, Mittlemark, Bracht, & Luepker, 1984). In short, we felt strongly that both the research process and the use of our study outcomes should foster empowerment of the participants (Marti-Costa & Serrano-Garcia, 1983).

Our primary mode of data collection was a two-part in-depth interview with 71 respondents. However, the interviews took place within the context of a growing set of community activities designed for, and increasingly by, grandmother caregivers. As a result, our data came from a number of sources: interviews, observations, and hundreds of hours of field notes over a 2-year period of involvement with grandparent caregivers.

**The Research Team**

The project began with the assembling of a research team that would be well equipped to engage in the in-depth and often sensitive interviewing process that the study would entail. Four African American graduate students from the University of California at Berkeley and San Jose State University were selected as team members. Each had extensive community experience in the fields of health education or social work, and three of the four had already worked in the area of substance abuse and African American families. All four had excellent interpersonal skills, and all were committed to the need for and potential contributions of the planned research.

In addition to the graduate students, the team included a community liaison whose role was to help bridge potential gaps between insiders and outsiders, between the universities and the community, and between the white co-investigators and the African American women who would be participating in the study. A field placement supervisor at U.C. Berkeley's School of Public Health, the individual chosen to fill this role was already heavily involved in the Oakland community both through her work and through her own church-related activities. As an older black woman herself, she was able to play an integral role as "cultural guide," helping us think through the many ethical and practical questions that the research entailed, as well as how best to conduct the research in a way that would be empowering to all involved.

The community liaison also played a key role in helping us establish a Community Advisory Group. She joined us in meeting with representatives of two key community-based organizations in Oakland—the West Oakland Health Center and United Seniors of Oakland—explaining and eliciting feedback on the proposed study, and seeking their help in identifying key agencies and individuals to be included in an advisory capacity.

Based on that initial feedback, and on a series of informational interviews conducted with other local health and social service professionals, community organizers, and individuals working with grandparents or young children in Oakland, 14 individuals were invited to serve as part of the Grandparent Caregiver Study Community Advisory Group. Of the original invited members, 12 became actively involved in almost all phases of the research, and met regularly with us for more than a year and a half.

One of the first tasks of the Community Advisory Group was to assist us in developing the overall design of the research process. Their input was invaluable in helping us work out the mechanics of arranging for and conducting interviews, developing our recruitment and outreach strategy, identifying appropriate compensation for respondents, and gently teaching us the crucial points of etiquette and sensitivity when working in this community. Members of the Advisory Group also provided critical moral support: They were unwavering not only in their belief that the study was important, but also that we, as a large team of researchers and community advisors, were equal to the task.

The Community Advisory Group continued meeting regularly for a period of several months after the data collection was completed, discussing policy implications of the study, critical next steps, and how best to make the findings accessible and meaningful both to study participants and to the broader Oakland community. As will be noted later, moreover, several of the Advisory Group members have subsequently helped form a community coalition on grandparent caregiving, which continues to meet monthly and was a direct outgrowth of the Grandparent Caregiver Study.

**Selecting a Theoretical Sample**

One of the crucial decisions we faced early on regarded the kind of sample and sampling strategy that would best meet the goals of our study.

We were well aware of the potential value of case finding research, especially because no one in Oakland, or anywhere else, seemed to know exactly how many grandparents were the sole or primary caregivers for their young grandchildren. Nor were there any current and reliable estimates of how many children were permanently living with their grandparents. We knew that these numbers would be important for policymakers and others advocating for the health and welfare of families.

We also knew, however, that it would be premature to begin counting when no one was exactly sure what we should count. The prevalence and difficulty of grandparent caregiving under the unique and complex circumstances of the crack epidemic had introduced too many unknowns into the more familiar patterns of extended family care. Therefore, we decided that an open theoretical sample (Glaser & Strauss, 1967), specifically designed to identify, investigate, and describe as many different caregiving experiences as possible, would be most useful at this point.

Open theoretical sampling is a standard component of qualitative research. *Open sampling* may be defined as a strategy used to find the variabilities and commonalities within the phenomenon under investigation (Miles & Huberman, 1984). These "discoveries" are made progressively, through a reflexive process of sampling, contrasting, comparing, and sampling again (Mullen, 1985-1986).

*Theoretical sampling* begins by casting a wide net, looking for any persons, places, or situations that might inform and orient the researchers. As simultaneous data collection and analysis continue, the sampling becomes increasingly discriminate and focused on those areas of particular importance to the emerging understanding of the phenomenon (Strauss & Corbin, 1990). Over time, a dense and rich sample can be developed as the researchers move between minimizing and maximizing differences in the subjects and situations they select. The end result is new knowledge: a "re-presentation" of what has been shared by the respondents from their own lived experience and in their own words (Hayes-Bautista, 1976), understood, developed, and expressed from the unique perspective of the researchers.

In our case, we continually sought difference and variation in our sample through constant comparison of who we had talked to and what they had told us. We initially sought to compare older and younger grandmothers, married versus single women, those who worked outside the home and those who were unemployed, women caring for only one child and those caring for more than one, and grandmothers embedded in an active support system compared to those who were more isolated. As we interviewed, we discovered new experiences that led to new comparisons, extended our outreach, and, as time went on, led to more deliberate selection of respondents. We continued recruiting, interviewing, comparing, and recruiting again until we reached "saturation"—the point at which, despite the important differences in every family's story, the core themes were being raised by every new respondent (Glaser & Strauss, 1967).

We knew that choosing a theoretical sample, rather than one that was random or even statistically representative, would limit our ability to generalize any patterns of distribution that we found within our sample. As suggested above, the strength of open sampling, and its chief advantage in exploratory research like ours, would be its ability to capture a greater range of experiences than would be possible with a similarly sized random sample. However, even within a theoretical sampling frame, the greater the number of cases, the greater is the power to count, rather than merely describe, the phenomenon being explored (Strauss & Corbin, 1990). With this in mind, we sought as rich and as large a sample as possible.

We arrived at our final sample of 71 based on our recognition of saturation and our need to synthesize all that we had learned. Although it was not our primary goal, we were pleased that the final count was sufficient to legitimize some basic descriptive statistical analysis of our quantitative data. Later, we learned that the sample was even more representative than we had either thought or intended. Once completed, the demographic profile of our respondents was found to correspond well to the profile of grandparent caregivers recently identified through a large random sample ($N = 1,377$) of 50% of the clients attending three child health clinics in New York City (Brouard & Joslin, 1991). In that study, the 118 grandparent caregivers identified were all grandmothers, great grandmothers, or great-aunts who ranged in age from 39 to 77 with a median age of 55. In our own study, the range was a very similar 41-79, with a median of 53. In both samples, moreover, well over half of the women were caring for two or more young children.

## Sample Recruitment and Selection

The Community Advisory Group played a central role in the construction of a rich and varied sample. Their advice, community experience, and design and dissemination of an invitational flyer brought our efforts to the attention of a wide group of people. Based on their assistance, the final sample was recruited through a dense network of community contacts, active referral from local health and social service providers, wide dissemination of the flyer, and snowball referral from study participants. The latter two strategies were especially effective in helping us find caregivers who were without phones, were not well connected to health and social services, and, in other ways, most likely would have been missed through more traditional sampling methods.

To be included in our sample, potential respondents had to have assumed full caregiving responsibility for at least one youngster under the age of 5 due to the crack involvement of the child's parents. In order to develop a picture of caregiving within a situated context, sampling was restricted to black women living in Oakland or near its borders. For the purposes of this research, the term *grandmother* was used broadly to include great grandmothers and great-aunts, as well as biological grandmothers.

The recruitment appeal invited women who were interested in the study to contact a designated Advisory Group member who explained the study in more detail and, if the woman was still interested and met the sample criteria, facilitated phone contact with a member of the research team. As time went on and the study became well known in the community, the intermediate contact with an Advisory Group member became less frequent. Respondents were informed that participation was entirely voluntary and that their decision would not effect their status with social service or community agencies in any way. They also were told that they would not be identified by name, that their responses would be held in the strictest confidence, that they had the right to refuse to respond to any questions, that they could terminate the interview at any time, and that they would be paid $50 for their participation in the two interviews.

If the invitation to participate was accepted, the interviews were conducted, usually a week apart, at the time and place most convenient to the respondent. The interviews, which were tape-recorded with the respondent's permission, lasted an average of 3 hours. Interviewing occurred between July 1990 and September 1991.

## The Study Sample

A total of 129 women were referred to us during the recruitment period. Of the 129, 80 women met the sample criteria and were invited to participate in the study. Six women refused for a variety of reasons, including scheduling conflicts, illness, or "going through a bad time." Of the 49 who did not qualify, reasons for exclusion included temporary caregiving, children over age 5, caregiving for reasons other than the consequences of crack use, or residence beyond the Oakland area. Completed interviews with 3 of the remaining 74 participants had to be later disqualified for the same reasons.

The great majority of respondents (86%) had assumed primary re-sponsibility for one (25%), two (37%), or three (23%) children under the age of 5. One grandmother had seven and one set of grandparents was caring for 10 of their grandchildren, three of whom were 3 years old. Ten respondents (14%) were caring for at least one great grandchild; five were caring for the young children of their nieces or nephews.

More than half of the respondents (54%) had at least one of their own children still living at home; the others had been living without children in the household, often for a number of years, when they had to assume primary caregiving for a grandchild. Respondents had been in this new role from 6 months to 5 years at the point of interview. At least nine of the respondents (13%) had raised other youngsters, usually their grand-children.

All but three respondents reported receiving some governmental support for the grandchildren they were raising; 81% reported receiving Aid to Families with Dependent Children (AFDC) for at least one child and 15% specified receiving Foster Care support. Ten women (14%) reported that they did not receive either.

Self-reported financial status ranged from "okay" (13%) to "very poor" (35%), with more than half of the respondents reporting that they were "not doing very well" (52%) and no one reporting doing "very well." Although respondents lived across 13 Oakland zip code areas, 72% of the sample ($n = 51$) lived within 10 zip codes in which at least 40% of the population had annual household incomes of less than $15,000 (National Planning Data Corporation, 1989). The 1990 poverty line for a family of four was $13,359.

Three quarters of the respondents (78%) reported that their income had decreased since they had assumed responsibility for their grandchildren, with the remaining 22% reporting that their income had remained the same since caregiving began. The majority of the sample (69%) felt that their income was inadequate to meet their needs.

## The Interview

As noted earlier, each participant was interviewed twice, usually one week apart, at the time and place of her choosing. Most interviews were conducted in the woman's home, but we did meet women at the local mall, at local restaurants, and even after hours at a beauty salon if they preferred. Although it was possible to complete the interviews within 2 hours, we quickly found that they tended to last much longer.

The interviews followed a format designed specifically for this study. The two interview schedules incorporated quantitative and qualitative assessments in a variety of areas including physical and emotional health, daily routine, social support and coping, the economic costs of caregiving, combining work and child care, relations with other family members, and parenting at this point in their lives. We also spent considerable time exploring the grandchildren's needs with particular attention to areas that place unusual strain on the primary caregiver. In almost all cases, we learned quite a bit about the adult child involved with crack, especially when that child was still using drugs, living on the streets, and/or involved or "interfering" with the grandmother's caregiving. We asked participants about their dreams for the future and their advice for policymakers, community leaders, and service providers. And we always left plenty of time to discuss anything else that they wanted to share.

Because the principal investigators were both white women, an interviewing strategy was selected that involved a team interview, conducted by one of the researchers and an African American Research Assistant, and a shorter, follow-up interview conducted 1 to 2 weeks later by the Research Assistant alone. We had anticipated that study participants might be more comfortable, and therefore, perhaps, more candid, at the second contact, and built in checks for reliability by including many identically worded questions in the first and second interviews. As will be discussed later, however, comparison of the data obtained from the sessions revealed a high degree of consistency of response, and the sharing of considerable amounts of often deeply personal information and feelings in both interviews.

The first interview lasted an average of 3 hours and covered the areas that we considered to be absolutely essential to understanding the story and exploring the key variables. The second interview enabled us to probe areas we had missed or not fully explored the first time. As noted above, it also provided a chance for us to ask some of the questions—in areas such as physical and emotional health and social support and coping—a second time as an indicator of reliability. But most important, the second interview was set up to allow the respondent to have some time after the initial meeting to reflect on what she had told us and add or change anything she might feel was important.

We were committed to leaving study participants with something tangible at the end of the interview so we always went out with a variety of supplies. The financial support from our Foundation sponsor enabled us to pay the respondents $25 for each interview. We brought that money, in cash, in an envelope and always gave it directly to the grandmother at the end of the session. We also brought a small library of resources: the women were each given handouts on local support groups; information on health care, substance abuse, and recovery programs; and notices of upcoming community events. On the advice of our Advisory Group, we also left each woman with a small handmade gift as a more personal token of our thanks, followed up with a hand-written thank-you note.

At the end of the first interview, each respondent was told that we would hold a special event at the conclusion of the study to honor those who had participated and to share the initial findings. We felt strongly that the results of this study "belonged to" the community, and prior to disseminating those results through professional meetings, journal articles, or policy briefings, we wanted to give the data back to study participants, and to involve them in deciding how the findings should be used.

## Qualitative Data
## Collection and Analysis

The exploratory goal of this study, and its emphasis on caregiving as perceived by the caregivers themselves, meant that the heart of our methodology was qualitative. In asking women about adjusting to their new role and their daily routine, their relationships with their adult children, about the trigger events that led to their taking primary responsibility for their grandchildren, their expected life trajectory, their relationships with their own grandmothers, and their advice for policymakers, we relied on open-ended, semistructured interviews. Called "conversations with a purpose" (Kahn & Cannell, 1957), these interviews allowed the respondent to tell us as much as she could, or as much as she wanted to, about the areas of concern to her, first and foremost. The use of "multiple in-depth conversations" (Rheinharz, 1983) facilitated the sharing of areas of concern between the respondents and the research team. Our open-ended approach, and the deliberate leisure of plenty of time to converse, meant that we were able to listen carefully to not only the words that were said, but to the way in which the respondents were framing and structuring their responses.

All interviews were tape recorded. The tapes were transcribed, and both tapes and transcriptions were reviewed many times by various members of the research team. The presence of two interviewers and the availability of tape transcriptions decreased the risks of distortion, misinterpretation, or introduction of personal bias on the part of the researchers. The multiple comparisons also enabled us to check for implausible or significantly incomplete information and to make attempts to verify, substantiate, or further explore any individual respondent's account.

Qualitative analysis occurred concurrently with data collection. As interviews were conducted, core themes were identified, particularly rich quotes were recorded and shared, case study accounts were developed, and further sampling needs were determined. As is standard practice in qualitative analysis, what we were coming to know about grandparent caregiving was continually related back to what we did not yet know, in a constant "interplay of figure and ground" (Rheinharz, 1983, p. 183). Our ongoing analysis of the interview and observational data was designed to be interactive, fostering dialogue between the members of the research team, the Advisory Group, study participants, and community leaders, practitioners, and activists.

Assessment of the validity of qualitative data requires the incorporation of a rigorous process of checking facts, accounts, and interpretations throughout all phases of the research (Whyte, Greenwood, & Lazes, 1991). To us, coherence, resonance, and usefulness to participants, practitioners, and policymakers were the criteria against which we measured the validity of our qualitative findings.

In our study, the respondents were the key to making sure that our data, and what we did with it, were honest, coherent, and appropriate. We structured respondent participation into the study in several ways. First and foremost were the interviews, in which respondents were encouraged to tell us anything they felt it was important for us to know. In addition to the open-ended nature of much of the conversation, each respondent was asked at the end of each interview if there were other questions or areas she thought that we should explore with other grandparent caregivers. Their recommendations were invaluable in helping us zero in on areas we might have overlooked or deemed unimportant. Participants also provided valuable suggestions of ways that we might better probe responses that were vague or incomplete.

Respondents were asked to refer us to other caregivers they knew, particularly those we might miss through our normal recruitment channels. As they told us the stories of women they thought we should talk to, we began to piece together a richer picture of their sense of context, which, in turn, helped us validate their information and our interpretations.

As we began to identify core themes, we actively brought those back to women we had interviewed before, or to new interviewees, presenting what we were hearing, what we made of it, and eliciting their reaction. In these interactions, we were particularly interested in their assessments of the accuracy and utility of our interpretations, and their sense of the generalizability of what we were finding.

As a broad check for validity, we frequently took our emerging understanding of grandparent caregiving to others who might have been eligible for the study but, for a variety of reasons, were not going to be directly involved. We also responded to many requests to share emerging findings with community groups, health care providers, and policymakers. Official presentations, telephone requests for information from us, informal social gatherings, and fortuitous conversations, all provided opportunities to share what we were learning and to measure its resonance against the experience of others. These varied and interactive activities served to increase our confidence in the integrity and validity of our qualitative data.

## Quantitative Data
## Collection and Analysis

A number of areas, such as physical health, emotional health, and social support, did lend themselves to the use of quantitative, as well as qualitative, methods. In these domains, we took full advantage of the opportunity to blend methodologies.

The quantitative portions of our interviews drew upon items from a variety of sources. Wherever possible we included the use of questions and measures that had been previously validated and used effectively with African American populations and/or with older adult samples. In exploring the women's perceptions of their physical health and how it had changed over time, for example, we utilized a variety of global self-rated health measures that have been used with African American samples and shown to correlate well with objective health indicators (Andersen, Mullner, & Cornelius; 1987; Kaplan & Comacho, 1983).

Global self-ratings of emotional health were utilized along with an emotional health scale validated for use with older adults (Moriwaki, 1974). By enabling us to look quantitatively at how many of our sample members had experienced any of a variety of mood states over the past week, the latter provided an important complement to more qualitatively oriented questions about the caregivers' perceptions of emotional health and well being (see Chapter 5 this volume).

There were other important areas of emotional health in which specific quantitative measures were available for incorporation into the interviews. In examining the social support and social networks of grandparent caregivers, for example, we were able to benefit from the existence of a variety of previously validated questions and scales that have been used effectively across ethnic and age group lines. Berkman and Syme's (1979) social support index and portions of the Lubben Social Network Scale (Lubben, 1988) were among the instruments used in this regard.

Responses to the standardized quantitative questions provided an important context within which to understand the unique accounts of each grandmother's situation. For example, a particular grandmother's qualitative account of how depressed she had been last week, when her adult daughter came over high on crack and demanded to see the children, took on added meaning when we learned that fully 72% of the women interviewed had been "depressed or very unhappy" at least part of that week. Together, these findings alerted us to the prevalence of depression and gave us various points from which to engage the respondent in discussion of this crucial topic. Similarly, qualitative information often sensitized us to areas we might probe with more structured, albeit unvalidated, quantitative questions. The resulting picture of grandparent caregiving thus was able to provide the depth and power of individual accounts against a backdrop of the distribution of that experience across a larger group of caregivers.

## LIMITATIONS OF THE STUDY

None of the quantitative methods used in this study could alone have told the complex stories we hoped to capture. But neither, of course, could the qualitative methods. As Brewer and Hunter (1989, pp. 16-17) have pointed out:

> Our individual methods may be flawed, but fortunately the flaws in each are not identical. A diversity of imperfection allows us to combine methods not only to gain their individual strengths, but also to compensate for their particular faults and limitations. The multimethod approach is largely built upon this insight.

There are, of course, several important limitations to this study of grandparent caregiving. Our study, and its sample selection strategy, were designed to explore and describe experiences, rather than count caregiving households or compare this group of caregivers to any other population. As a result, we are unable to tell, based on our own data, how often the experiences we heard about occur in other families, nor are we able to claim that our specific findings are generalizable beyond the 71 women in our study. Our selection of a theoretical sample also restricts our quantitative analysis to the use of descriptive statistics and, necessarily, precludes multivariate analysis and hypothesis testing.

Qualitative methodologies, so appropriate for a new phenomenon such as grandparent caregiving in the crack epidemic, have their own limitations that are certainly relevant to this study. We relied almost exclusively on the words and actions of the caregivers whom we came to know as we collected and analyzed our data. Other than our judgment of people, the triangulation of perspectives, and the benefit of repeated contacts, there is no way to guarantee that our respondents told us the truth. We did not search records, we did not request verification of information, and we scrupulously protected the confidentiality of what we had been told; as a result, we can only stand on the informed intuition of our entire research team that what we heard, and saw, and learned is indeed true.

We also know that we did not hear every story. Our saturation point may have been premature and based more on our own needs to synthesize what we had learned than an accurate assessment that we had learned all that was there. We know, for example, that we did not reach any grandparents who were currently living on the streets, and we know, from our conversations with caregivers and social workers, that there are homeless grandparents who are fully responsible for the care of their young grandchildren. We also know that we did not speak with anyone who was severely dysfunctional due to alcohol or other drugs, illness, or other circumstances. Given the distribution of those events in the general population we have to assume that there are grandparent caregivers in those situations as well. And we also know that we did not talk with anyone who was not, at some level, "ready to talk." The experience of all of these "missing cases" will be important to add to the growing picture of grandparent caregiving.

Another important addition to the overall picture will be the experiences of those explicitly left out of our study. Anecdotal data strongly suggest that the drug epidemic in the United States has shattered families of all ethnicities. Their stories need to be added to our initial account of the experiences of African American families. And so must the stories of grandparents who, for reasons other that the drug involvement of their children, have become the primary caregivers for grandchildren of all ages. Indeed, this initial study gave rise to a subsequent effort intended to understand better the experience of grandparent caregiving across the country (see Chapter 12 this volume). Each of these additions will add to our growing understanding of the experiences, needs, and contributions of grandparents raising grandchildren.

## COMMUNITY ACTIVITIES

It is impossible to end a discussion of the methods of the Grandparent Caregiver Study without including the community activities that became such a central part of our experience. Somewhat naively, we initially imagined that our primary contact with the grandmothers would begin and end with the interviews. As noted above, we planned to have an event after we had completed the analysis in which we would formally thank each one for participating, and present initial results. We did not anticipate, nor did we plan for, any other significant activity beyond the seemingly formidable tasks of recruitment, interviewing, and analysis over the 9 months in the field. But that was before we met the grandmothers.

Our experience of interviewing grandmother caregivers was far more intense than any of us anticipated. Day after day, we found ourselves in the homes of women who shared some of the most intimate details of their lives with us. Our interview schedule called for us to probe personal areas such as coping, stress, marital relationships, loneliness, vulnerability, and unexpected change in middle or later life. However, the women in our study shared much more than that with us. On their own, they offered accounts of their parenting experiences, their disappointments and losses, their own perceived failures or the failures of the social system to nurture and protect their children. In response, we offered support, validation, resources and referral when we could, and, sometimes even our own experiences of parenting, caregiving, or family life. The words of other researchers (Watson, Irwin, & Michalske, 1991) nicely echo our experience of this study:

> It became increasingly difficult and less desirable as the study progressed to remain completely detached from our respondents. . . . Our role as researchers did not exempt us from feeling empathy, and it went a long way toward allowing our respondents to see us as real people living in the real world who could relate to them as human beings. (p. 510)

From our perspective, women we met through the study have become friends and colleagues in a deeply personal way. From what respondents have told us, many felt that being interviewed was the first time that anyone cared to listen to their experience, and the first time that they felt able to confide some of their feelings to another person. Indeed, several said that the most important thing in their lives in recent years was taking on the care of their grandchildren but that the second most important thing was participating in the Grandparent Caregiver Study.

As much as they have enriched our lives, the by-products of the study go far beyond individual friendships. From the very first interviews, we knew that this was a group of women of unusual courage, spirit, and humor. Their love for their grandchildren was seemingly boundless. Their energy was already stretched to the limit but they could summon up strength for anything that would provide security or opportunity for their grandchildren. And they were interested in helping each other. For all of these reasons, the scope of our activities grew.

The event we had planned for the end of the study became a much more significant celebration. Through the generosity of community merchants, local organizations, the study's Foundation sponsor, and a local medical center, we were able to host an elegant luncheon at a waterfront restaurant in one of the city's most popular entertainment areas. Child care and transportation were provided, there was entertainment, a lovely lunch, and a chance for grandmothers to dress up (which they did!), meet each other, and enjoy an afternoon in their honor.

An important part of the luncheon event was a brief formal program. During this time, we presented the preliminary results of the study and heard the grandmothers reflect on the experience of participating in a research project. As noted above, we also used this opportunity to ask participants what "next steps" they'd like to see taken, and how they hoped the study findings could be used in informing policy and in other ways helping to meet the needs of grandparent caregivers.

Every woman received a corsage, a certificate of participation, a resource manual for grandparent caregivers (Legal Services for Prisoners with Children, 1990), a booklet of preliminary study results, and personal thanks for her contribution. Members of the research team and the Advisory Group also were able to get 71 gift donations from local merchants that allowed us to have a drawing in which every woman received a personal gift. The gifts were all things stimulated by comments the grandmothers had made in the interviews: certificates for a half day of respite care, manicures, trips to the beauty salon, picture frames, albums, books, and even a trip for two on a national airline.

In order to make sure that the celebration reflected the special desires and wishes of the grandmothers, we asked several of the respondents if they would like to help us plan the event. This group became an official subcommittee that met with us biweekly for 2 months, planning not only the luncheon celebration but also a children's party to be held the month before. Subcommittee members pointed out to us that, although the grandmothers needed a day away and would enjoy the luncheon, they would not be able to relax unless they felt that they had done "something special" for their grandchildren, especially with the holidays approaching. And so, the celebration stretched into two events: the January luncheon for grandmothers and a Christmas party for the grandchildren.

Through the planning committee's efforts, an elaborate children's Christmas party ensued, with more than 135 grandchildren, and their grandmothers, in attendance. In addition to pastries and punch from local stores, enough gift donations were gathered to enable the party's Santa Claus—one of the grandfathers—to distribute an age-appropriate toy and book to each child by name.

Although the parties brought sparkle and some much needed relaxation to the holidays, we were keenly aware that the more critical and longer term need was for ongoing support and assistance for grandparent caregivers. Another important by-product of the Grandparent Caregiver Study, therefore, involved the support it was able to provide for several community interventions that either were in the planning stages or had recently been initiated when the study got under way.

One of these, the warm line for grandparent caregivers described in Chapter 12, had been started informally by a member of the study's Advisory Group shortly before our data gathering began. Operating out of a concerned city supervisor's office, the warm line was designed to provide emotional and other needed support for local grandparents raising their grandchildren. Although its founder began by handling all of the calls herself, she hoped to recruit and train grandparent caregivers as peer counselors who could help staff the phone line and provide important empathic support for other grandparents who called in. As we came to know the participants in the Grandparent Caregiver Study, we were able to discuss the warm line with several who had expressed an interest in doing something to help other grandparents who suddenly found themselves parenting again. Several of the women we spoke to subsequently undertook the training and became warm line volunteers.

The study also was able to assist a community-based project, Families United Against Crack Cocaine, with the production and dissemination of a newsletter for and by grandparent caregivers and their grandchildren (see Chapter 12 this volume). The project director of Families United, a member of the study Advisory Group, was beginning work on the newsletter as the study got under way, and hoped to find grandparents interested in contributing articles or editorial assistance. Our early interviews underscored the potential importance of the newsletter project: Many grandmothers spoke of the need for more information, and more than one even brought up the need for a newsletter or similar vehicle that would help local grandparents feel less isolated. Research team members from San Jose State University were able to secure seed money from their university to help support the newsletter project, recruit grandparents interested in working on the newsletter, and participate in editorial meetings as the newsletter became a reality.

The Grandparent Caregiver Study also provided direct and indirect assistance to a church-based group in its efforts to lay the groundwork for a respite center for grandparent caregivers. As discussed later in the book, respite care was described by study participants as second only to financial assistance in terms of its importance to grandparents raising grandchildren. The lack of such child care had forced many women to quit their jobs, and posed a tremendous financial burden to almost all of the grandmothers we interviewed.

By sharing with the church-based group our preliminary study findings on the need for respite services, we were able to provide the documentation they needed for their efforts in both consciousness raising and fund-raising. Members of the church group met with the study Advisory Group to share and receive input on their plans for developing a respite program, and members of the research team also helped directly with the church group's fund-raising efforts.

Finally, an important policy outgrowth of the study involved the creation of a community coalition to support legislation and other advocacy efforts by and for grandparent caregivers. In keeping with our goal of giving study findings back to the community, the first formal presentation of findings was made to members of the local Gray Panthers chapter as part of a larger panel on grandparent caregiving. The interest in "doing something" generated at this meeting was great, and study team members therefore worked with the Panthers to co-found a broad-based community coalition on grandparent caregiving. Termed the "Coalition for Grandparents Parenting Grandchildren," the coalition is composed of grandparent caregivers, legislative aides, community activists, health and social service providers, and others who meet monthly at a local senior center (see Chapter 12 this volume). Many of the Coalition members also are helping in the creation of a statewide coalition in support of grandparent caregivers.

Participating in these and other community activities has enabled the Grandparent Caregiver Study's research team members to help local groups and organizations utilize and build on the study's outcomes in a way that can ideally help influence policy and/or assist in the development of needed community interventions. Equally important, however, participation in such activities enabled the researchers to "give back" to the community of women who had so willingly and openly shared their lives, thoughts, and experiences and made the research possible.

* * *

Sociologist Robert Bellah and his colleagues (Bellah, Madsen, Sullivan, Swidler, & Tipton, 1985) have argued the importance of making research moral, by making participants collaborators and taking seriously the charge to "public responsibility" contained in the original meaning of the word *profession*.

The Grandparent Caregiver Study, on which much of this book is based, represents an attempt to meet Bellah's charge, by honoring and respecting the integrity of participants, bringing forward their authentic voices, grounding the study in principles of interactive community-based research, and trying to ensure that both the process and the results of the study foster empowerment of the participants. In addition, by discussing with the women and with Advisory Group members the potential policy and practice implications of our findings, and by helping concerned individuals, groups, and organizations access and utilize these findings to support community interventions and policy changes that would assist grandmother caregivers and their families, we attempted to increase the study's capacity to "give back" to the community of women who made the research possible.

The combination of qualitative and quantitative research methods employed in this study helped provide richness and depth, and further helped compensate for some of the limitations of any one approach used in isolation (Steckler, McLeroy, Goodman, Bird, & McCormick, 1992).

The Grandparent Caregiver Study did not seek to document the prevalence of grandparent caregiving, nor to examine a large random sample so that it might provide findings that would be generalizable. Rather, this exploratory study attempted to capture the lived experience of a diverse group of grandmother caregivers within one ethnic group and one geographic area, and to "re-present" what they shared with us in a way that could contribute to policy and practice, as well as further research.

The limitations of our study, described in this chapter and elsewhere in the book, underscore the need for much additional research in this complex and critical area. In writing this book, however, it is our hope to contribute to a process of illuminating the perceptions and experiences of a particular group of "forgotten caregivers" in a way that will stimulate greater attention to the special strengths, and the critical unmet needs, of grandparents who are raising the children of the crack epidemic.

# 4

---

# Assuming the Caregiver Role

In their examination of the African American extended family, Martin and Martin (1978, pp. 43-44) described several alternate routes by which black grandparents and other relatives most typically become the primary caregivers to young children. Assumption of the caregiver role was seen to occur "mainly out of economic necessity," when the children's parents lacked adequate resources due to their young age, lack of work, or an already large number of children.

But informal adoption by grandparents or other relatives also was seen as desired by some of these individuals because of the status and respect it brought within the family or because it was the only means available to prevent a child's being put up for adoption. For some grandmothers, raising their grandchildren offered a constructive way of dealing with their profound grief and helplessness over the circumstances of their adult child's life. For others, it provided a second chance to raise a child, and therefore ease the guilt they experienced over their earlier child rearing that some now felt, in the words of our own study participants, had been "too strict," "too permissive," "too reserved," or "too indulgent." Finally, grandparent caregivers were seen to take on this role sometimes out of a felt obligation, either to their own sons and daughters in need, or because as children, these grandparents had themselves been taken in by relatives (Martin & Martin, 1978).

Each of these motivations or reasons for the assumption of caregiving was mentioned by at least one, and usually more than one, of the women in our study. Yet for each, the primary motivation was to provide a safe and nurturing home for one's grandchildren, great grandchildren, or grandnieces or -nephews while their parents were involved with, or sought recovery from, crack cocaine.

A theme of the present book is that although grandparent caregiving has a long tradition in the African American community, those grandmothers who are raising grandchildren as a result of the crack epidemic are encountering an experience that is often substantively different from that of either their foremothers, or of their contemporaries who are caregiving for grandchildren under different circumstances. As will be described in more detail in Chapter 11, the often extreme neglect and abuse suffered by many children of crack involved parents, family and neighborhood violence in areas hard hit by the epidemic, the pain of watching the deterioration of an adult child on crack, societal labeling and treatment of "crack babies," and even "crack grandmothers," and the physical and behavioral problems experienced by some (though not all) cocaine exposed children are among the dimensions of the new caregiving that may contribute to both its complexity and its difficulty.

In this chapter, we will explore the circumstances surrounding women's assumption of a caregiver role for their grandchildren in the crack cocaine epidemic, and how the new role was taken on and reconciled with preexisting roles and responsibilities. The trigger events that catalyzed the assumption of full-time caregiving, and grandmothers' perceptions of how their own lives had changed because of the new role are examined, as are both the perceived pluses and minuses of their new positions as surrogate parents.

## ROUTES TO CAREGIVING

Several patterns emerged from our data with respect to the assumption of caregiving. The first of these involved a small minority of women for whom becoming a full-time caregiver for one's grandchildren happened quickly and often without warning. Fifty-nine-year-old Lucy Thomas was among the women whose experience fit this pattern. Although her daughter Kasandra had been involved with crack at one time, Mrs. Thomas was convinced that the young woman had straightened out; she was, after all, attending church regularly once again, and appeared to be caring for her four children, aged 3 through 12. Mrs. Thomas thought nothing was out of the ordinary when Kasandra dropped the kids off "for a couple of hours" one afternoon, asking that grandma baby-sit. Two hours quickly stretched into 2 months, however, with no word from Kasandra. And to Mrs. Thomas's chagrin and astonishment, the grandchildren never cried for their missing mother, and "didn't seem to care" when living with grandma became permanent.

For 56-year-old Ronda Leeds, the catalyst to becoming an "instant caregiver" occurred when her 2-year-old granddaughter was taken from her mother after the young woman's live-in boyfriend, who was also involved with crack, was accused of molesting the child. Like other grandmothers confronted with situations like this one, Mrs. Leeds stepped in quickly to take her grandchild and "keep the family together," rather than risk having the child placed with strangers through foster care.

Another version of this first pattern of a sudden assumption of full-time caregiving involved grandmothers taking in their grandchildren when an adult child was incarcerated. According to the U.S. Department of Justice (1991), more than three quarters of women prisoners are mothers, and two thirds of these have children under age 18. In most cases, it is the maternal grandmother who becomes caregiver during the period of incarceration (Barry, 1991; Dressel & Barnhill, 1991). Although many of the women we interviewed had had a drug involved child in and out of jail, the first incarceration of a young parent was often the time when the grandmother suddenly found herself a full-time caregiver for her grandchildren.

For several of the grandmothers we interviewed, an abrupt onset to full-time caregiving occurred when a hospital called to say that a daughter or niece who had just given birth had left the facility and abandoned the infant in the process. Fifty-six-year-old Mary Byrnes was at work when such a call came. "I didn't want to quit work," she said. "I didn't know the baby was drug exposed at first, so I just took a leave of absence, then ended up quitting." In such cases, the shock of sudden parenthood was often second only to discovering the extent of an adult child's drug involvement, and the toll it was taking.

A second and more frequent pattern in the assumption of caregiving involved a grandmother, great grandmother, or great-aunt negotiating informally with a crack involved relative to have the children come and stay with the grandmother while the substance abusing individual went into treatment or "straightened out." In many of these cases, the grandparents reported that their adult children or nieces had been "relieved" when the grandmother suggested the arrangement, and they freely admitted that it was in the best interest of the children. Fifty-seven-year-old Gayle Street's daughter was one of these, and as Mrs. Street put it, "I took them so she could get herself well."

In such cases, there was often continuing contact between a grand-mother and her adult child or other relative, with the latter often either living with the grandmother too or simply maintaining frequent contact while she made a genuine effort to "get clean." Forty-four-year-old Laura Shipley was among the grandmothers who reported letting a drug involved daughter or niece live with her and her grandchild "on a trial basis" while the young woman tried to stay off cocaine. Mrs. Shipley's niece and her 9-month-old baby had both moved in with her when they became homeless 4 years ago, and for a while the niece did try to stay away from drugs. When her efforts failed repeatedly, however, and she refused to get professional help, Mrs. Shipley insisted that she move out, and there has been little contact between the young woman and her aunt and child since then.

The majority of grandmothers who had informally arranged with their drug involved relatives to serve as primary caregivers to their children reported that money was never an issue. In these cases, it was assumed by all parties that any financial support, such as AFDC, coming in for the children would be handled by the grandmother. In a few cases, however, a financial arrangement lay at the base of an informal negoti-ation regarding the grandmother's assumption of caregiving. The grand-mother thus agreed to allowing her drug involved child to continue to receive the welfare check, and in exchange, that child permitted the grandmother to take the grandchildren into her care.

Fifty-four-year-old Sarah Thompson was one such grandmother, and had to stretch a small monthly paycheck of $650—her total source of income—in order to meet expenses and raise her 4-year-old grand-daughter. The girl was badly learning delayed and had a host of physical and emotional problems when Mrs. Thompson brought her back from her daughter's home in Nevada. And although things are "very tight" financially now, giving up access to AFDC seemed to Mrs. Thompson a small price to pay for the chance to "catch the girl up on her learning" and help her get a decent start in life.

Although this type of experience was not common among partici-pants in our study, it was reported often enough to help illuminate the complexity of the negotiation and the range of feelings it evoked. Grandmothers in this situation were almost always uncomfortable with the arrangement, expressing concern about enabling their child's con-tinued crack use or the diversion of already precious resources to the wrong person. Most were angry at their child's demands, or at a welfare system that they felt doesn't "pay attention to who's getting what and who really needs it." Some, such as 67-year-old Alice Clark, felt that they were doing something wrong by allowing their child to receive money meant for the grandchildren:

> I worked every day of my life for over 45 years and I never cheated the government or anybody else. I know this isn't right—she's out smokin' up the money somebody thinks is going for the babies—but I can hold my head up because it was the *only* way to get the babies out of that situation. If I had left them there they'd be dead or even worse by now.

We have looked so far at two patterns in the assumption of caregiving, the first involving a sudden and unanticipated thrust into the new role, and the second, an informal negotiation for caregiving responsibility with the adult child.

The third and by far the most prevalent route to caregiving typically began, like the second one, with a grandmother's growing awareness of and concern over the extent of an adult child's drug involvement, and the toll it was taking on the grandchildren. For grandparents fitting this pattern, assumption of the caregiver role often came after a difficult and sometimes protracted period of trying in vain to help the crack abusing relative to conquer the drug habit, "checking up" on the grandchildren, and providing more and increasingly lengthy informal care to ensure their well-being. This period usually came to a head when the grandparent felt forced either to take the child(ren) directly or to call the police or Child Protective Services to have them removed from the parents' home.

Some of the grandparents whose experience fit this pattern told of how the discovery of an adult child's drug habit (or the worsening of that habit) began a long process of taking increasing amounts of responsibility for the grandchildren. Vera Mullholland, a 44-year-old food service worker, talked of going to a daughter's apartment on her lunch break and on the way home from work each day to be sure her young grandchildren had food to eat and clean diapers and clothes to wear.

Evelyn Cross, a 57-year-old grandmother, watched weekend respite for her 3- and 4-year-old grandchildren stretch to weeks at a time, increasingly unannounced and open ended. For 49-year-old Dorothy Scott, it was hard to remember "how it happened. [It] just seems like they used to live with their mother and then they lived with me. I never dreamed it would be forever."

Sooner or later, an adult child or other relative "crossed the line," engaging in behavior that triggered, for the grandmother, the need for more drastic action.

For 53-year-old Sandra Young, the trigger came when she went to see her infant grandniece and found her having a severe asthma attack and in need of hospitalization. The gas and electricity had been shut off, and Mrs. Young's niece, high on alcohol and crack, had resisted her aunt's attempts to take the baby to the emergency room. The infant, who was also badly undernourished, "nearly died" on that occasion, and Mrs. Young realized she had no choice but to intervene and try to get custody. The trigger event for 58-year-old Sharon Lane is still almost too painful to recount. With tears in her eyes, she told of driving down a large street in downtown Oakland and being stunned to see her 1- and 2-year-old grandsons, dirty, disoriented, and only partially clothed, alone on the sidewalk while their mother was inside with a crack dealer.

For several of the grandmothers, the trigger event telling them that they had to step in happened when the parents of infant or young grandchildren took them to crack houses, or left them unattended for hours, and in some cases, days at a time. Sixty-three-year-old Shelley Henderson spoke in low tones of how her granddaughter had gotten evicted after using the rent money for drugs, and how she had left her baby unattended for long periods. "She was taking the baby to crack houses. . . leaving the baby at this one's house and that one's house—leaving the baby with no food, no diapers."

Other grandmothers spoke of their pain, anger, and incredulity on learning that a crack involved child had sold food stamps, diapers, or baby formula for crack. When the grandmothers confronted such realities, however, and took the painful step of reporting the children's parents to Child Protective Services, their nightmare often simply took a turn for the worse. Indeed, one of the hardest parts of the assumption of caregiving, according to many of the women we interviewed, was getting the authorities to take their concerns and warnings seriously.

Sally Fairlane, who now has custody of her 3- and 5-year-old great grandchildren, recounted her anger and frustration at trying in vain to get the social welfare people to intervene when she discovered just how badly the youngsters were being neglected by their crack involved mother:

> I was talking to social workers, trying to get them to *do* something for these children. I would send them over to where she was staying and tell them

the kids didn't have any food. And they'd go over and find a box of crackers and they'd say, "well, she's got food—as long as we see food in the house, there's nothing we can do." That's what they'd tell me. I told the social worker how she was selling the food stamps to buy drugs. He told me there was nothing he could do, that all he was supposed to do was give her the food stamps. I had to sit here and watch her get the money and walk out the door, down the street, and when she comes back she has no money, no diapers, no food stamps, nothing! . . . I had to let them go down to where [the social workers] had to step in, and the little baby almost died.

Forty-four-year-old Wanda Kehoe told a similar story:

The parents had no place to live, both were on drugs. I'd bring them Pampers and baby food and they'd sell them for drugs. The little boy was nearly starved when I got him. I asked [the Department of Social Services] "do you have to wait until there's a death?" They said, "Basically, yes." I finally just went and took them. The baby was nearly starved to death by then.

In short, then, the third and most commonly described route to the assumption of caregiving often entailed a lengthy process of growing disillusionment on two fronts. Grandmothers became disillusioned first with a crack involved child who appeared unwilling or unable to kick the habit and care for his or her children. Yet at least as disillusioning for many were their interactions with a social services bureaucracy mired in rules, and in an interpretation of child welfare that sometimes ends up hurting the very people it's meant to protect. As one grandmother put it:

Protective services! For years I phoned them, trying to get them to check up on my daughter and her kids. Nothing happened, nothing! Until she abandoned them. I don't know why they call them "protective services!"

As we shall see in Chapters 12 and 13, the anger and frustration many grandparents feel around their dealings with the bureaucracy as they attempt to assume caregiving often stay with them. For some, these experiences have served as the catalyst for mobilization in different parts of the country to change the system in order to better protect the rights of grandparents and the grandchildren in their care.

## LIFE CHANGES WITH
## THE ASSUMPTION OF CAREGIVING

Just as there were different routes to the assumption of the caregiver role, three patterns emerged from the data with respect to the type of life change that assuming the new role entailed.

For the majority of women, surrogate parenthood involved a major and abrupt disruption of mid- or late-life activities, as well as their plans and hopes for the future. Several subgroups of women fell into this category, including working women who had to quit their jobs in order to become full-time caregivers; elderly women whose long awaited "leisure time" was now filled with raising children all over again; and women in their forties and fifties who had recently completed their own child rearing, or who had only older teenage children at home when they took in their grandchildren.

Although such women were at different stages of the life cycle and faced varied life circumstances, the assumption of caregiving represented for each an abrupt transition necessitating major and often unwanted changes in how they lived their lives, and in what they anticipated would lie ahead.

For many women in this first category, the sudden loss of freedom and of being able to "do what I want to do," was a persistent theme. A 41-year-old grandmother raising three preschoolers lamented:

> I got a taste of freedom a year ago. I was just finished raising my children. I'd go around everywhere, get up whenever I wanted to. I didn't have any more babies to tend. Now when I go out, they come too.

A 62-year-old, who had prided herself on her meticulous housekeeping, commented:

> I thought I could take things easy. Once the house was clean, it stayed clean. There was no extra cooking or cleaning or washing. Everything is stress for me now because I can't relax or do what I want to do.

And for 48-year-old Gwen Eaker, raising five of her grandchildren:

> [My children's] responsibility has become my headache. I feel I've been cheated. I'm not ready for the rocking chair, but if I want to go out with friends, I can't. I feel like something has been stolen from me.

The theme of "feeling cheated" by the need to assume a new caregiving role came through in many of the interviews and supported earlier findings by Burton (1985) and others (Burton & Bengtson, 1985; Ladner & Gourdine, 1984) suggesting that many black grandmother caregivers would prefer a more tenuous grandparental role.

Although grandmothers in our study most often reported feeling cheated by their adult children ("I raised my kids, why can't they raise theirs?"), the failure of other family members to shoulder part of the responsibility for caregiving also led some to feel they had been taken advantage of. Paternal grandmothers raising their sons' children sometimes complained that the maternal grandparents should be playing more of a role. And several women who were raising their great grandchildren reported feeling cheated since the responsibility to provide care really should have fallen to the younger grandmothers (see Chapter 10 this volume). As Burton (1991b) similarly discovered in her research on black grandmother caregivers, there was sometimes a tendency for caregiving responsibility to be "pushed up the generational ladder" by younger grandmothers for whom the "off timing" of entry into grandparenthood made full-time caregiving for one's grandchildren a task they were unwilling to undertake.

For several of the women interviewed, the assumption of caregiving involved a perception of being cheated out of private time and of long anticipated leisure activities with a husband or partner. Comments like Wanda Kehoe's—"We used to travel a lot. Now we can't, we feel tied down"—were frequently expressed by such women. And for two, assumption of caregiving robbed them of the marriage itself, serving as the last straw that broke an already troubled relationship apart, culminating in separation or divorce (see Chapter 7 this volume).

Unmarried grandmothers also frequently brought up the loss of time to travel and to live the kind of life they had anticipated in their later years. Jacqueline Peters, a 58-year-old grandmother caring for three of her daughter's five little girls under 5 years old, spoke wistfully of "that restless feeling a woman gets when she turns 50—that get-up-and-go feeling." Mrs. Peters added that she had planned to live with her suitcase "half packed and always waiting by the door," once her youngest child was grown. But taking on the responsibility of the three grandchildren had changed that forever.

When asked to describe their life since the assumption of caregiving, many women for whom the new role had abruptly and negatively impacted on their life plans spoke of not really *having* a life of their own at this point: "I put my life on hold since I got the kids," "My life is at a standstill," "I have no life," and "I feel like I'm filling a vacancy," were among the comments made in this regard.

For other women, including many of those who had quit work in order to be full-time caregivers, life was not simply frozen in the present but actually moving in reverse. "I feel like I'm going backwards," one grandmother explained. Like many others, the job that had given her income, dignity, and a chance at a decent retirement had been permanently relinquished when she took in two of her grandchildren. A grandmother who had recently had to declare bankruptcy, and another who could no longer afford the expense of a car and was back to riding buses, were among others for whom "going backwards" was a frequent and unwelcome sensation.

Although most of the women we interviewed described the assumption of caregiving as having profound effects on their current activities and life plans, there was a smaller group for whom the new caregiving role fit relatively easily within a life that had often revolved around caregiving. As discussed in more detail in Chapter 10, nine of the women we interviewed had already engaged in "second time around parenting" when they became caregivers for grandchildren, great grandchildren, or grandnephews or -nieces as a consequence of the crack epidemic.

One example of this pattern was particularly poignant. Lily Atkinson, a 66-year-old single woman, had decided to devote this time in her life to caring for babies of crack involved African Americans. Although she didn't have any direct experience with the crack epidemic, she felt strongly that this was something she could do to help her own community deal with its devastating effects. She felt that with her own children grown, working, and living their own lives, she had "a lot of love still to give." She planned eventually to take in three children and, after she retired, began studying, taking parenting classes, and equipping her home for small children. She had just become the legal guardian for a 12-month-old girl, her "first baby," when her only daughter, 9 months pregnant, was arrested and eventually sent to prison for a crime committed because of her recent addiction to crack. Ironically, Lily Atkinson's "second baby" thus turned out to be her own grandchild.

For some grandmothers, a lifetime of caregiving had been the norm, made easier in part by a large and well-functioning extended family. These women described raising a sibling's children as well as their own, and having nieces, adult daughters, cousins, and others living in their households, and all helping out over the years with household chores, finances, and child care. Although the grandmothers in our study were all, by definition, sole or primary caregivers for at least one grandchild, many of those in this second category experienced the new role not as a radical life change but rather as a new variation on an old life theme (see Chapter 10 this volume). Claire Shawcross, 58, provides full-time care for two grandchildren and regular part-time respite and baby-sitting for at least five others:

> There's always kids here—always has been. I don't treat these two any different than the others and I don't want them to feel any different. They're all family, no matter how they got here or how long they'll be staying. They really aren't a problem—if it wasn't these two, it would be two others!

For a small minority of women interviewed, the assumption of caregiving, although tragic in what it stood for in terms of an adult child's crack involvement, was nevertheless a very positive life change. Included in this category were several great grandmothers for whom an infant or young child in the home meant companionship and sometimes a new lease on life. Seventy-six-year-old Lena Johnson spoke about the positive change that caregiving for her 9-month-old great grandchild had made in her own life. Although her initial reaction was one of anger and despair—"It was a low down dirty shame! My youngest is 22 years old, and then up comes this whippersnapper!"—she quickly saw the new role as providing an important new sense of purpose:

> I've changed my way of thinking. Sitting down eating a lot of greasy food like you did at those senior centers, that isn't getting you anywhere. I like [raising my great grandson] because I can educate him, make available numbers and things.

For 54-year-old Sarah Thompson, whose own children "didn't turn out very well," raising a young granddaughter, and being able to help her overcome the emotional scars of early abuse and neglect, provided an important sense of pride and accomplishment. And for 73-year-old Shelley Henderson, having a 2-year-old great grandson in the house had an unexpected positive effect on her marriage by necessitating improved communication between herself and her husband.

Yet even among grandmothers for whom the assumption of caregiving represented a positive life change, the long-term consequences of taking this step were often hard to think about. As one grandmother put it, looking down at the giggling 3-year-old in her care, "I can't imagine my life without her now. But I can't imagine life *with* her as a teenager!"

* * *

Although the grandmothers we interviewed all had become primary caregivers for their grandchildren because of the crack involvement of the children's parents, the actual routes to the assumption of full-time caregiving took several different forms. Some of the grandmothers became surrogate parents suddenly and without warning, as when a grandchild was abandoned or the grandchild's parent incarcerated. For other grandmothers, an informal negotiation with a crack involved adult child took place, and enabled the grandmother to take over caregiving for her grandchildren. Finally, for still other women, the assumption of full-time caregiving was the culmination of weeks, months, and sometimes even years of steadily increasing concern over and involvement in the grandchildren's care.

Yet regardless of the route that led them to the assumption of the role of surrogate parent, the grandmothers we interviewed frequently shared in common anger, shock, and frustration at a social services bureaucracy that thwarted, rather than assisted them in their efforts to help their grandchildren. Giving up jobs, privacy, leisure time, and the prospects of economic security in later life, the women had almost all made major sacrifices in order to provide a safety net for their grandchildren. And although they did not expect thanks from the government for the sacrifices they were making, neither did they expect to be mistrusted, stigmatized, and obstructed by a "bureaucracy of care" that seemed to care little for them, or for their grandchildren.

# 5

## The Health Status
## of Grandmother Caregivers

The 1980s and early 1990s saw a dramatic increase in research directed at the health consequences of family caregiving. Concepts such as "caregiver burden" and "caregiver strain" were developed and operationalized to measure the physical, emotional, social, and financial problems associated with providing informal care (George & Gwyther, 1986; Pearlin, Mullan, Semple, & Skaff, 1990; Scharlach, Sobel, & Roberts, 1991). Similarly, terms like *the hidden patient* came into being, in reference to the fact that caregivers frequently had significant physical or emotional health problems of their own that tended to go undetected and/or untreated (Fengler & Goodrich, 1979).

Research on the physical and emotional health of caregivers has included a look at younger caregivers, including the parents of mentally disabled or terminally ill children, and family caregivers for cancer patients or persons with chronic illnesses (Biegel, Sales, & Schulz, 1991; Jenson & Whitaker, 1987; Kessler, McLeod, & Wethington, 1985; Wortman, 1984). For the most part, however, the literature has focused on the middle-aged and older caregivers of disabled elderly spouses or parents (Biegel & Blum, 1990; Brody, 1985; Cantor, 1983; George & Gwyther, 1986; Scharlach et al., 1991; Schulz, Visintainer, & Williamson, 1990; Stone, Cafferata, & Sangl, 1987).

National survey data suggest that approximately a third of such caregivers perceive their own health to be only fair or good (U.S. House of Representatives, Select Committee on Aging, 1988), with other research demonstrating that 30% have health problems causing some activity limitations (Stephens & Christianson, 1986). And although a number of studies have demonstrated that caregiving for the elderly is stressful (Zarit, 1989) and may effect the physical health of caregivers (Rabins, Mace, & Lucas, 1982; Scharlach, 1987; Stone et al., 1987), the most consistent finding is of emotional strain and related problems (Brody, 1985; Cantor, 1983; Gallagher, Wrabetz, Lovett, DelMaestro, & Rose, 1989; George & Gwyther, 1986; Schulz et al., 1990).

The burden of caregiving for a disabled elderly spouse or parent differs in important ways, of course, from caregiving for infants or young children, particularly when the latter are in reasonably good health. As Pilisuk and Park (1988) have suggested:

> Children, despite the objective burden, represent a daily fascination and an unfolding potential. However, when a person who has been a life partner becomes a source of daily disintegration, the psychic representation is frustration, a deep sense of loss and death. (p. 436)

As noted in Chapter 2, however, caregiving for grandchildren bears some important similarities to caregiving for the elderly. Grandparent caregivers themselves are typically middle aged or older and, like caregivers for the elderly, may have chronic health conditions that are exacerbated by frequent lifting and carrying, emotional stress, and the myriad demands associated with the caregiver role. Moreover, although children are indeed "a daily fascination," caring for infants and young children who may suffer hyperactivity, learning delays, and other health and behavioral problems resulting from prenatal drug exposure or early neglect and abuse may well bring with it some of the same symptoms of depression and high-level stress experienced by caregivers who are watching the deterioration of an elderly spouse or parent. And it may also be the case that the promise of a child's "unfolding potential" is laced with fear, or at least significant stress and anxiety, when the surrounding social context is violent, unpredictable, and just beyond the grandmother's door. In short, grandparent caregivers, and particularly those who are raising children of the crack cocaine epidemic, may be vulnerable to a host of physical and emotional health problems.

It should be noted, of course, that health may well be a selection factor in determining whether grandparents take on the caregiving role in the first place. A "healthy grandparent effect," similar to the "well worker" bias in retirement research (Haynes, McMichael, & Tyroler, 1977), would suggest that grandparents who are ill or disabled would be less likely to take responsibility for grandchildren, leaving a pool of grandparent caregivers who are in better health, overall, than a random sample of individuals in their age group.

On the other hand, the low socioeconomic status of many grandparent caregivers, including most of those in our study, and the well-documented relationship between social class and illness (Kaplan, Haan, Syme, Minkler, & Misynski, 1978; Syme & Berkman, 1976) suggest the likelihood of significant health problems in this population.

Some of the earliest signs of the potential physical and emotional consequences of grandparent caregiving were observed by health care providers at San Francisco General Hospital. In the late 1980s they began to notice a pattern of broken appointments, stress-related conditions, and exacerbations of chronic health problems among middle-aged and older women attending their adult medical clinic and satellite health center. The women had in common the fact that they had become primary caregivers for their grandchildren. Their health problems included insomnia, and sudden flare-ups of previously controlled conditions such as asthma, hypertension, and arthritis (Miller, 1991).

More recently, providers at other clinics and hospitals around the country have begun reporting similar findings. However, these new reports are mostly based on anecdotal accounts rather than on systematically acquired data.

In an effort to learn more about the health status of women who were raising their grandchildren, the Grandparent Caregiver Study examined the physical and emotional health of participants as well as their perceived changes in health and personal health behaviors since the onset of caregiving. A variety of structured and semistructured questionnaire items was used to gauge self-rated physical and emotional health, illness symptoms and conditions, health behavior, and perceived changes in health and health behavior both over the last year and in the period since caregiving began. To measure the reliability of responses, most such questions were asked in both the first and the second or follow-up interviews.

In order to situate the participants' quantitative responses in a richer and more complex rendering of their perceived health status, a series of probing and open-ended questions also was asked. The resulting combination of quantitative and qualitative data offered a more complete and in-depth picture of the health of study participants than either form of data gathering could have achieved in isolation (Minkler, Roe, & Price, 1992).

## PHYSICAL HEALTH

Individuals' perceptions of their own health status frequently are assessed using questions such as, "Overall, how would you rate your health: excellent, good, fair or poor?" As noted in Chapter 3, such global self-rated health measures have been shown to correlate well with physician ratings and with objective health indicators (Ferraro, 1980; Kaplan & Comacho, 1983; Mossey & Shapiro, 1982). Although as Gibson (1991) has noted, the literature is contradictory on whether self-reports of health among blacks systematically contain more or less bias than those of whites, research by Andersen and his colleagues (1987) suggests that self-ratings accurately portray the health status of African Americans.

When asked to rate their overall physical health, the great majority of women in our study reported that it was either good (44%) or fair (39%), with just five women saying that their health was poor and seven, or 10%, rating it as excellent. No significant differences were found by age, but employment status did appear to make a difference, with employed women significantly more likely than nonemployed women to rate their health as excellent or good (see Chapter 9 this volume). A significant difference in self-reported physical health also was observed in relation to marital status. Interestingly, the 11 women who were not married but reported a steady relationship with a man or boyfriend had significantly higher self-rated physical health status than either married women or single women without a male partner.

When the same self-rated health questions were asked at the follow-up interview approximately a week later, almost identical ratings were given, suggesting high reliability of the responses in this area (see Chapter 3 this volume).

Approximately half of the 71 study participants ($n = 35$) reported that they were "concerned about their health right now," with 16% reporting that they were "very concerned." Close to 44% of respondents ($n = 31$) stated that they were in pain at the time of the interview, and high proportions reported having experienced physical problems in the last 6 months including stiffness or swelling (51%), back or stomach pain (49%), heart trouble (25%), and other physical symptoms and conditions.

Not surprisingly, one of the most frequently mentioned physical health problems was exhaustion. Among the comments made in this regard were:

I'd love to just lay down and sleep because physically I'm wore out!
Seems like my energy got up and went out the door.

It's all the up and down, this and that, getting up in the night, never a break. These old bones are tired and so am I!

With great humor, 45-year-old Claire Potts told the story of being so tired that she crossed town on the bus, carrying her two infant grandchildren in her arms, to take advantage of a grocery store sale. She bought seven bags of groceries—not realizing until she had paid for them that she had no way to carry them home on the bus.

I went through the checkout line and everything and then it dawned on me—Claire, you got no car! I was so wired up with kids, kids, kids I just couldn't think anymore. You should have seen me gathering up those bags, stacking them up, trying to balance babies and groceries out of the store and on to the bus . . . I was dropping things right and left! And you know, that's when it clicked to me that I was just too tired.

Despite their frequent reports of pain, exhaustion, and other physical symptoms, fully 45% of the women *(n* = 32) stated that their health "never" got in the way of things they wanted or needed to do, with only eight women saying that it "frequently" got in the way.

Many of the women reporting that their health never got in the way, however, qualified their response by adding statements like, "It can't— I don't let it," "I don't have the luxury of being sick," "I use my asthma pump and keep going," "I just take my medication and keep on," or "I bandage my leg, grab my cane, and keep going."

Ann Stevens, a 65-year-old great grandmother, working part time at a local school and caring for two great grandchildren under 2 years old, was among those who reported that her physical health was "good" and "never got in the way." However, she qualified her response, saying:

I've been blessed. Oh sure, I've got arthritis and I had a bladder infection last week. I have high blood pressure and diabetes, I have sleepless nights, but I'm not concerned about my health. What does worry me lately is this pace I'm trying to keep up.

Comments like Mrs. Stevens's illustrate the utility of a research strategy that supplements quantitative health measures with more open-ended investigative approaches. For although more than half of the women in our study reported that, like Mrs. Stevens, their health "never got in the way," and although half stated that they were in good or excellent health, their answers to our more open-ended questions suggest that their quantitative ratings may well overstate the case.

There is no doubt that the women in our study were well accustomed to challenges that strain their physical and emotional resources. Indeed, many of their physical problems predate the assumption of caregiving for their grandchildren. In the words of 73-year-old Mae Morton, a great grandmother caring for her 5-year-old grandson, "There's not a time in the last 10 years that I haven't felt some degree of pain." Or, as stated by Clarice Bond, another grandmother in her early seventies caring for eight grandchildren,

> I've been working since I was 3 years old. My bones been tired since I was a little girl. The only thing new about this is the pain from the [recently diagnosed] cancer and the lifting of the babies.

The qualitative findings also suggested another reason for the high overall physical health assessments. Even though most of the grandmothers were committed to raising grandchildren for the next many years, they were very concerned about the stability of their formal, or informal, caregiving arrangements. Many shared an intense desire to protect the children in their care, and their authority to care for them, which may have led them to down play their own health problems. Mrs. Stevens spoke for many when she said "I'm pretty old for this but it's alright—I'm equal to the occasion." For many of the women, the very real fear that their grandchildren might be placed in foster homes if they were perceived as unable to care for them themselves appeared to contribute to the likelihood of inflated physical health ratings.

In short, the women in our study appeared often to be dealing with some significant physical discomfort, complicated by the physical challenges of caregiving, but saying, in essence, "I can handle this." As Burnette (1991, p. 175) has noted, "There is an important distinction between unconscious denial of disease and reframing the illness experience within the context of daily life." Although the grandmothers admitted to a variety of health problems, some of which were quite debilitating, they for the most part refused to dwell on their symptoms, or to let them get in the way of their caregiving activities.

## CHANGES IN PHYSICAL HEALTH

When asked to compare their physical health to before caregiving began, close to half of the women interviewed ($n = 33$) stated that there had been no change, whereas about a fifth ($n = 14$) reported a change for the better, and just over a third ($n = 24$) said that their health was worse now.

The only statistically significant difference that emerged in this study with respect to perceived changes in physical health status since caregiving began was a surprising one: The small group of women ($n = 9$) without a confidante, or someone they could "tell anything to," were significantly more likely to report an improvement in health status since taking in their grandchildren than were women who had such confidantes. As discussed in Chapter 7, this finding appears to contradict the literature on the importance of having a confidante for one's health and well-being (Lowenthal & Haven, 1968; Schulz & Rau, 1985). On closer analysis, however, the fact that most of the women without confidantes had very small social networks suggests that the addition of children to the household may have added important new sources of affective and reciprocal support (see Chapter 7 this volume).

Although not reaching statistical significance, the greatest perceived decline in physical health status since caregiving began was reported by great grandmothers and great-aunts, those caring for four or more children, caregivers over 60, employed women, and those who were "not doing very well" financially.

As noted earlier, an interesting finding of this study was that often, even among women reporting a worsening of what was already poor health, there was an intense desire to convey that "I can handle things," including, importantly, the added caregiving responsibilities. Ann Stevens, the 65-year-old great grandmother with two little ones, reported that she has developed chronic tendonitis due to the constant lifting and carrying of active babies. "I ache to where I think my hands are going to snap off. . .but I wear a brace and pick them up any time they need me."

The response of a 48-year-old grandmother caring for three pre-school-aged children illustrates the determination we observed in so many grandparent caregivers. Her chronic and often disabling back pain requires that she lie on the floor much of the time, yet in her words:

If they don't take me out of here in an ambulance I'll care for them. I've
had to almost crawl to the kitchen sometimes but they've never gone
without a meal.

Several of the women who reported improved physical health since
caregiving began attributed the change to the decreased stress they
experienced when they simultaneously ended or sharply reduced contact with their drug involved children. For women like Claire Potts, this
meant "cleaning out the house" by having her crack abusing offspring
move out:

> My kids had me under so much stress. . . . I had pinched nerves, I had blood
> pressure problems, I had a light stroke. I was almost a drug addict myself,
> I was on pills for this, pills for that—and it was all nerves! I went to my
> doctor and he said, "Mrs. Potts, when you get rid of the problem, come see
> me." He couldn't help me. But when I got my house cleaned out, my blood
> pressure went down, everything cleared itself right up. And I don't take
> pills for anything now.

In such cases, it wasn't the onset of caregiving per se but rather a
concurrent and often related change—the lessening or curtailing of
contact with the drug involved parents of the children—that the grandmother perceived as making a positive difference in her physical health.

Since study participants became primary caregivers for their grandchildren at different times, we asked them to compare their physical
health at the point of interview to what it had been a year ago. Close to
half of the 71 women ($n = 33$) reported that their health status was the
same now as it had been a year ago, with approximately a quarter
reporting improved health. Of the latter, 6 women said that their health
was "much better" now, with twice that number stating that their health
had improved only "somewhat." About 28% of the sample ($n = 20$) reported that their health was worse now than a year ago, with 7 of these
women saying that their health had become "much worse" in the last
year.

Among the quarter of the sample reporting improved overall health
compared to a year ago, many attributed this to improved health behaviors as a consequence of their new caregiving responsibilities. An
overweight 57-year-old raising two grandchildren reported that she had
cut back from two packs a day to almost no cigarettes and had lost 30
pounds because she takes the grandchildren for long walks and bike
rides and because "there's no time to sit and enjoy food!" Another care-

giver reported giving up smoking entirely because of the baby's respiratory problems, and a 56-year-old with an infant grandson remarked:

> I realized I was neglecting myself so I started seeing a doctor, losing weight and taking care of myself, because I'm the only one he has now.

And 50-year-old Jewell Champion, now raising two granddaughters, said that:

> Before, I was always going and I didn't care much about different things. But now, I got to think. I got to be prepared. I got to preserve myself for them.

Among grandmother caregivers who reported that their health had deteriorated over the past year, changes in health and social behaviors as a consequence of caregiving also were frequently cited as having been at least partially responsible. A 62-year-old diabetic woman commented that she had missed four medical appointments in the last year. Each one had been important, and each one was missed because of caregiving, or because the disarray and confusion in her household, with two young children and a crack involved daughter, caused her to forget her own needs. A 44-year-old raising two toddlers reported that she and her husband "drink and smoke more than we should now," because of all of the additional responsibilities. And several older grandmothers stated that they no longer took their prescription medications because they needed to "stay alert all the time" for the grandchildren.

For a 79-year-old great grandmother who described her health as poor and as having worsened since taking in a 2-year-old great grandson, the lack of time and the lack of respite care that would enable her to attend to her own health needs was described as taking a toll:

> I'd like to get myself under the care of a doctor, because I'm feeling this soreness in my back. I can feel myself failing. I'd like to get some teeth in my mouth. That would help my image so much. If I could just get myself some things I need. I need glasses and don't have any. . . . Glasses are available, it's just having someone to watch the baby so I can get an appointment.

Among the women reporting a worsening of health status over the last year, only employment status appeared to be significantly related to the change. As noted earlier, employed women were significantly more likely to rate their health as good or excellent than were nonemployed women. But employed caregivers were also significantly more likely to report that their health had deteriorated over the last year: "I've slipped a little," "I'm more tired and I'm not catching up," "I'm real tired—This is a lot of demands on me." These comments, together with the quantitative findings noted above, suggest that employed women may merit special attention from health care providers and others when they take on the caregiver role.

## EMOTIONAL HEALTH

Studies of African Americans in mid-life and older age groups have demonstrated that mental or emotional health tends to improve in successively older cohorts. Blacks at age 65, for example, report better emotional health than do blacks at 45, with those at 80 rating their emotional or mental health more positively than those aged 65 (Gibson, 1982).

No significant differences in self-rated emotional health by age emerged from the findings of the Grandparent Caregiver Study. Overall, however, the mid-life and older participants tended to offer fairly positive assessments of their emotional health status. Almost 3 times as many women reported themselves to be in excellent emotional health as had rated their physical health to be excellent (28% vs. 10%). Yet it should be added that many of those reporting excellent emotional health qualified their rating with comments like, "It has to be excellent or I'd be in a nut house" and "I guess it's excellent or how could I deal with all this?"

Finally, even among those rating their emotional health as good or excellent, there were frequent reports of feeling depressed, or of having other potential symptoms of emotional distress. In examining the emotional health of participants, we utilized an abbreviated version of Blackburn's Affective Balance Scale, which had been validated for use with older adults (Moriwaki, 1974). Using this scale, which measures mood states experienced during the past week, we found that 72% of the total sample had felt "depressed or very unhappy" at least some of the time during the past seven days. Seventy percent reported feeling that they "couldn't get going," with 78% feeling "totally exhausted even though it was still early in the day," and 47% reporting feelings of loneliness during the past week.

It is, of course, difficult to interpret these rates without comparable data on a demographically similar sample of noncaregiving grandmothers. Moreover, although high self-ratings on items such as "feeling depressed" in the last week may be suggestive of emotional problems in some caregivers, they should not be used simplistically as evidence of psychiatric morbidity. As Schulz et al. (1990, p. 1) have pointed out:

> Periods of grief, despair, helplessness and hopelessness may be much more common among caregivers. However, these periods of extreme distress are usually circumscribed enough to enable caregivers to retain a reasonably problem-focused orientation in coping.

For many of the women we interviewed, feelings of depression or exhaustion were understood as being normal and natural responses to an often extremely difficult situation. Jasmine Price provides a case in point. A 48-year-old grandmother caring for her 3-year-old granddaughter, Miss Price was among the women who rated her emotional health as excellent but also reported feeling very unhappy at times during the last week:

> I get depressed. I'm a realist. People who get depressed can be in excellent emotional health. Sometimes, I feel a great deal of grief and pain but that's legitimate.

The far greater tendency for respondents to report excellent emotional health than excellent physical health may suggest that many of the women in the study had a greater perceived reserve of emotional strength than of physical resources. Yet at the same time, the high rates of feeling depressed, lonely, or "like I couldn't get going," over the past week, together with qualitative findings of often immense stress and worry, underscore again that simple self-ratings of emotional health may present an overly optimistic picture. In the words of 49-year-old Veronica Paul:

> I get depressed a lot. Hell, this is a depressing situation! If I didn't get depressed I'd be really worried about myself.

Forty-eight-year-old Elaine White provides a good example of the inadequacy of quantitative ratings alone in capturing the range of feelings the women had about their emotional well-being. Working full time as a nurse and raising two young grandchildren, Mrs. White rated her emotional health as "excellent." But she qualified this by adding, "It's excellent considering what I have to deal with." Mrs. White then went on to admit that she had frequent migraine headaches, "a stressed-out back," and had recently developed an ulcer. She reported that she is sometimes depressed, and that her emotional health, although still "excellent," has become considerably worse since she took in the grandchildren.

Perhaps 54-year-old Letitia Franklin summed it up best when, after rating herself as being in excellent emotional health, she added that she feels depressed and she feels rage every day. "But then," she said, "depression and rage are completely appropriate responses to what has happened to me and my family."

As noted earlier, research on caregivers for the elderly has demonstrated that although such caregiving may negatively impact on the physical health and economic circumstances of caregivers, the most consistent consequence is that of emotional strain (Brody, 1985; Cantor, 1983; George & Gwyther, 1986; Scharlach & Boyd, 1989; Schulz et al., 1990). Without ignoring the important differences between caring for disabled elderly relatives and raising infant and preschool-aged grandchildren noted above, the important potential role of emotional strain reflected in both our qualitative and quantitative findings is worthy of attention.

A subgroup of women for whom the emotional dimensions of caregiving often appeared particularly stressful consisted of those working women for whom the nature of one's paid employment tended to mimic work at home. Teacher's aides, school bus drivers, and food handlers who were constantly around children, and nurse's aides who gave care in their jobs, only to perform many of the same tasks at home, frequently described the emotional drain involved in having work and home lives blur into each other without much of a break (see Chapter 9 this volume).

A second subgroup for whom the perceived emotional costs of caregiving were often especially high were those women who were combining caring for their grandchildren with service as the primary caregiver to a frail or disabled parent or other elder. Although only eight of the women in our sample fell into this "dual caregiver" category, our qualitative data suggested that such women often felt "stretched to the limits" by the overwhelming nature of their responsibilities. As will be discussed in Chapter 10, although such women usually reported that they were glad to be able to help out their elderly parents, they also made clear the impact that this added caregiving responsibility was having on their emotional health and their ability to cope.

## CHANGES IN EMOTIONAL HEALTH

Respondents were almost equally divided between those who reported "no change" in their emotional health since caregiving began (34%), those who reported a change for the better (30%), and those who said that their emotional health had worsened since the assumption of full-time caregiving (36%). Of those reporting improvement in their emotional health, three quarters reported that their emotional health was "much better" now than before they took in the grandchildren. In contrast, the majority of those reporting worsened emotional health said that their emotional health was only "somewhat worse" now, with just nine women reporting that it was "much worse."

The earlier mentioned significant difference in physical health associated with the presence or absence of a confidante appeared again in relation to emotional health. Women without a confidante were far more likely to report that their emotional health had improved since caregiving began than were women who reported having someone in whom they could confide. In addition, great grandmother caregivers rated their emotional health now as significantly better than did grandmothers.

When comparing their emotional health now to a year ago, approximately 42% of the 71 women ($n = 30$) reported no change, with about 28% and 30%, respectively, reporting better and worse emotional health. As was true when comparing their emotional health now to before caregiving began, women who said their emotional health had improved in the last year were likely to report that their emotional health was "much better" now, whereas those reporting worse emotional health were most likely to state that their emotional health was only somewhat worse than before.

Once again, a significant difference was observed based on employment status, with employed women reporting greater perceived decline in emotional health over the past year than nonemployed women. Although not statistically significant, the greatest decline in emotional health over the past year was reported by women over 60 and by married women (see Chapter 7 this volume).

Of those women reporting improvement in their emotional health since before caregiving began, many attributed the change to knowing that the grandchildren were finally safe and cared for now that they were in the custody of the grandparents. Others, such as Jewell Champion, found that their emotional health improved due to the demands of the grandchildren:

> I don't have to worry about my daughter and the drugs now . . . because I have something to keep me busy. I don't have time to focus on the drugs or where she might be, if this ambulance or that police siren is for her. . . . Now, I just focus on the girls.

For other caregivers, the daunting task of bringing a seriously ill infant "back to life," or helping a learning delayed child to "catch up on what she missed," gave a sense of renewed purpose, with consequent improvements in a woman's perceived emotional state. A 48-year-old grandmother raising three young grandchildren told of how the poor physical condition in which her first grandchild had come to her helped her pull herself out of her depression:

> My emotional health is better now. Tina really brought me out of my depression because she was so sickly I thought I was going to lose her. She got me that urge to where you've got to get up and do things. She really was good for me.

For still other grandmothers, coming to terms with the crack addiction (and in some cases, the death) of an adult child or grandchild on drugs, had resulted in improved emotional health. Sixty-year-old Henrietta Stillman describes herself as having been "very upset" and "an emotional wreck" when her second daughter went on crack, but adds, "I accept it now. I haven't cried in a couple of years." And for 59-year-old Lucy Thomas, learning to accept what you "can't do anything about" was a major factor responsible for the marked improvement in her emotional health:

> The older I get, the calmer I get. I realize I can't make anybody change. The Lord's going to take care of it. If she's going to die out there in the streets, they'll tell me and I'll bury her.

In contrast, many of the women who reported that their emotional health was worse now than before caregiving began, or worse than it had been a year ago, stated that watching the deterioration of an adult child on crack was the main factor responsible. In the words of Jacqueline Peters:

> I remember when I had my [own] babies. I knew they were God's gift, God's little angels, just loaned to me for a while. They were the most important thing in the world to me. . . . So that when this [crack addiction] happens, it hurts twice as bad. It's a hurt inside that just never goes away.

For Mavis Jenkins, a 61-year-old great grandmother, raising two toddlers was not nearly as difficult as watching the deterioration of their mother, who Mrs. Jenkins had also raised from the time the girl was 11 years old. Fighting back tears, Mrs. Jenkins described the pain she felt as she picked her granddaughter up from the hospital after a recent stabbing, knowing that this probably wouldn't be the last time. For women like Mrs. Peters and Mrs. Jenkins, it wasn't caregiving per se that caused a perceived worsening of their emotional health, but rather living with the tragedy that had necessitated the caregiving that made the burden so great.

## THE BROADER CONTEXTS
## OF PHYSICAL AND EMOTIONAL HEALTH

The many women in our study who linked their physical and emotional health status to the experiences of their adult children, and their concerns for the grandchildren they have taken in, remind us that we must consider the needs of grandparent caregivers within the context of the larger family unit.

As we shall see in Chapter 13, the most effective support for caregiver health may actually be support for family members. A number of women specified, for example, that the expansion and improvement of crack treatment programs may be as important to the emotional well-being of grandparents as counseling and other interventions directed at the caregivers themselves.

The women in our study also remind us of the importance of understanding their experience within the even broader social context within which they raised their original families and within which they are raising this next generation. Almost everyone mentioned the ever-present drugs in their environments and the escalating violence that has accompanied them (see Chapter 11 this volume). In the words of Claire Potts:

> There's so much drugs and killing going on in the street. Right outside! It's like cops and robbers every night—pow! pow! pow! and I get so worried.

As Mrs. Franklin said, the grandmothers' feelings of rage and despair are perhaps quite appropriate toward a social system that provides increasingly fewer opportunities and resources to those who need them the most.

*  *  *

Earlier studies of caregivers for the elderly have suggested that perceived caregiver burden may be less among African American women, for whom cultural attitudes and beliefs, and the nature of the extended family system, may strongly impact upon their interpretations of burden and strain (Young & Kahana, 1991). In our study, participants' repeated indications that they were glad they could be there for the grandchildren, and that the new caregiving role was well worth the costs, similarly suggested that any negative physical or emotional effects of caregiving may be viewed as less important and troubling than might otherwise be the case.

As our data have suggested, however, grandparent caregivers may also inflate their self-reported health ratings or attempt to downplay specific problems in order to underscore their ability to cope with the new caregiving role. The use of qualitative research methods enriches our understanding of the grandparents' health status by situating their self-ratings in a more complex portrait of their physical and emotional health and well-being.

The special vulnerabilities of particular subgroups of grandparent caregivers, such as employed women and women who are combining grandchild care with eldercare, were underscored in this research and suggest important avenues for further investigation. In addition, clinical studies of the functional health status of grandparent caregivers are needed, as are longitudinal investigations that could highlight changes in physical and emotional health and in perceived caregiver burden over time.

Finally, it is important to acknowledge and address the multiple potential threats to caregivers' physical and emotional health caused by the intersecting demands of small children, possible prenatal drug exposure, the spiraling effects of the adult child's crack addiction, the related deterioration of a beloved child, and the effort needed to raise children who have been already hurt in a social environment that puts them at continued risk.

Grandparent caregivers and the children of the crack epidemic experience daily the intersection of private troubles and public issues (Mills, 1959). The lack of recreation programs for their growing youngsters, violent streets and dangerous neighborhood parks, respite that is inconsistent at best, inaccessible health care, poor public transportation, and inflexible work policies will come up over and over in coming chapters as structurally caused burdens that grandparents caring for grandchildren struggle to transcend. It is these systems-level failures that pose perhaps the greatest threat to the physical and emotional well-being of grandparent caregivers.

# 6

# The High Cost of Caring: Economic Considerations

As Hilda Scott (1984, p. 129) has argued, "the personal is not just political, it is also economic." For grandparents who become the primary caregivers of infants and young children, the personal decision to care often has profound financial consequences.

The high costs of caring may be particularly pronounced in African American communities, where economic vulnerability is already a frequent fact of life. This vulnerability is increasingly concentrated in female headed households; by the mid-1980s, 70% of all black families in poverty were headed by women, and just over half of all black children lived in these families (Simms, 1986). Indeed, with the exception of families headed by Hispanic women, families headed by African American women continue to have the lowest incomes and the highest poverty rates of any family type in the United States (Simms, 1986).

Although poverty rates in female headed households are highest in families whose head is young (age 24 and below), grandmother heads of households are also at high risk for poverty, particularly if they are elderly. Black single women aged 65+ constitute the poorest group in American society (Grambs, 1989), and many such women are stretching their already meager resources to cover the costs associated with raising grandchildren.

As noted in Chapter 1, most of the participants in our study lived in East and West Oakland—areas characterized by high rates of poverty and unemployment. Close to three quarters of the women lived in 10 zip codes in which at least 40% of households had an average annual income of less than $15,000 (National Planning Data Corporation,

1989). In 1990, the year in which our study data were collected, the poverty line for a family of four was $13,359.

Despite these economic realities, however, less than a quarter (*n* = 17) of the women in the study reported that they were "not doing well" financially before taking in the grandchildren, with only one reporting that she had been doing poorly prior to becoming a caregiver. The women who reported financial difficulties before becoming caregivers for their grandchildren cited a variety of sources for their financial hardship, ranging from long-term financial struggles to recent crises such as loss of work, divorce, family emergencies, or other often unexpected financial disasters.

Almost two thirds of the study participants (*n* = 45) stated that they had been doing "okay" financially before the grandchildren came. Many of these women mentioned that they had had enough to meet their needs, or that even though they hadn't had much, they also hadn't needed much prior to caregiving. Finally, 9 women reported that they had been doing "very well" financially, and cited some savings, their homes, or recent trips as examples of the comfort level they had experienced prior to assuming the responsibilities of caregiving.

In sharp contrast to the generally optimistic picture described above, not a single caregiver reported that she was doing "very well" financially at the time of the study interviews, and only nine reported that they were doing "fine" or "okay." The vast majority of respondents (87%) reported significant financial difficulty since assuming full-time caregiving, often saying that they were "spending down to the last penny" or "getting by each month on prayer alone." Half of the sample said that they were "not doing very well" financially now, and 35% said that they were doing poorly.

Contrary to political arguments suggesting that single mothers, and in this case, grandmothers, may be profiting financially from government child support payments, not a single woman in our study reported that her economic situation had improved since taking responsibility for the grandchildren, and many had experienced a substantial financial decline. A 58-year-old grandmother raising the 5-year-old daughter of her deceased son commented, "We were doing so well before—now it's a disaster!" And a 62-year-old who has had her young grandson for 4 years now similarly remarked, "Before we were fine, we finally had plenty. Now, we can just barely make the basics, and it's getting worse!"

Fifty-three-year-old Sally Forester, married at the time of our interviews and raising two young grandsons, was among the women who had been "doing very well" financially before caregiving began. Her husband held a prominent professional position, and they had a lovely and financially comfortable life together. To Mrs. Forester's shock and dismay, however, their entire nest egg was spent in the first 2 years of caregiving. Reflecting back, she remarked:

> It never crossed my mind to get outside help—we just used everything up so fast! They were puny babies and they needed special milk and so many different things—we just had to get the things they needed and didn't even think about how we were going to make it in the long run. We spent everything we had. . . . At first, I didn't notice it was so expensive because I could just cut out the little things that were extra. I stopped getting my hair done, getting my nails done. . . . But then I noticed that I couldn't even go shopping for myself because they always needed something . . . I had to always have my eye out for what I could get now at a bargain that they might need later on. Before I knew it, everything was gone.

The impact of sudden full-time caregiving also took a toll on Mrs. Forester's marriage, and her subsequent separation from her husband has added still further to the high costs of raising grandchildren. Although she and her husband have worked out the financial arrangements, "the boys are my responsibility—he is very clear that he doesn't have to support them, and I can understand that. They are my responsibility. I'll be taking care of them myself."

For study members who had been financially strained before becoming caregivers, the added costs of child care made things harder still. As one grandmother remarked, "I wouldn't say it was great before, but this is impossible."

In view of the relatively negative assessments that most of the women had of their current financial situations, and in view of the frequently major changes in perceived economic well-being since becoming caregivers, it is not surprising that fully 69% of the sample ($n = 49$) reported that their income was not adequate to meet their needs. For many, this meant, in particular, not being able to meet the needs of the young grandchildren in their care. As one grandmother caring for three little ones put it:

> I don't have needs anymore [since caregiving began]. But they have needs, terrible, terrible needs and I don't have near enough money to meet them. That hurts me, and I'm afraid it's hurting them already.

Even among those who did report that their current income was adequate, nearly all qualified the option to "just barely adequate" or limited the statement to refer only to meeting "basic needs." Even the meeting of basic needs seemed contingent for many on having nothing go wrong. As a 69-year-old great grandmother put it:

> I have what I need day to day, but I'm used to having a few pennies to put away. . . . Now there's nothing to fall back on . . . I ask the Lord every day to keep my car running and my babies healthy. If anything happened to me or them, I don't know how we'd make it.

This combination of relatively optimistic assessment of the present with deep concern for the future was common among the caregivers who felt their income was adequate. But among the almost 70% who reported that their current income was inadequate to meet their needs, worries about both the present and the future were often pronounced. The experiences of these women warrant a closer look, because they represent caregivers with a particular burden. It is to some of their stories that we now turn.

## LIVING ON THE EDGE

Without adequate income, and without anything in reserve, the physical and emotional strain of grandparent caregiving may be greatly amplified. The Martin family, with their 10 grandchildren under 13 and their 17-year-old son, were recently without a car for 6 months. Their lack of transportation further compromised Mr. Martin's already limited ability to pick up odd jobs—their only earned income and, once, their full and adequate financial support. Using public transportation, the almost weekly medical visits for the three 3-year-olds took 3 or 4 times as long and infinitely more patience and energy.

Without a car, they were also severely limited in what they could do for the older grandchildren. "We couldn't give them rides anywhere or pick them up at friends' houses in the evening," Mrs. Martin remarked, which strained relations with the young teenagers. Grocery shopping, laundry, and other routine chores for their household of 13 became full family projects and often exhausting ordeals for everybody. "But there just was no money to fix the car so we did the best we could."

For some of the women in our study, living on the edge meant that their current ability to just get by financially was viewed as only a temporary preface to more difficult times ahead. Lily Roberts, a young grandmother with legal guardianship of three preschool-aged grandchildren, prides herself on her ability to make ends meet by passing down or remaking clothes, shopping the sales, thrifty cooking, and cutting corners. But she worries that this will change as the kids grow older:

> We're making it now because with them being so small they don't eat as much as older kids. And I can get their clothes pretty cheap by catching the clearance sales. . . . What with three of them, they can share clothes pretty well. . . . But pretty soon they're going to need preschool or day care. I would need extra money. I couldn't do it with what I have now.

Mrs. Roberts *is* making it now, although her concern for the future is very real. Others, like Lena Johnson, are already in more desperate situations. Poor to begin with, 76-year-old Mrs. Johnson says that she has been "pushed to the edge" physically, emotionally, and financially, by the strain of caring for an infant great grandchild, and by the precariousness of government support:

> When you have to live off benefits such as SSI and Social Security and nothing goes wrong, that works fine, but if anything goes wrong, then you're in real trouble because you can't earn anything. That has worried me a lot lately. When you get older and you don't qualify for loans, the pressure sets in. You have to extend yourself and your children. You take your little resources and you suffer behind them because you're not able to pay your water bill and things like that, and that's the situation I'm in.

Mrs. Johnson was at a particularly difficult point financially when she took in her great grandson. Like several other grandmothers we interviewed, her home had suffered significant structural damage during the Bay Area's major earthquake in October 1987. Her crack involved granddaughter, who was not living with her at the time, took the earthquake relief forms, filed them herself, collected the government relief money, and spent it all on drugs. Unable to repair her home, and in trouble with government authorities for her inability to account for the thousands of dollars her granddaughter had spent, Mrs. Johnson was feeling shaken and stressed:

> I don't want the prettiest house in town, but I want this house comfortable so the water don't leak. . . . If I could just get my house in shape and the earthquake damage fixed, why, I could kinda relax.

Without a financial cushion, and convinced that no further resources were available to her, Mrs. Johnson couldn't "relax," and talked about the severe insomnia she often experienced as a result of her financial worries.

Lena Johnson's concerns are felt by many others. For some, the combination of no resources, no support, and the sense of having no options drives them to do things that they previously would have thought unimaginable. Fifty-two-year-old Doris Watson's story provides a poignant case in point.

Living in a crowded East Oakland apartment, Mrs. Watson sleeps in the living room so that her 3-year-old granddaughter, Diana, can have the only bedroom. Because she does not have legal custody of the girl, there is no AFDC, and Mrs. Watson's only income is an SSI (Supplemental Security Income) check of about $600 a month. She hopes to supplement her meager government allowance by cooking in her home to make extra money, but so far that is just a dream.

Mrs. Watson's granddaughter was in very poor condition when she came to her home nearly a year ago: Diana was anemic; had frequent, terrifying nightmares; cried a lot; and had regular "screaming fits." The child was also constantly thirsty and prone to frequent and long lasting colds, which doctors at the local health center attributed to her prenatal drug exposure.

Mrs. Watson's financial situation has deteriorated badly since she took in her granddaughter, but she is determined to get off of government assistance, getting herself and Diana "out of the system." She is a proud and deeply caring woman.

But recently, both Mrs. Watson and Diana had bad colds, and the grandmother had no money with which to buy the medicine they needed. As the little girl's condition worsened, her grandmother made a desperate move:

> I did something I shouldn't have. I was low on funds and I went to the store and took something for (her fever) and I got caught for it. That was some-

thing I did a long time ago, when I was a little girl. But we were both sick that time and needed something. I just went to the drugstore and did it and got caught.

As Doris Watson tells this story, her eyes fill with tears and her shame and her pride are laid out side by side. She knows that her story is about much more than shoplifting and getting caught. Her story is about the desperation that one can feel when there is no help, and no money, and your child is ill. Her story is about a responsible woman taking a huge and perhaps foolish risk because she cannot see any other way to care for the child in her trust. And her story is about the inadequacy of the "safety net" that is supposed to keep American families from this kind of despair.

## CARING NOW, PAYING LATER?

Although low-income women like Doris Watson and Lena Johnson illustrated what were often the most tragic stories of life on the edge, the experiences of several of the middle-income women in our study also portray the increased economic vulnerability occasioned by caregiving. Forty-nine-year-old Betty Driscoll's job as a legal assistant, for example, had enabled her to live fairly comfortably, to visit new places, and to "socialize a lot" before she took in her 3-year-old granddaughter.

But the high costs of caring for a toddler, and particularly one with significant physical and behavioral problems, changed all that:

I used to travel a lot, spur of the moment. . . . I had money to shop to take care of myself, to fix the car. Now, we take the bus. The highlight of my life now is going to see *The Jungle Book.*

Although Betty Driscoll has been able to keep her job while caring for her granddaughter, many grandparent caregivers are not so fortunate. As discussed in Chapter 9, for example, fully a third of the non-employed women in our study had been forced to quit their jobs in order to become full-time caregivers for their infant and young grandchildren. Still others had passed up promotions or the opportunity to apply for new jobs with better benefits in order to accommodate the demands of their new caregiving responsibilities.

For still other women, progress toward a college degree, or completion of literacy courses or a computer training class came to an abrupt halt when the grandchildren arrived. For such women, the high costs of caregiving must be measured not only in terms of current needs and expenses, but also in terms of the impact of caring on their future economic prospects—their access to better jobs, educational opportunities, and to an adequate retirement income (Scott, 1984; see also Chapter 9 this volume).

Like caregivers for the elderly, grandparent caregivers not currently "on the edge" financially may be placing themselves in jeopardy of future economic vulnerability by making what they feel is the only decision they can make—the decision to care.

## FINANCIAL SUPPORT
## AND THE EXTENDED FAMILY

Studies of African American extended families have shown "making ends meet" to be a persistent theme (Hill, 1971; Martin & Martin, 1978; Simms & Malveaux, 1986; Stack, 1974). As Martin and Martin (1978) note:

> The economic interdependency of family members is a major element of the extended family structure. Many have no choice but to depend on relatives for economic assistance. Others maintain a stance of economic dependency out of habit or to ensure that aid will be available if they need it. The built-in mutual aid system in black extended families . . . is a major survival component. (p. 29)

As Martin and Martin (1978, p. 37) go on to point out, however, "Though the mutual aid system gives family members the assurance that they will not be deprived of basic necessities, it can do little to move them beyond a decent survival level." Further, accounts that stress the effectiveness of the extended family as a mutual aid system sometimes give "distorted accounts" by underemphasizing the serious strains and problems that occur when members are unable or unwilling to contribute, or when certain segments of the network become a severe drain on already scarce resources (Aschenbrenner, 1978; Martin & Martin, 1978). As Lesnoff-Caravaglia (1982, p. 113) has suggested, "The constant and frequent sharing with other family members limits the ability of a particular family segment to maintain material advantages."

Describing such limitations, and the impossibility of getting ahead when so many family members depend on you, a 62-year-old grandmother in our study commented:

> This is the way it's always been with black folks, we look out for each other. Just like sand, you can't get ahead because others need you and are below so you can't come up.

All of the women in the Grandparent Caregiver Study belonged to extended families because, by definition, households consisting of grandparents and their grandchildren traditionally fall within this category and are, indeed, its most prevalent form (Hatchett, Cochran, & Jackson, 1991). For many of the women, too, close relationships with siblings, mothers, cousins, nieces, and nephews, and often, "fictive kin," contributed to a sense of strong extended family ties (see Chapter 7 this volume).

For a few of the women, mutual aid and support within the extended family included regular financial assistance. Fifty-seven-year-old Mary Harte's family provides a case in point. Three of her grown children, a son-in-law, and until recently, Mrs. Harte's elderly father all lived with her and her three young grandchildren in a large old East Oakland house. The rent and all household expenses are divided equally, and members of the household also chip in with baby-sitting and chores according to their work schedules.

For 56-year-old Ronda Leeds, a great grandmother raising two preschoolers, extended family members also help out financially when they can. Her niece lives next door, and her mother, sister, and several other relatives all live within a few blocks of each other. Until his recent layoff, Mrs. Leeds's son helped out with a modest but regular contribution to her rent. "We're a big family, but everybody works together. I wouldn't trade my family for anybody's," she remarks with pride.

Sixty-two-year-old Carol Innis also benefits financially from the mutual aid system within her extended family. She shares her house with two daughters and their children, a grown son, and an adult nephew who is temporarily in need because his Army checks have been interrupted. All of the adults contribute to the meeting of household expenses, and although Mrs. Innis is the primary caregiver for one of the grandchildren, family members also help out with child care. "In my family none of our kids ever went to foster care," she remarks. "We chip in and help each other out."

For Mary Harte, Ronda Leeds, and Carol Innis, financial assistance is indeed one of the ways family members "chip in" and help each other make ends meet. For the great majority of women in our study, however, such direct financial assistance from family members was not available, except on special occasions or in an emergency. Instead, family members often freely helped each other with things like baby-sitting, transportation, and sharing kids' clothes ("I have 10 grandchildren, and out of the 10, we keep the clothes movin' ").

Fifty-nine-year-old Lucy Thomas is an example of a grandparent caregiver whose extended family is helpful in many ways other than with finances. She gets help from her sisters, her niece, and one of her sons in raising the four children in her care, and other extended family members sometimes help with house cleaning and respite. In turn, Mrs. Thomas is heavily relied on for transportation because she has the only car, and she frequently also provides baby-sitting for two of her grand-nieces. "My family is good and supportive," Mrs. Thomas comments, "but they can't help out financially. Welfare is just enough to get by."

Comments like Mrs. Thomas's are reflective of the fact that the mutual aid system—once the "cornerstone" of poor black families—is becoming "a custom of the past" as extended family networks experience greater economic scarcity (Ladner, 1986; Martin & Martin, 1978).

All but 9 of the 71 women in our study reported that they had a family member or friend from whom they could ask to borrow money in an emergency. Yet the realities of life in many of the low-income extended families we examined were such that even the closest of family members were sometimes helpless to come up with financial assistance. When Mrs. Thomas's crack involved daughter recently smashed the new car she had purchased and on which her mother was a cosigner, Mrs. Thomas was forced to declare bankruptcy. The family, always there for her emotionally, was helpless to assist more tangibly in this emergency, and as a consequence, her financial situation is even more precarious than before.

The inability of most of the women's extended families to provide regular financial aid, and the lack of adequate personal income and other resources, left most of the grandmothers in need of government assistance to help them support their grandchildren. As we shall see below, however, the costs of such support in terms of one's pride and dignity were often significant.

## STIGMA AND SUPPORT:
## THE VAGARIES OF GOVERNMENT ASSISTANCE

Of the many topics discussed by the women we interviewed, few generated as heated a response as government support (or lack of support) for children being raised in the care of grandparents or other relatives. At the heart of the controversy was the fact that although all but 10 of the women were receiving some government support for the children in their care, that support was limited to "welfare" (Aid to Families With Dependent Children), or at best AFDC-Foster Care (AFDC-FC), an additional support program for relative caregivers. In contrast, nonrelative caregivers were receiving considerably higher levels of support, without any of the stigma that attached to AFDC.

The largest cash benefit program in the United States, AFDC is a federal/state program that, like its predecessor, Aid to Dependent Children (ADC), provides dramatically different amounts of support to poor families in different states, as a result of differences in both local economic situations and prevailing ideologies and values (Katz, 1989; Sidel, 1992b).

Although AFDC rates vary by region, in no state are they high enough to bring families above the poverty line (Sidel, 1992b). The value of AFDC in terms of purchasing power, moreover, dropped 42% between 1970 and 1990 (Sidel, 1992b), with further deep cuts being enacted in many regions of the country in the early 1990s (see Chapter 13 this volume).

In California at the time of this study, parents and grandparents receiving AFDC were allocated an average of $326 for a single child, $536 for two children, and correspondingly lower rates for each additional child. Grandparent caregivers who qualified for AFDC-Foster Care received a slightly higher payment—$345 for a child zero to 4 years old, with greater amounts for older children (County of Los Angeles, 1991).

To qualify for AFDC-FC, however, a child had to have been removed from the parents or another relative and placed with the grandmother *by court order*. In addition, the child had to have lived with the parent or relative from whom he or she was removed for at least part of the prior 6 months, and those parents or relatives had to have received or been eligible for regular AFDC payments (County of Los Angeles, 1991). Not surprisingly, most grandparent caregivers fail to meet these stringent requirements, and hence are ineligible for the higher AFDC-Foster Care rates (Barry, 1991).

Moreover, although the U.S. Supreme Court has prohibited the arbitrary exclusion of relatives from participating in foster care (*Miller v. Youakim,* 1979), it does *not* require the states to assist grandparents and other relatives in qualifying for the program, or in overcoming such obstacles as the lack of a required extra bedroom in their home for the grandchild. Consequently, as Takas (1992, pp. 5-6) has pointed out, states that follow only the bare bones requirements specified in *Miller v. Youakim* may find themselves facing an "ironic and unintended" consequence. Relatively stable and financially secure families, able to act assertively in pursuit of the superior benefits provided through AFDC-Foster Care, thus would probably have a good chance of being accepted into the program. In contrast, more impoverished and less stable families, which provide care for grandchildren but fail to meet state foster care standards, would be more likely to be restricted to the considerably lower AFDC payments, and to receive less in the way of protective supervision. "In effect," Takas (1992, p. 6) points out, "the less needy family would receive more, in terms of both financial assistance and supervision, while the more needy received less."

Our own study corroborated this observation, with the very poorest families generally also the most likely to be receiving only the minimal AFDC support and assistance.

The biggest difference in benefits for caregivers, however, is not between AFDC and AFDC-Foster Care, but rather between AFDC in either of these forms and "real" foster care. For although grandparent caregivers eligible for the former programs were receiving $326 and $345, respectively, for a preschool-aged grandchild in their care, a nonrelative foster care parent was receiving $450 per child (Bates, 1989).

Nonrelatives raising foster care children, moreover, are eligible for a variety of special services and programs—"extras" such as counseling and clothing allowances. Some, though not all, of these are available to AFDC-FC grandparents, but none of them are available to those receiving only the minimal AFDC benefit (Barry, 1991).

The difference in benefits favoring nonrelative caregivers limits the resources of grandparents at the same time that it angers and dumbfounds them. In the words of one grandmother caregiver:

> They would rather pay some stranger to take care of my grandchildren than pay their own grandmother. I'm kin! They are my flesh and blood! These children need so much love. And they're tellin' me a stranger can give that to them better than their grandmother? No way! That's just plain crazy!

As noted earlier, apart from the superiority of the tangible economic and other benefits connected with foster care, enrollment in the program comes without the stigma and labeling of a welfare program. In contrast, AFDC recipients are heavily stigmatized as "welfare mothers" or grandmothers, and frequently feel themselves to be "second-class citizens" in the eyes of government. A 58-year-old grandmother raising three young grandchildren as well as her own two youngest children voiced the resentment of many others we spoke with:

> They make you fill out forms, save receipts, justify everything you do. They tell you what you can and cannot buy and they even question my judgment when I buy something for the babies they don't think is necessary. It's insulting!

The discrimination against relative caregivers that is built into the discrepancies between the AFDC and Foster Care programs was deeply resented by many of the women in our study. A 57-year-old grandmother caregiver of three echoed the sentiments of others when she lamented:

> They don't give grandmothers the recognition they should. They recognize foster care parents and give them more money, which isn't fair. Why no help for the grandmothers?

Apart from the inferior treatment accorded grandparents by the AFDC program, however, the logistics of simply getting into the system were described by many as making for a daunting task. A 53-year-old grandmother raising two preschool-aged children summarized the feelings of others when she remarked:

> I went through hell just trying to get the welfare check changed to my name. It wasn't my fault I had the kids. I was willing to give up my life and they make me fill out a thousand pieces of paper!

For other grandmothers, the stringent rules and regulations that surround the receipt of AFDC or AFDC-Foster Care benefits left them ineligible, even if they had been willing to fill out "a thousand pieces of paper." As O'Reilly (1989) has pointed out, a grandparent's eligibility for foster care payments under the federal foster care program is determined by parental eligibility or receipt of AFDC in the 6 months prior to intervention by the Department of Social Services. But crack involved parents often fail to follow up on their initial AFDC applications, or lose eligibility when they fail to return the necessary paperwork to AFDC each month. As a result, the grandmother and the grandchildren in her care may later discover that they are automatically ineligible to receive benefits (O'Reilly, 1989).

The uncertainty of the situation of an adult child on crack also sometimes causes grandparent caregivers to put off applying for assistance, thereby making them ineligible when they finally *do* apply. Grandmothers whose grandchildren were abandoned by their parents, or simply left in the grandparents' care for long periods of time, thus often fail to approach public agencies about assistance, in the hope that the parents will "straighten out" and resume caring for their children. Because there is only a 6-month window of eligibility for AFDC enrollment, however, such grandparents often find that they have waited too long to come forward, and as a result, cannot receive benefits for their grandchildren (O'Reilly, 1989).

Of the 10 women who were receiving neither AFDC nor AFDC-FC monies, 3 were in situations where the welfare payment was continuing to be made to the drug involved daughter. Many other grandmothers reported that, although resolved now, they, too, had been in situations where AFDC money intended for the youngsters in their care was going instead to their adult daughters who were not currently involved in raising the children. Although in one case this was done by tacit agreement with the adult child (in exchange for the grandmother being able to keep the grandchildren with her), in the other cases, the grandmothers expressed their anger and dismay that the state continued to "support" an adult child's drug habit through misdirected AFDC payments. A grandmother raising three of her grandchildren, all under age 4, angrily remarked:

> You know the shocking thing to me? Here *she* is on the streets, doing drugs. And she can go and apply for welfare and they give it to her, but not to me! I don't understand it. The system is messed up. . . . Here they are saying the state is broke, and what are they doing with the money? They're giving to these able-bodied men and women who are lined up on the corner, drinking and doing drugs, and the state is paying for it! But when it comes to our little children, they don't want to give us anything. They need to think about our children, and about people like myself, because we're the ones who are going to have to take care of them.

Whether the issue is getting AFDC for one's grandchildren, or accessing food stamps or other needed programs and services, some grandmothers are familiar with and able to navigate the maze that constitutes the government health and welfare bureaucracy. They know who to talk with, how to persist, what to say, and how to get the resources they need. Others have more difficulty, sometimes spending crucial months, or even years, unaware that the children may be entitled to MediCal cards, additional counseling, or supplemental food stamps.

Yet as with AFDC, the very system designed to help low-income women access needed supplemental services like food stamps or MediCal often exacerbates the problem.

This was certainly the case for Margaret Peterson, a single, 57-year-old woman working 40 hours a week as a cook and raising two granddaughters, ages 2 and 3. Miss Peterson was able to get food stamps for the girls, which, although only $55 a month, helped ease her tight budget. The food stamps were cut off, however, when the welfare worker reported that Miss Peterson was feeding the family together and not cooking separate meals for the girls. The repeal of assistance, and the insult to her dignity as a manager of her home and her responsibilities, made this grandmother understandably furious:

> The system stinks. The system is messed up! They want to know about every little penny they know you got . . . [then] they want to take everything away from you!

Miss Peterson's outrage is felt by other grandmother caregivers who feel not only that their contributions and sacrifices are dismissed but that their motives are often suspect as well. As a result, they slip into deeper financial trouble as they try to provide the home, food, clothes, and other resources that their grandchildren so desperately need, without much help.

For several of the women we interviewed, staying off of AFDC, or getting off of it as soon as possible, was a matter of principle. For a low-income 59-year-old grandmother raising five of her grandchildren without welfare, this meant standing in lines for government surplus cheese and other items, often 3 times a day. The standing in line is work, she says, but adds that she doesn't mind because, "anytime they're giving you something you gotta work for it. I have no problem with that. I stand in the butter and cheese lines, it's a way of life."

For 63-year-old Martha Holt, government surplus food, like AFDC payments, are a form of the dole, and hence an insult to one's dignity and sense of self worth. "I try to catch all the sales," she remarks proudly. "I will not go on welfare!"

Forty-one-year-old Ellen Strickland is another grandmother who chooses to forgo the benefits to which she knows she and her grandchildren are entitled. Like others, she is tired of the bureaucracy, the hassles, and the not-so-subtle insults that getting assistance involves:

> All that paperwork and denials. They discourage me and it's like, I don't have time for people to be putting a lot on me. I got enough problems as it is! And I know money makes the world go round, but I'm not one that goes "money, money, money!" I'm managing.

Yet Mrs. Strickland worries a lot about the future and wishes that she made more money, or that more resources were available to her family without all of the indignities of welfare.

> It would ease my brain. It would keep me from, like they say, stiffin' Peter to pay Paul. It would ease a lot of fears that I have like, am I going to pay this bill or that bill?

So the grandmothers find ways to manage, borrowing from Peter to pay Paul, buying poorer cuts of meat and seasoning them well, shopping the sales, working at night, taking on baby-sitting or cooking or sewing from the home, and mostly doing without themselves in order to provide for the children.

But their financial resources are not as elastic as their spiritual and emotional ones. They know their grandchildren's immediate material needs and anticipate a time, not so far off, in which those needs will be greater and their own abilities to meet them further diminished. These women know, because they have seen it before, that the hardest times lay ahead.

*       *       *

The economic costs described by grandparent caregivers range from having to give up travel and leisure time pursuits to losing jobs and incurring heavy debts, being suddenly unable to afford anything but the basic necessities, and, in some cases, lacking even enough money for food at the end of the month. Although the financial hardships imposed by such caregiving have been described by women of diverse income and social class levels, the high costs of caring are often particularly acute for women of low and modest income.

The majority of participants in the Grandparent Caregiver Study fell within the latter categories, and for these women, the added costs of taking in one, and typically more than one, grandchild as a consequence of the crack epidemic took a tremendous toll. Indeed, more than a third of the women reported themselves to be doing poorly financially since taking responsibility for the grandchildren, and more than two thirds said that their income was inadequate to meet their needs.

Yet in the face of the often significant unmet needs these women described, public assistance programs, such as Aid to Families with Dependent Children, were far from providing a true safety net. Grandmothers receiving AFDC, or the slightly higher compensation provided through AFDC-Foster Care, described the miserly benefits offered, the stigma and shame that frequently went with them, and the seemingly endless forms and red tape involved in gaining access. Particularly when contrasted with the more substantial financial benefits and other services available to "real" foster care parents, the support received by relative caregivers was cause for high levels of anger and resentment.

As we shall see in later chapters, however, efforts on both the state and local levels to improve the support available to grandparents raising grandchildren have met with little success. The politics of retrenchment in economically lean times, combined with a deeply rooted ideology stressing women's duty to care, have effectively thwarted such needed policy changes. As the stories and statistics presented in this chapter graphically point out, however, such changes are critical if grandmothers and other relatives are to be able to provide adequately for the children in their care, without suffering serious economic deprivation in the process.

# 7

## Support Networks
and Social Support

Studies dating back to the turn of the century have documented what human beings have long known: that people need people to be healthy (Cobb, 1976; Cohen & Syme, 1985; March, 1912). Both social networks, or the web of interpersonal relationships in which individuals are embedded (Cohen & Syme, 1985), and the supportive resources they give and receive through those networks, bear an important relationship to health and well-being. The presence of social ties and social support thus has been shown to protect people in crises from a wide variety of pathological states, to increase recovery rates from illness, and to effect self-esteem and life satisfaction positively (Berkman, 1985; Cassell, 1976; Cobb, 1976). Conversely, the absence of support has been linked to depression and other mental health problems, and also may have a depressive effect on the immune system, increasing susceptibility to illness (Kiecolt-Glaser et al., 1987).

Assuming the role of grandparent caregiver may have profound effects on women's support networks and social support, adding new and often very dependent persons to the center of the network, dramatically changing marriage and family relationships, potentially isolating the women from former co-workers and friends, and in some cases providing an important new network of friends and confidantes through support groups and other activities related to the demands of caregiving.

Women's roles as support *givers* may also be radically transformed as they find themselves with less time for other family members and friends, and with the demands of new children interfering with their ability to give the quality and quantity of instrumental assistance they formerly may have been providing for an elderly parent or neighbor, or

99

their other children or grandchildren. For women who had been heavily involved in church or volunteer activities, the demands of their new life may also take a toll on these key dimensions of their support systems.

## HUSBANDS AND PARTNERS

As Gibbs (1990, p. 331) has noted, "Contrary to conceptions of the black family as a matriarchal or matrifocal arrangement, historians have documented the preference for a two parent family before and since the days of slavery." Moreover, except during slavery, when marriage among blacks was forbidden, and during periods like the present, characterized by economic recession and/or high unemployment among black males, black families have traditionally been headed by two parent couples.

Although all but 10 of the women in our study had been married earlier in their lives, only 20 of the 71 (28%) were currently married and living with their husbands. This relatively low rate of current marriage reflects in part the older average age of sample members (mean = 53) because black women have the highest rates of widowhood in the population: For example, 27% of black women aged 55-64 are widowed, compared to just 16% of white women in that age group (Grambs, 1989). But the low rate of currently married women in our study also reflects the higher rates of marital instability and dissolution found among black couples as a consequence of poverty, racism, unemployment, and related factors (Gibbs, 1990).

In addition to the 20 currently married women in our study, another 8 reported having a man regularly involved in their lives. Of those 28 women with husbands or male partners, 17 (28%) stated that the men were "very supportive" of the grandmother's role as caregiver, whereas 7 said they were "somewhat supportive," with only 4 men being characterized as somewhat or very unsupportive.

Yet the perceived support of husbands and male partners was not matched by reports of more concrete forms of involvement. Only 10 of the 28 women described their husbands or male partners as being "very involved" in actual caregiving, with 16 others stating that the men were "somewhat" or "occasionally" involved, and 2 reporting little or no involvement at all.

Studies of caregiving for the elderly have routinely documented gender differences in the quantity and quality of care provided. Although male caregivers typically provide assistance with things like errands, repairs, and finances—things that can be done on their schedules—women are far more involved in the day-to-day provision of help with feeding, bathing, and other time-consuming tasks (Abel, 1991; Berk, 1988). When caregiving and work roles conflict, moreover, it is women rather than men who are likely to take time off work, to cut back on hours, or to rearrange their work schedules (Stone et al., 1987).

The sexual division of labor around caregiving also appeared in our study. Although a few of the women with husbands and male partners reported that they helped with a variety of tasks, none felt that there was an equal division of labor, or that their men really shared with them the responsibility for caregiving. The tasks with which men were most likely to help out were not the arduous daily chores such as feeding and bathing the children, but rather the specific and somewhat sporadic activities such as taking them to the doctor or on outings, paying the bills, or providing occasional baby-sitting. This distinction is important, for as Webber (1991, p. 87) has noted, there is a "curious paradox" that "although the emotional burden may be the most difficult part of the caregiving experience, instrumental assistance is best at alleviating it."

This paradox is clearly illustrated in the words of Helene Wheaton, a 63-year-old married grandmother caring for the 5-year-old grandson she lovingly calls Little Gerald:

> My husband helps, but on his time. What I really need is someone else that I could count on regularly, even for just a period of time every day or so. Someone I knew loved little Gerald and would take care of his needs that afternoon—give this heart a rest. Because I'm wearing down, emotionally and physically, and I'm not catching up.

For most of the married women in our study, husbands and partners were not generally perceived of as a source of consistent help with the most basic instrumental caregiving activities. This finding supports Burton's (1991b) observation that grandmother caregivers tend to report a lack of significant involvement in caregiving by the men in their lives. Yet as in Burton's research, the use of more probing questions, and our observations of the families in which we interviewed, often revealed a higher degree of male involvement in child care than was initially reported by the grandmothers.

Because of the strain that new caregiving can put on a relationship, we were interested in married caregivers' assessments of their marriages at this point in time. We knew that assuming full-time caregiving would impact both life and relationship satisfaction, but we also knew that satisfaction with marriage is a complex state, affected by a wide range of contextual factors.

Although studies among white populations have consistently demonstrated a positive relationship between marriage and higher levels of life satisfaction, this finding has not held true among blacks (Campbell, Converse, & Rodgers, 1986; Gibbs, 1990). Ball and Robbins (1986) have demonstrated, for example, that once income and other factors were controlled for, black married women reported no higher levels of life satisfaction than single women.

As Gibbs (1990) and others point out, a variety of factors help explain this phenomenon, among them the pervasive and continued racism that undermines both the confidence and the competence of black men, the latter's greater difficulty in finding jobs that enable them to support families, and the frequent tendency for black women to marry men with lower educational and occupational levels than they themselves have attained.

Finally, a significant relationship has been found between marital status and economic well-being in black couples. Black women who are very poor thus tend to report the lowest levels of satisfaction with their marriages (Belle, 1982) and among blue-collar women, marital satisfaction is also significantly lower among blacks than among whites (Blood & Wolfe, 1960).

In light of these facts, it was not surprising to find that only 5 of the 20 married women in our study reported that they were "very happy" with their marriages. Another 8, or 40% of the 20 married women, stated that they were "somewhat happy" and 7 reported that they were "somewhat" or "very unhappy" with their marriages.

None of the married women felt that their marriage had greatly changed for the better since taking in the grandchildren, whereas more than a third ($n = 7$) said that there had been "some change" or "a great change for the worse." For two of the women, taking on the role of primary caregiver had in fact been the final straw in ending a marriage. A 53-year-old nurse, separated from her husband for 3 years, described how taking in her 7-month-old grandson had proven too much for the marriage to absorb: Her husband moved out shortly after the baby moved in. The 52-year-old wife of a prominent judge was "shocked, but not really," when he couldn't handle the embarrassment of their daughter's deterioration. One year after assuming responsibility for the daughter's two little girls, the grandmother's husband of more than two decades filed for divorce and moved across the state.

For women who were happy with their marriages, diminished time alone with their husbands and decreased opportunities to get away together were often mentioned as a "downside" of their new life. A 56-year-old grandmother, married for more than 30 years, remarked, "My husband had just retired from being a merchant seamen, and we had planned to travel." Looking down at her 10-month-old grandson she added wistfully, "This is my travel right here!"

In a number of cases, the pluses of taking in grandchildren seemed to counterbalance the negative effects on their relationships. A 63-year-old great grandmother described her marriage as having "good days and bad days," noting that "Sometimes [my husband] gets depressed because he says I don't take enough time for him." But, she added, the marriage is generally better now than before the kids came "because his concern is for me, and that makes me feel a lot better."

Several women also noted that taking in the grandchildren had the effect of improving communication within the marriage. A 44-year-old with two crack exposed grandchildren and her own youngest child all living at home reported, "Sometimes my husband and I drink more than we should now, but we've become closer and better able to communicate" since the grandchildren came. Communication also improved in some marriages that were described by the women as generally unsatisfying: A 63-year-old great grandmother noted that she and her husband had had little to say to each other before their 2-year-old grandson came to stay: "I had really tuned [my husband] out." The marriage "has improved some" since they became caregivers, however, because communication now is required, as least where the child is concerned.

## FAMILIES AND FRIENDS

As McAdoo (1982, p. 479) has noted, "One of the traditional and continuing stress absorbing systems for blacks and other minorities has been the wide supportive network of their families." Among troubled black families, including many of those that have been hard hit by the crack cocaine epidemic, such networks often play an especially important role, offering emotional support and serving as "therapeutic communities" during times of severe psychological stress (Belle, 1982; Gibbs, 1990). For nearly all of the women in our study, nuclear and extended families, sometimes including close nonrelative "fictive kin," were very much a part of the fabric of daily life.

Only 3 of the 71 women reported having no close relatives, and 2 of these were elderly sample members who had outlived most of their kin. Nineteen women (27%) reported being close to 1 or 2 family members, while the majority (42%) were close to between 3 and 9, and close to a quarter stated that they were close to at least 10 of their relatives.

The women reported that they were in frequent contact with their families. Two thirds ($n = 47$) reported seeing their other grandchildren on at least a weekly basis, and half of these saw them daily. Seventy-one percent of the entire sample had visited or spoken with a family member or friend within the last day, suggesting again a high frequency of contact.

Research on social support suggests, however, that although contact with families is important, it is frequency of contact with friends, rather than relatives, that is associated with improved life satisfaction and other measures of subjective well-being (Kane & Kane, 1981; Schulz & Rau, 1985). The particular importance of nonfamily contacts among certain subgroups within the black population also has been demonstrated (Chatters & Taylor, 1990; Gibson, 1982; Ladner, 1971). Gibson's (1982) comparison of mid-life and older blacks and whites, for example, found blacks at both of these life stages to be more likely than whites to use friends and neighbors in coping with psychological stress.

All but 6 of the women in our study reported having close friends, with the largest numbers (27 and 24, respectively) having between one and two or between three and five close friends. However, even though nearly all of the women reported frequent contact with their friends, a number indicated that their time with friends had been sharply cut back as a consequence of their child-care responsibilities.

Close to two thirds of the women ($n = 44$) related that they had meals with friends less often now than before they took in their grandchildren. And more than half ($n = 36$) had, in the last year, ceased having much contact with someone they used to be close to. In the majority of these cases, caregiving was the direct cause of the loss of contact. For 54-year-old Sarah Thompson, inability to afford baby-sitters, and pride in not wanting a handout, have made social outings with friends a thing of the past: "My girlfriends used to pay a baby-sitter sometimes for me to be able to go out with them, but I don't let them anymore."

For 49-year-old Betty Driscoll, friends were at first not interested in visiting anymore because "those days were behind them," and because her 3-year-old granddaughter Sandra "was slobbering and had other medical problems when she first came, and my friends didn't like to be around her."

For many of the women who had quit work in order to be full-time caregivers, the sudden lack of contact with co-workers and friends at work was also stressful. On the plus side, however, caregiving had resulted in the development of new friendships for a number of the grandmothers. Twenty-nine women (41%) reported having made new friends in the last year. Although this was particularly true for the women who had joined support groups, even those who had not reported a tendency to seek out the company of other grandparent caregivers. The sometimes instant affinity born of their common bond was captured by a 61-year-old who remarked:

> If I'm out in public and people are with their grandchildren we walk up—we don't even know each other's name—and we just start talkin.' And I bet out of 10 fingers there's about 1 that doesn't have the same problems as I do!

For a 57-year-old raising two preschoolers in a large housing project filled with caregivers, mutual support is similarly forthcoming, because, "All the grandmothers I've talked to, we're all in this together."

## CONFIDANTES

Of the many aspects of support networks, only size has been consistently demonstrated to have predictive value (Gore, 1985; Webber, 1991). Individuals with larger networks thus appear to live longer, to have better self-esteem, and to cope more effectively with stress and illness than their more socially isolated counterparts (Arling, 1987; Biegel, Shore, & Gordon, 1984; Cobb; 1976; Cohen & Syme, 1985). Yet as several researchers have demonstrated, the most important size difference appears to involve the difference between zero and one, or more specifically, between the presence or absence of a confidante (Lowenthal & Haven, 1968; Schulz & Rau, 1985; Specht, 1986).

All but six of the women we interviewed reported having a close friend or relative they could confide in or "say anything to." Such confidantes were typically sisters or mothers, women friends, or adult daughters, and less often husbands, male partners, brothers, or sons.

The gender factor in confidante status is in keeping with the findings of several earlier studies. Belle (1987) has demonstrated that men are more likely to confide in their wives than women are in their husbands, suggesting an unequal allocation of emotional support resources within the marriage (Abel, 1991). Studies among different ethnic groups also have shown that women tend both to receive and to give more support to others over the life course, with most of the support they obtain coming from other women (Abel, 1991; Antonucci, 1985; Belle, 1987; Rubin, 1985; Stack, 1974).

In our own study, more than half of the women with a confidante ($n = 33$) reported seeing or talking to their confidantes at least once a day, with another 26% ($n = 16$) reporting contact several times a week, and only 3 women stating that they were in contact less than once a month. Contrary to expectation, no significant change appeared in the proportion having less contact since becoming a full-time caregiver: Well over half of the 65 women with confidantes ($n = 36$) reported no change in their amount of contact, and only 13 stated that they saw or talked with their confidantes less than before. Indeed, 16 women (25%) reported that contact with their confidante had increased. In short, although grandmother caregivers tend to have less "social time" now with friends and relatives, their closest confidantes remain in frequent touch and provide a critical supportive resource as the women cope with their own new support roles.

Although many of the women who had confidantes stressed the importance of this relationship for their emotional well-being, a paradoxical finding of this study was that the nine women *without* confidantes were significantly more likely than those with them to report improvements in their physical and emotional health status since caregiving began.

As noted in Chapter 5, this finding contradicts earlier research demonstrating the importance of the presence of a confidante for physical and mental health (Lowenthal & Haven, 1968; Schulz & Rau, 1985). Yet closer analysis reveals that the women without confidantes also tended to have very small social networks: two were elderly great grandmothers who had outlived husbands, siblings, and most of their friends and relatives; others reported estrangement from family members and/or a life history in which their closest and most meaningful relationships had been with the young children they were raising. A 79-year-old great grandmother was among those who described herself as lacking much contact with others, let alone having someone in whom to confide. She had outlived her husband and several of her children, and reported that:

> I don't mix well with other people my age. I'm a loner because I don't understand people and they don't understand me. Most people stand outside and talk. I've been living here for 40 years and I still don't know the people living on this side of me, or on that side. I don't make friends easily.

Yet this elderly woman, who had recently taken in a great granddaughter, went on to describe how much she enjoyed "teaching her things" and just having the youngster around.

For such women, the addition of young grandchildren or great grandchildren to the household may well have provided an important new source of affection and support, and one that would overcompensate for the lack of a confidante. Although the number of women without confidantes in our study was small, the findings in this area do suggest an important avenue for further research.

## SUPPORT GROUP MEMBERSHIP

Although the concept of self-help and social support groups has been traced to preindustrial civilizations (Kropotkin, 1972), its contemporary popularity dates to the 1960s. Dissatisfaction with traditional social institutions, a rebirth of interest in individual and community autonomy and control, and the 1973 recession ushering in a climate of fiscal conservatism and cutbacks in health and social services all contributed to the genesis and mushrooming of a self-help movement unparalleled in scope and magnitude (Gartner & Riessman, 1984).

Defined by Katz and Bender (1976, p. 9) as a "voluntary small group structure for mutual aid in the accomplishment of a specific purpose," the self-help or social support group has gained special prominence in the area of caregiving for the elderly. More than 200 support groups for caregivers of persons with Alzheimer's Disease currently exist, for example, as loose chapters of the Alzheimer's Disease Association (M. Bergland, personal communication, March 1992). And throughout the country, less formal groups have been developed for, and often by, family caregivers who derive emotional as well as informational and other instrumental forms of support through these intentional networks.

Mellor, Rzetelny, and Hudis (1984, p. 98) have outlined a number of reasons why self-help or social support groups are particularly appropriate for caregivers of the aged. Many of these factors, however, appear equally relevant to the phenomenon of grandparent caregiving. To paraphrase these investigators:

> [Grandparent] caregivers are a recently identified population, whose needs the professional service network is only beginning to recognize. Caregivers themselves possess the necessary expertise and hold many of the solutions to their own problems. Group meetings can be a conduit for this knowledge between caregivers. . . . A self-help group approach enables the group's duration. This in turn sets the stage for the development of a self-help network of caregivers that people can turn to in times of crisis and on an "as needed" basis.

Studies based on self-reports and/or participant observation suggest that support groups for family caregivers may play an important role in increasing sense of control and improving coping ability (Clark & Rakowski, 1983; Lazarus, Stafford, Cooper, Cohler, & Dysken, 1981). Yet more rigorous experimental studies have, for the most part, failed to find significant differences between support group members and non-members along these and other dimensions of psychological or physical well-being, or of caregiver burden (Biegel et al., 1991; Toseland & Rossiter, 1989). Moreover, as will be discussed later, support groups cannot begin to compensate for inadequate institutional and societal supports that devalue caregivers and deny them critical resources needed to cope with complex health and social problems.

Despite the limitations of support groups, however, and the equivocal nature of findings concerning their effectiveness (Biegel et al., 1991; Toseland & Rossiter, 1989; Webber, 1991) such groups are often highly valued by their members, and the women in our study were no exception.

Thirteen of the 71 women we interviewed were current members of grandparent support groups run by churches, hospitals, and other formal and informal organizations. Most of the support group participants had learned about their group through social workers, physicians, or other providers, with others citing a family member, friend, or the mass media as a referral source.

Roughly half of the 13 group members attended a support group that met on a weekly basis, with the others in monthly or bimonthly groups.

Nearly all of the women, however, mentioned having to miss sessions at least some of the time because of lack of child care. Only one of the groups provided on-site child care for its members. One member stated that, although child care was available in her group, she didn't bring her grandchildren to the meetings because, "It's my time. That's *my* time!" However, the other 12 members of support groups enthusiastically endorsed the idea and stressed its importance in enabling more caregivers to get to the meetings.

Even without child care, the incentives for attending grandparent support groups were great. The cathartic value of the groups was mentioned by a number of women as being extremely important to them. A 49-year-old grandmother who tends not to confide about her home situation to anyone except the group members remarked, "I think that's what we go for—to holler and scream and cry!" Similarly, a 57-year-old commented:

> The grandparents really open up and let it out. They cry, they really explode. You sit there with them and they're cryin' and you cry with 'em, and they're wipin' their eyes and you're wipin' yours. It just all sort of comes out.

For several of the grandmothers, being among people with similar problems and life situations "relieves a lot of stress" because "they can understand and relate to what you're saying and you don't have to feel bad or embarrassed about it."

For the majority of support group attenders, however, the thing most liked about the groups was the chance they provided to hear about other people's problems and put one's own situation in better perspective. A 56-year-old caring for her elderly mother and two grandchildren under age 2 thus remarked, "When I listen to other people's problems I don't feel so bad because they're worse off than I am." And an older grandmother similarly reported that: "At first I was crying more than anybody. I had the worst problems of anybody. Then others came with worse problems." As will be discussed later in this chapter, the ability to compare one's own situation favorably with that of others emerged throughout our study as a critical coping strategy, and one that helps explain the importance of this aspect of the support group experience.

Second only to their perceived importance in affording an opportunity for favorable comparison of one's situation to that of others, several support groups were highly valued by their members for the instrumental assistance they provided. In particular, group leaders who went out of their way to help grandmothers track down needed services or deal with the bureaucracy were cited for the direct service and support they provide. Fifty-four-year-old Sarah Thompson commented:

> [The group facilitator] gives us leads to things we need. I didn't think I'd ever get MediCal for [my granddaughter] because she didn't have a card, but she ran that down for me. She helped me find places to go to when I run out of food. They get us tickets to different places so we can have outings. They give us baby-sitting while we're in the group.

The importance attached to the instrumental assistance received through support groups is consistent with earlier research by Morycz (1985) suggesting that instrumental or tangible aid is the form of support most appreciated by caregivers for the elderly.

The need for support group members to themselves work on accessing increased instrumental support, rather than simply having group leaders provide it, also was discussed. Fifty-nine-year-old Belle Anderson expressed this view emphatically:

> It's been more than 2 years now and we're still talking about how we got the children and what the parents are doing. I want to talk about how we get better housing for the children . . . better child care. [The group leader] did a lot for us by opening up doors for us, but she's not the grandparents, we are. She opens the door and then we walk through. That's the only way we're going to get anything done!

Echoing Mrs. Anderson's sentiments, two of the four women in our study who reported that they had formerly been in support groups but had ceased going cited the lack of attention to issues like child care and an overemphasis on talking about the "depressing" aspects of grandparent caregiving as the reasons they had stopped participating.

All of the 13 women currently attending grandparent support groups reported that they believed such groups to be a "very important" resource. For the majority of women we interviewed, however, support groups were not an option, sometimes because of embarrassment ("who wants people to know your baby's drug addicted?"), but more often because of lack of information, time, child care and/or adequate transportation. In short, like other forms of informal support, the availability and accessibility of grandparent support groups appears to be heavily dependent on the more formal support resources that, in predominantly low-income communities, are often in short supply.

## THE ROLE OF CHURCHES

The important role of the church in the life of African Americans has been well documented (Poole, 1990). A place of affirmation, celebration, and recognition, the black church has been described both as a unit of *identity* (black controlled and operated, and able to confer honor, respect, and a sense of achievement), and as a unit of *solution,* offering insights into life's meaning, providing members with "a structured response" for dealing with life changes, and serving as both a stabilizing force and a force for positive social change (Eng, Hatch, & Callan, 1985). As Eng and her colleagues (1985, p. 90) suggest, "The uniqueness of the Black church as both a unit of identity and solution makes it a potentially effective unit of *practice* for addressing health and social problems."

For most of the women in our study, church was indeed a vital unit of identity and, at least in part, a unit of solution. As noted earlier, only one grandmother described herself as having no religion, whereas close to 90% were Protestant, chiefly Baptist, and the remainder Catholic and Muslim. More than three quarters of the women ($n = 54$) were church attenders, with close to a third ($n = 22$) attending at least once weekly and more than half going to services at least once a month.

Approximately one quarter of the women reported taking part in other church activities, such as Bible study and singing in the choir. And of the 40 women who reported that they do some volunteer work, the majority added that their volunteering was church related.

Given the important role that church and formal religion play in the life of the community of grandmothers we interviewed, it is significant that 45% ($n = 32$) stated that they had attended church less in the last year than previously, with only 7 women reporting that their church attendance had actually increased. Eighty percent of those whose church attendance had decreased, moreover, said that the change bothered them, with half of these stating that it bothered them "a great deal." For women like 61-year-old Jerry Wills, "not being able to go to church when I want to" is in fact the single most difficult thing about being a great grandmother caregiver.

For several of the women we interviewed, the church's role as a unit of solution and a unit of practice had extended to church involvement in providing critical emotional and instrumental support to grandparent caregivers. Lucy Thomas, a 59-year-old member of a Missionary Baptist congregation, related that when she first got custody of her grandchildren the church gave her food and people from the congregation helped buy clothes for the two girls. "So many grandmothers in the congregation are affected that the pastor let us set up programs," including outings for the kids and tutoring for the growing numbers who have learning disabilities.

More often, however, the women commented on what they saw as the church's disappointing lack of involvement in supporting grandparent caregivers in the congregation. For Helene Wheaton, the church she has belonged to for more than three decades has become another source of stress for her—a place where she feels she has to hide what has happened in her family:

> I feel so much pressure when I'm there—I just don't know how to let people know. You [the interviewers] are safe because you don't know me, but I can't tell people who know me. At church, especially. I have been going to the same church for over 30 years. Lots of people have me up on a pedestal. They know how much I love my family and how proud I was of my boys. They would never believe it if they found out what has become of [my son]. . . . And people talk. I don't think I could bear that.

A 70-year-old great grandmother who was in church every Sunday before taking in two toddlers remarked, "The church hasn't been helpful. I can't often go now but they don't call to see what's happened."

A number of the women argued that churches, although logical sources of instrumental support for grandparents and their families, have been particularly slow to help in tangible ways. In the words of a 44-year-old grandmother:

> You give your $5.00 or $10.00 every Sunday. They take collections, but they don't do anything. This is a religious thing. They should get together and be involved.

Or a 59-year-old great-aunt:

> I don't think the churches do enough to help and encourage the grandparents. Baptist churches especially, they have what they call "collections for

the community." But they don't offer any help. You know, churches could set up child-care centers, they are the ones that really could do that. But they don't offer any help for the grandparents of these children, even if they're members of the church.

Several grandmothers also remarked on the churches' tendency to ignore the drug wars raging in their communities and largely responsible for the high rates of grandparent caregiving. A 57-year-old raising two preschoolers echoed the sentiments of a number of the women when she argued that the churches need to

educate the young folks. Instead of preachin' to 'em about the devil and Jesus Christ, tell them about crack. Instead of having Sunday school, have a class where they can learn about drugs.

In sum, the church's role as a unit of identity and as a partial unit of solution was not matched by the institution's role as a source of practical, instrumental aid and/or special emotional support around the issue of grandparent caregiving. As will be discussed in Chapter 8, however, although many of the women we interviewed were disappointed with their church's lack of involvement in supporting grandparent care- givers, their religious faith remained by far the most important coping strategy for seeing them through the problems and challenges of the caregiving role.

## GROUP MEMBERSHIP AND VOLUNTARISM

Sociologists repeatedly have demonstrated significant social class differences in formal group membership, with lower income individuals far less likely to be "joiners" than their higher socioeconomic status counterparts (Lowenthal & Robinson, 1976). At the same time, a growing body of research suggests that when socioeconomic status is controlled for, blacks have significantly higher rates of social participation and voluntarism than their white counterparts (London & Giles, 1987).

Well over half of the women in our study ($n = 39$) reported belonging to a social organization, group, or club apart from their church. As noted earlier, 13 women were regular members of grandparent support groups, with others belonging to neighborhood organizations, senior centers, unions, social clubs, and religious groups.

Rates of voluntarism were also high among the grandmothers interviewed. Close to 30% ($n = 20$) reported doing some form of volunteer work, with all but 4 of these stating that they volunteer at least several times a month. Although most of the volunteering was done in conjunction with church, unpaid service activity for hospitals and convalescent homes, unions, tenants' organizations, and other groups also was reported.

For women with a history of heavy involvement in voluntarism or group participation, one of the hardest things about the new caregiving role was the decreased time for such activities. A 63-year-old grandmother remarked that she used to be a leader of the active tenants' association in her housing project but now rarely had time even to attend the meetings. Similarly, a 59-year-old who had prided herself on her active union involvement and her volunteering on behalf of a host of social causes lamented not being able now to fulfill this aspect of her identity:

> If I didn't have the kids, I'd go out and do volunteer work. Maybe somebody got a petition, "we need the water to be better," I'd go take some petitions and get 'em signed and stuff like that. I have plaques for all kinds of volunteer work I did for the schools. . . . What do I miss most now? The chance to volunteer!

* * *

In their study of teenage motherhood and its intergenerational impacts, Ladner and Gourdine (1984) observed that the majority of grandmothers interviewed looked primarily to their daughters for emotional support. Most of these grandmothers, they concluded, were "somewhat isolated" from other relatives, had few female friends, and had no significant man in their lives.

For the women in our study, an adult child's cocaine use and its attendant problems had often driven a wedge between the grandmothers and the parents of the children in their care. Yet contrary to Ladner and Gourdine's (1984) findings, the grandmothers we interviewed were, with few exceptions, embedded in a dense network of other family and friendship ties, and many were also heavily involved in churches, social organizations, and voluntary activities.

Of these, support group membership appeared particularly important in helping women cope with the new role, whereas churches, contrary to expectation, were often seen as less helpful to grandparents and other family members coping with the crack crisis in their communities.

Although family and friendship ties played a central role in the lives of most of the grandparents interviewed, when asked how they coped with difficult situations, or what they did when upset, few reported seeking out or talking to a friend or relative, or in other ways drawing upon their support networks. Instead, the women tended to utilize a variety of alternative coping strategies, and it is to these other means of coping that we now turn.

# 8

---

# Coping With the New Caregiving

As suggested in the preceding chapters, grandparent caregivers face an array of problems, issues, dilemmas, and crises every day. In addition to the normal and predictable crises of raising small children, the women we interviewed found themselves confronting the often unpredictable crises that may be involved in raising children of the crack epidemic (see Chapter 11 this volume).

Trouble with an adult child who is still using crack, worries about elderly parents, financial troubles, conflicts at work or in family relationships, and problems with the bureaucracy also were described as contributing to the high levels of stress they experience.

In this chapter, we will focus on how the grandmother caregivers cope with these problems. We will highlight in particular five strategies that emerged in the study as primary methods used by the women to help them cope both with specific problems and difficulties, and with the daily stresses arising from their multiple and often competing role demands. These five strategies were: coping through prayer or personal religious faith; coping by comparing; coping through focusing; coping through making the situation fun; and coping through reframing the burden.

We will attempt to demonstrate in this chapter the effectiveness of grandparent caregivers in coping with what are often significant problems and stresses in their lives. At the same time, however, we will end the chapter by underscoring that the grandmothers' personal coping strategies, however effective in helping them "get by," cannot significantly improve the lives of these caregivers and their families unless broader community- and societal-level supports and interventions also are put into place.

Kessler, Price, and Wortman (1985) have suggested that coping strategies can be examined along three key dimensions: (a) attempts to impact directly on the problem; (b) efforts to change one's own perspective on the problem or difficulty; and (c) attempts to manage the stresses that the problem has generated. A similar model, developed by Pearlin and Aneshensel (1986) proposes that coping with life problems may take the form of managing the *situation* giving rise to a stressful life problem; managing the *meaning of the situation,* and hence reducing the threat that it poses; or managing the *symptoms* of the stress to which the situation gives rise.

Typologies like these have proven useful when applied to explorations of the coping strategies of older blacks (Chatters & Taylor, 1989), and provide a helpful framework for the current discussion.

The literature on coping strategies and resources among African Americans has tended to stress two primary areas: family or kinship networks and exchange patterns, and the role of prayer and religious behavior (Chatters & Taylor, 1989; Gibson, 1982; McAdoo, 1982; Slaughter & Dilworth-Anderson, 1991). Both may involve mobilization along one, two, or all three of the dimensions noted above.

As Chatters and Taylor (1989) have pointed out, for example, prayer may be used in an attempt to seek direct intervention in a problem; it may be called upon to help change one's perspective on the problem, for example, by "accepting God's will"; and/or it may help the individual manage the stresses associated with a difficult situation (Gibson, 1982). In a similar manner, the mobilization of a family support network may help one directly confront and address a problem, and simply talking to a close family member or confidante may help one get needed perspective on the difficulty, or better manage the stresses that it is causing.

The findings of our study strongly support the literature on the importance of prayer as a coping strategy among older African Americans (Chatters & Taylor, 1989; Gibson, 1982; Neighbors, Jackson, Bowman, & Gurin, 1983; Taylor, 1986). In contrast, however, and contrary to expectation, the grandmother caregivers in our study did not appear to draw heavily upon a family support system as a primary coping strategy.

In making this observation, we do not mean to discount the very significant roles of confidantes and family and friendship ties in the lives of the women interviewed. As illustrated in the preceding chapter, most of the women were immersed in strong family networks and had frequent contact with confidantes, who were most often sisters, mothers, and women friends, and slightly less often husbands and partners or adult children.

When asked specifically how they cope with a difficult situation however, the women tended not to mention talking to a confidante or mobilizing a family support network, but spoke instead of turning to prayer, or calling upon internal strengths and resources. These frequently articulated coping approaches, along with several others that emerged from the data, now will be examined.

## COPING THROUGH PRAYER

Middle-aged and older African Americans turn to prayer more frequently than do older whites of similar ages, educational backgrounds, and incomes (Gibson, 1982). And, although a decline in prayer among blacks since the 1950s has been noted (Veroff, Douvan, & Kulka, 1981), this behavior remains a traditional means of handling difficulty among African Americans, and especially among older black women (Gibson, 1982).

In our own study, prayer, reading the Bible, and turning to God were the most frequently cited means of coping. One in five participants identified the Bible or prayer as her primary coping strategy. And almost everyone told stories of the number of times that their strength, their courage, their will to go own, their patience, or their perspective was renewed or sustained through spiritual reflection. In the words of a 69-year-old great grandmother raising two infants, "I pray really hard —that's the only way I get through."

The women in our study have long traditions of spiritual expression and often find comfort for the new challenges of caregiving in familiar verses or stories. A 56-year-old grandmother who had been forced to quit her job to care for two young grandchildren said that when she's in need, "I remember the words of a Jesus song my father used to sing to me. That was 50 years ago!" Another grandmother remarked that she turns to a motivational radio program every morning, because "If I don't start the day with the Lord, I'm starting out lost."

Several women spoke of scriptures or passages that had been meaningful to them all their lives but that had taken on new relevance now. For some of these women, there was a sense of having recently understood what God had been trying to prepare them for. In the words of a grandmother raising five of her young grandchildren:

I always knew that the Lord wanted more of me. I thought that I had met
my obligations and that now I could rest. I guess I underestimated His plan.
But I accept it because He has prepared me. And I *know* that the Lord does
not impose a burden that we cannot bear.

Many women remarked that they had found the strength they needed
in the Bible when all else had failed them. A 45-year-old grandmother
raising a 5-year-old while working two or three jobs, described how she
had "hit rock bottom" when her husband of 20 years walked out:

I didn't know how I would survive . . . I was in the bathtub and crying. I
was so tired. And I said to the Lord "I know that you say that there's something for everyone in the Bible but I know that there's nothing in there for
me." . . . I was sitting there and my Bible was on the floor. So I picked up
the Book and the Book fell open to Isaiah 54th Chapter . . . and it was like
a flashlight was shining down on me—like that verse was highlighted. And
the verse said "Fear not for I am with you." I cried—it was scary—it was
weird—but I believe that that was what He wanted me to understand.

For this woman, and so many others, God is their confidante—accessible,
understanding, and supportive. As one grandmother put it:

I just sit down and talk to the Lord. I talk to Him just like I'm talking to
you all, because He knows how much I can bear. It's like a weight being
lifted off my shoulders. I just don't have anyone else to talk to *but* Him.

For many grandmother caregivers, this confidante serves as coun-
selor, helping them understand the significant losses and tragedies of
their lives. For example, a 79-year-old respondent has outlived most of
her children and now must accept the death of a daughter who had been
clean for 2 years but died because of the damage that drug use had done
to her heart. Sadly, she interprets what happened through the Bible:

You can't go up against it. You can quit doing what you're doing and be
good and everything, but it's more or less going to catch up with you!

Or in the words of a 43-year-old, trying to live with her daughter's murder
last year: "I remember what God's promises are. It gives me the relief
I need."

Through our interviewing, it became clear that the mainstream models
of family dysfunction, codependency, and enabling behavior (Beattie,
1987; Schaef, 1986; Sorensen & Bernal, 1987) that have helped many

families cope with the harsh realities of drug abuse and addiction do not yet resonate with the respondents' experience. Whether that is a flaw in the models themselves, a matter of vocabulary or phrasing, or merely a lack of exposure and dissemination is difficult to determine.

But it was clear that the grandmothers were struggling for a way to understand what had happened to their families, what had happened to their children, and how to relate to a child who "is *not* the child I raised."

And, in many cases, they found their answers through prayer. Many women spoke of their relationship with God as the single most important factor in developing the necessary distance from an addicted and abusive child. Many spoke of their years of listening to sirens, calling the hospitals, and having nightmares, not to mention being robbed, verbally abused, or publicly humiliated by adult children who were high on crack or in need of money or drugs.

Trying desperately to balance the demands of the abusive children, the grandchildren, and often other children or grandchildren, it was not uncommon for grandparent caregivers to maintain close contact with a child using crack, even when the emotional or physical consequences were devastating (see Chapter 11 this volume).

But several of the caregivers with the greatest clarity about how to cope with the crack abuser in the family spoke of a new understanding, an epiphany, that had come to them through prayer:

> He sent me a vision and I started praying for me. And that's what turned it around. For a long time, I was praying the wrong prayer. I was praying for her. Lord, keep her safe, Lord, help her quit, Lord, take care of her. . . . And then one day I said Lord if you need to, take her, but give me the strength to go on. And that turned it around.

And lastly, many reported that their relationship with God gets them going when all else has failed. In the words of a 61-year-old grandmother with two preschoolers: "Sometimes I go to bed at night and I say 'I don't care if I never get up in the morning.' And then, the next morning, the Lord just pushes me right out of bed and says 'You're not through yet!' and I get up stronger."

## FOCUSING

In her study of the stress absorbing systems of upwardly mobile African American families, McAdoo (1982) found that calling upon one's own resources was second only to turning to other family members as a means of coping with problems. Close to a quarter of the 300 adults in her study reported that their most frequent response to a problem was to "think about it myself, stay calm, and do what was needed" (McAdoo, 1982, p. 485).

In the Grandparent Caregiver Study, calling upon one's own resources most often took the form of reaching deep inside and finding an inner peace or focus. Nell Gibson, a 65-year-old grandmother raising three very active preschoolers, illustrated this strategy:

> I've had a place inside me that no one has ever found. It's there waiting for me, whenever I need it. All I have to do is find me a few quiet moments and I can go there in a minute. Sometimes in the bath, even doing the dishes or standing over the rice on the stove. If I didn't have that little place, I couldn't get through some of the days I'm facing.

Several grandmothers spoke of this kind of solace and comfort as different from that found in prayer. These inner spaces didn't seem to provide answers or direction as much as a chance to think, an escape, and, sometimes, a release.

For a number of women, "going to myself" or "talking to myself" when upset were a critical means of calming down and "regrouping" in order to go on. As one grandmother put it:

> I get tired, I really do—I'm human! And then I say, "oh why do I suffer like this?" But then I just talk to myself and try to get myself out of the rut. Because if I don't do it, nobody else is going to do it, so I just gotta keep on going.

Naomi McFarland finds her chronic insomnia to be "a blessing" for it gives her time alone, deep in the night, to reflect and to write the poems that have been her passion for many years. A 62-year-old grandmother with two 4-year-olds in her care, and a crack-involved adult daughter who is in and out of the house, told of getting away alone, even for a short while, in order to get a quiet time for such regrouping: "I get in my car and just go somewhere, sit in my car and think." Another grandmother, who has three grandchildren and three of her own teenage and young adult children at home, spoke of taking a 45-minute bus ride down to the Oakland waterfront. Once there, she has her own special rock that she sits on to "feel the wind and the water and cry my heart out."

For many grandmother caregivers, being physically alone was almost impossible, so they found ways to escape in the presence of their families. Going into a bedroom, closing the door, and sitting quietly for a few moments, or using the ironing time to think about a problem, or to forget one's troubles for a while, were among the strategies mentioned in this regard. But whatever the external circumstances or the inner processes involved, the ability to go inside of one's self and focus frequently was used as a strategy to enable the grandmothers to "keep going."

A variant of this coping method, mentioned by a number of women, involved focusing on and thinking about the grandchildren. When asked what she did when upset, for example, 54-year-old Sarah Thompson looked at her 3-year-old granddaughter and said simply, "I think about her." Using almost identical language, a 45-year-old grandmother with four of her grandchildren and one of her own teenagers still at home said, "I think about them. That makes me keep going."

For 49-year-old Betty Driscoll, coping by focusing on her 3-year-old granddaughter Sandra often involves thinking about what the little girl's life would be like if her grandmother weren't around. "I'm learning to cope," Mrs. Driscoll says:

> You can have a pity party for 15 minutes, then you solve the problem. You look at this girl who can't take care of herself and say, "what happens to her if you commit suicide or run away?" Little kids are so helpless.

For several of the women, focusing on the children in their care also meant consciously changing earlier coping styles and behaviors in an effort to role model positive ways of dealing with stress. Forty-seven-year-old Myra Lewis, the sole caregiver for her 4-year-old grandson, commented:

> I used to tell the world which train to catch. Now I have to be aware of how I'm behaving because it makes an impression on him. If I explode and lose my temper, he does too!

For 59-year-old Lucy Thomas, focusing on the children and their needs also meant changing her old ways of reacting to stress, but for a different reason: "Before I'd rant and rave and curse," Mrs. Thomas remarked. But since taking in her four grandchildren, "I stay calmer now, because I don't want the kids to know there are problems, like not enough money."

Coping by focusing on the grandchildren sometimes took the form of thinking about the contributions the youngsters were making to the grandmother's own life, in spite of the hardships involved in caregiving and the often tragic circumstances that had made their surrogate parenting necessary. A 60-year-old with two young grandchildren remarked:

> I look back on my life and realize I might have been bored with nobody after [my daughter] came out of high school. I might have stayed here and gotten old! But taking them on really did bring things back. One time before they came I was in the kitchen doing dishes and I thought, "I sure do miss the sound of little feet." And then those little feet started comin'! And I have them now!

And a 47-year-old similarly commented that when things get tough, she reminds herself of what she likes best about having the grandkids: "More or less, they keep me going. I don't have time to grow old. They keep me hopping!"

Finally, several grandmothers offered illustrations of the ways in which focusing on the grandchildren gives them the strength they need to go on. In the words of Joan Harrison, a great grandmother in her sixties:

> The kids bring you so much goodness. I can be ever so down and I can pick up Carmen [her great granddaughter] and she has a picture—just a simple picture, but she did it herself! And that picks me up and leaves me glowing!

And another grandmother described the strength she got through focusing on her 2- and 3-year-old grandchildren: "When I give them a bath and they say, 'Nana, I love you' and give me a big kiss. That makes my day and carries me over to the next."

## COPING BY HAVING FUN

Focusing on and taking joy in one's grandchildren often went hand in hand with another major coping strategy that emerged from the interviews, namely having fun. We discovered among many of the grandmothers a determination to reduce the stresses associated with caregiving by making the situation as enjoyable as possible under the circumstances.

Fifty-seven-year-old Nancy Cooper was among the grandmothers who talked about trying to make the new life fun both for her three young grandchildren and for herself.

> I don't have the energy I used to, I used to play ball with my children when I was in my thirties and forties. I used to love going to the park. I'd go across the street and play ball anytime! And now I try to play ball—and I'm not too bad! Just because I'm stiff doesn't mean I can't do it!

Another grandmother spoke of the fun she had with her older grandson on Christmas Eve, staying up all night trying to assemble a new bicycle for the younger boy. And Naomi McFarland showed us the song she had written and yearbook she had compiled for her grandson's graduation—from preschool!

Sometimes the fun is deliberate—a conscious attempt to mediate the pain of the circumstances in which the women and the grandchildren find themselves. Forty-four-year-old Eva Smith commented:

> I just had to make up my mind that I could do this. And I have to take breaks. So when I get the chance, I take a little vacation. We might even have to take the bus if I can't drive to where we want to go, but I just told Tyrone [grandnephew] that we're going to have some adventures, he and I. And that made me feel better.

Sometimes, the fun is designed to give a sense of the ordinary to their extraordinary situations:

> I let the oldest one have a slumber party for her birthday last week—I used to always let my kids do that. So we all slept right here and oh, they wore me out! But it was fun. We have lots of fun together.

And sometimes, the fun is purely spontaneous, based on the amazing reservoir of love and affection that these women feel for their families:

> We keep each other going by sharing the love that's between us. . . . And I give them plenty of love alright . . . especially in the night when they wake up and they've just got to play. I'll be kissing feet and butts, under the chin, and wherever the heck they need a tickle, at 3 in the morning! Sometimes the baby, he's just got to play. This baby hasn't ever needed a tickle he didn't get.

## COPING BY COMPARISON

Another frequently used coping strategy is one we have termed *coping by comparing*. Grandmother caregivers find tremendous strength in relating their situation to other events of their own lives, to the situations of others around them, or to their image of how much worse things could be. In making such comparisons, they are using a coping strategy that functions chiefly by changing one's perspective on the problem and managing the meaning of the situation, so that the threat it poses is reduced (Kessler et al., 1985; Pearlin & Aneshensel, 1986).

A 43-year-old woman raising two preschoolers remarked, "Some of these grandparents are older than me, with arthritis and all. How do *they* do it?" And a single woman living alone with her 3-year-old granddaughter commented, "Some women my age are worse off—in bad marriages *and* raising kids!"

For several of the grandmothers, even the heart-breaking crack involvement of an adult child could be placed in perspective when viewed in a broader social context. Reflecting on the high homicide rate among black males in the city, one grandmother said, "Both of my kids a lot of people wouldn't be happy with. But I have a son who just turned 25, and he's still alive—in Oakland!"

The comparison can be based on the severity of the crack problem of an adult child, economic or health considerations, or any one of a number of different criteria. But what emerged from the data was both the power of the comparative assessment as a coping strategy and the generosity and goodwill with which the comparisons were made. In the words of a married grandmother, whose husband helped out with the caregiving, "These women doing it by themselves have my complete respect—I don't know how they manage."

For 57-year-old Mattie Singer, watching what other grandparent caregivers had to go through not only made her own burden seem lighter but invoked a real desire to be able to help:

I can't complain or feel sorry for myself when I see how bad it is for others. It makes me want to try and help them in some way, which is sort of comical since I can hardly help myself! But you have to wonder how they're going to make it.

Ironically, even a lifetime of difficulties was seen by some grandmothers as giving them an edge over grandparents who were trying to cope with the new caregiver role without such background. In the words of a 79- year-old great grandmother raising an infant:

> My whole life has been trouble. I'm acquainted with hardship. So having Veronica [her great grandchild] isn't such a hardship for me as it is for someone who isn't used to it.

The objective circumstances of one's own situation appeared to bear little relationship to the ability to successfully invoke comparison with others as a coping strategy. One of the most economically disadvantaged women we interviewed, a 62-year-old grandmother with two grandchildren and a crack involved daughter living under her roof, compared her situation to that of a 75-year-old neighbor who had three of her children and more than a dozen of her grandchildren living with her. Describing in detail how this frail elderly neighbor would use her walker to cart the grandkids' clothes to the self-service laundry each day, the 62-year-old repeatedly pointed out that her own problems were minor by comparison.

For other women, the basis of favorable evaluations of one's own situation lay not in other people's lives, but in one's own life at some earlier time. A 54-year-old who had suffered ulcers and mental problems a decade earlier thus remarked, "I think about the times it was worse. Things were really bad then compared to now." And for a 61-year-old raising two preschoolers, the broken sleep suffered since her great grandchildren came is easily put into perspective by a backward glance: "I'm used to it. When I was working I had to be at work at 4 o'clock in the morning."

As discussed in Chapter 7, the critical role of grandparent support groups for many study participants appeared also to relate in large part to the groups' effectiveness in helping the women favorably evaluate their own situations. "You think you've got it rough until you hear about someone else's problems" was typical of the comments made by group members.

Finally, the importance attached to comparison as a means of better coping with one's own situation was suggested in several grandmothers' comments concerning how they were attempting to teach this approach to their grandchildren. In the words of a 48-year-old grandmother, "I try to get my grandkids to understand that no matter how hard their situation is, there's always someone out there who's worse."

## REFRAMING THE BURDEN

The fifth coping strategy that emerged from our data may be termed *reframing the burden*. Like focusing, reframing the burden appeared, in part, a means of coping by getting a new perspective on the problem, or on one's relationship to that problem.

Reframing may come about as a result of any or all of the previous four strategies: prayer, comparison, focusing, and having fun. When those strategies are mobilized, the women sometimes envision their lives differently. What is being asked of them becomes a challenge, an opportunity, even a sacred trust, and by reframing the burden in this way, they are better able to deal with it.

For several of the women we interviewed, reframing the burden involved viewing their new caregiving responsibilities as a "second chance" to "raise kids right." "I was a 'new age' mom to my kids," said a 43-year-old grandmother. "I wanted them to have independent minds, to make their own choices. I don't know about that now," she says, adding that her two children both ended up getting into trouble. When the task of raising a preschooler becomes overwhelming, she calms herself by reframing the burden so that it becomes less a chore and more an opportunity to raise this new child in her life with more discipline and "good values."

For 59-year-old Lucy Thomas, a similar reframing process takes place as she copes with the responsibility of raising four youngsters by reminding herself that this is her chance to "raise children as Christians." "The Lord is giving me a second chance to raise kids the way I should have raised mine in the first place," she says, noting that it's really easier this time because she is "born again."

For some of the grandmothers we interviewed, reframing took the place of putting one's current caregiving activities within the context of one's own earlier life. For Sally Fairlane and her husband, raising two great grandchildren was reframed as an opportunity to keep the little ones from experiencing what their great grandparents had as children. Remarking that she and her husband had both been raised in orphanages, Mrs. Fairlane spoke of their commitment to offering the grandchildren a better start, adding, "We both know what it's like to be without parents."

As described in Chapter 10, many of the women we interviewed had spent several months or years of their childhood in the care of their own grandparents. For some of these women, reframing the burden took the place of reminding themselves that "what goes around, comes around."

Finally, as noted earlier, prayer and religious faith were closely intertwined for many grandmothers with reframing the burden as a coping strategy. Such women frequently saw the new caregiving as a role the Lord had chosen them for, and they frequently reminded themselves of this special charge. "I tell myself, 'you're doing these things for God,' " 70-year-old Hedda Wilson remarked. "That gives me the courage to go on."

Most of the women who refocused the burden by means of their religious faith did so, like Mrs. Wilson, by thinking of grandparent caregiving as God's chosen work for them personally. Yet for at least one of the grandmothers, the Almighty's plan was on a grander scale. In this grandmother's words:

> There won't be a "lost generation"—no way! The Lord saw all of us Southern grandmothers, tired and ready to retire to our porches. But he knew that there was only one kind of person who could save these children—Southern grandmothers. And so He pointed to each of us and He said, "you and you and you—I've got one more job for you!"

\* \* \*

Grandmothers raising the children of the crack cocaine epidemic do indeed have "one more job" to do, and they are often doing it under tremendously difficult circumstances. The coping strategies described in this chapter were key among those that emerged in our study as enabling the women to deal with the problems and stresses faced, often on a daily basis.

As will be discussed in Chapter 13, however, personal coping strategies, regardless of how effective they may be over the short run, cannot take the place of broader community and societal strategies for dealing with the root causes of poverty and unemployment, the drug infestation of many low-income inner-city communities, and other factors that have contributed to the rise in grandparent caregiving. The intimate interdependence of "private troubles and public issues" (Mills, 1959) indeed makes even the best coping strategies severely limited in how much they can hope to achieve alone.

# 9

---

# Combining Work and Child Care

The proportion of mid-life and older women in the labor force has continued to grow dramatically since the 1950s, with projections now suggesting that 75% of all women aged 45 to 60 will be working outside the home by the year 2000 (Creedon, 1988). Among African American women, rates of employment have remained consistently higher than among white women, with the former also disproportionately represented in jobs having the lowest wages and status. As Sidel (1990, p. 187) has noted, "While black women are crowded into a few sex-segregated occupations, they are, to a significant extent, working in the least desirable, lowest paying jobs within these occupations."

For women of all ethnic groups, the need to combine work and caregiving is often a daily reality. Indeed, as Older Women's League President Lou Glasse has pointed out, if a woman's nest empties out at all, it tends to remain empty for a very short time, filling up again with elderly parents and other relatives in need of care (Weinstein, 1989).

As noted earlier, many of the women in our study were already engaged in caregiving—for their own youngest children, their elderly parents or other relatives—when they took in one or more of their grandchildren or great grandchildren. For the approximately one third of women ($n = 25$) who were working and remained in the labor force after taking on the grandchildren, the realities of conflicting demands and responsibilities were often particularly pronounced.

Approximately two thirds of the employed women in our study were working 40 hours a week or more outside the home, with the remainder working between 15 and 39 hours. Close to half (45%) were working in domestic service, janitorial, and other low-paying blue-collar jobs, with another quarter in clerical positions, 13% working as nurses aides or other health care technicians, and four occupying professional or managerial positions.

Like caregivers for the elderly (Stone et al., 1987), many of the working women in this study found that they had to rearrange their work schedules radically to accommodate their new grandchild caregiving responsibilities. Close to a third of the women (32%) had cut back their hours because of child care, whereas another five had added hours in order to make ends meet. Fully half of the women had rearranged their hours to accommodate caregiving, changing the days they worked or the hours, typically to include more graveyard shifts, earlier mornings, or weekends.

Despite the changes made, however, most of the working caregivers found themselves faced with severe time constraints, money pressures, and feelings that they often couldn't do justice to their jobs or their grandchildren as a result of the pressures of their conflicting roles.

Fifty-seven-year-old Frances Green personifies such conflicts as she struggles to juggle the competing demands of her two grandchildren, ages 10 and 3, her job as a data processor, and the needs of her partially blind, 94-year-old mother. Recently cut from full- to part-time work, Mrs. Green worries about her diminished income (less than $1,000 per month) and the fact that she can no longer pay all the bills, much less provide needed "extras" for the grandchildren. She is particularly worried about the lack of heating in the house since the earthquake, and about the special needs of 3-year-old Clarence, who suffers severe hyperactivity, nightmares, and other consequences of prenatal drug exposure. In her words:

> I feel like I'm supplying a place to stay and food to eat, but I'd like to do more. The kids need a counselor. I'd like to take them places but I can't afford to. I'm behind on the rent, and can't afford to fix the broken light fixtures.

Although Mrs. Green hopes for a return to full-time work so that she'll be able to do more financially for her grandkids, she also fears what the added time away from them may mean. Indeed, looking back on her strenuous work schedule as she raised her own children, she reflects that her good intentions—working two jobs to stay off welfare—may have hurt the children in the end by taking her away from them so much of the time. All four children were involved with drugs at some point, one has since died a drug-related death, and two daughters remain on crack. Determined to provide a better life for her grandchildren, Mrs. Green sees full-time work as both critical to achieving that end and detrimental to meeting the children's need for her presence and attention.

For 49-year-old Denise Briggs, putting her youngest child through college while caring full time for an older daughter's baby has elevated financial concerns to the top of the priority list. A postal worker for the past 16 years, Mrs. Briggs now gets up at 4 or 5 o'clock each morning in order to get her grandson to the baby-sitter and still get to work on time. She takes her lunch to work these days, since she can no longer afford to go out to lunch with co-workers, and she comes straight home from work in order to cook his dinner. Since taking the boy in a few months ago, she has worked overtime 2 to 3 days a week to cover her sudden added expenses. But the high cost of baby-sitting, added to her 17-year-old's college expenditures ("this term she had to pay $45 for just one book!") have made making ends meet all but impossible:

> Last week, for the first time since I had them, all of a sudden I started crying. After I got paid and paid the baby-sitter and all, I had only $41 left. It seemed like, "what am I working for?" I can't afford to even buy stockings anymore. Everything just came down on me.

Mrs. Briggs' sentiments were echoed by other working women, like 54-year-old Yolanda Davis. Divorced, and determined to stay off welfare and out of "the system," Mrs. Davis is a proud woman, struggling to make it on her own. But she has found her finances stretched to the limit by the combination of a daughter's college expenses and the high costs of child care for a grandchild. After experiencing the humiliation of having to borrow money from friends and family members, she has taken to working two and sometimes three jobs in order to manage:

> I think the hardest thing was that period when I just could not seem to make ends meet. I had expenses for [my grandson] and was helping my daughter through college, which was very important to me. And then having to pay for child care. I just didn't have the money and I was struggling. I was doing crazy things—I was borrowing from people, from friends and family —and I don't like to do that. I'm getting through that period now. With my extra jobs and my daughter going to school here instead of down South, it helps. I'm coming out of it.

Borrowing from family and friends, giving up "extras" like home repairs or a new pair of stockings, getting behind on the rent, and having
to take on extra jobs or longer work hours—these were just a few of the
economic costs of caring mentioned by the employed women in our study.
Not surprisingly, as we shall see later, many of the working women also
perceived themselves as paying a price physically or emotionally, for
the combination of roles they were attempting to fulfill.

## WORK OUTSIDE THE HOME:
## NEEDED BREAK OR ADDED STRESSOR?

In the field of informal care for the elderly, the question of whether
employed caregivers experience more or less caregiving strain than
their nonworking counterparts remains subject to debate (Brody, 1985a;
Giele, Mutschler, & Orodenker, 1987; Scharlach, 1987). As Scharlach
et al. (1991) have argued, however, the tendency of most studies in this
area to treat employment as a unitary construct, without attention to
working conditions and related factors, has lessened the utility of the
research findings. That work is more likely to have negative effects on
caregiving when the job involves long hours and inflexible work routines has been suggested (e.g., Archbold, 1983; Enright & Friss, 1986;
Horowitz, 1985), and underscores the importance of looking at the nature
of the employment experience in more detail.

In our own study, the fact that the majority of working women were
in low-status, low-paying jobs, frequently with lengthy shifts and inflexible schedules, suggested the need to determine whether work
outside the home under such conditions was perceived as providing a
relief from the stresses of caregiving or an additional burden in and of
itself.

Approximately half of the 25 working women in our study ($n = 13$)
reported that they generally enjoyed the break that work provided from
constant child-care responsibilities at home. For others, however, the
combination of work and child care made for a life without any time to
relax and catch one's breath. A 52-year-old food handler reflected on
her situation and commented, "If you're working, I wouldn't advise you
to keep your grandchildren, because there's no break at all!" In a similar
vein, a 43-year-old professional woman remarked, "I have two demanding jobs now. I need some social time. I just need 20 minutes a day to

myself. People at work say, 'Have a nice weekend,' and I think, 'I have 48 hours with a 2-year-old!' "

As Baines et al. (1991) have noted,

> The work women do within the family is often mirrored in their work outside the home: as child care workers, as domestic and office cleaners, and as waitresses and factory workers in food preparation plants. . . . In the home, the work is unpaid and undervalued; in the workplace it is poorly paid and undervalued. (p. 12)

For those women in our study whose paid work most closely resembled their responsibilities at home, the stresses of combining work with child care appeared particularly pronounced. In the words of a 59-year-old raising five grandchildren and working as a school bus driver, "There's kids at work and kids at school. Everywhere I go it's kids!" Fifty-six-year-old Ronda Leeds expressed a similar sentiment, though in her case the source of special stress lay in the similarity of the nature of caregiving tasks, rather than of the ages of those cared for: after an 8-hour grave- yard shift spent "changing people's diapers" and providing general custodial care as an aide in a convalescent hospital, she goes home by bus and stays up most of the day with her hyperactive and learning delayed great granddaughter, age 2. Work isn't something she enjoys, says Mrs. Leeds, "I just do it because I have to." Ironically, this woman, who recently switched to graveyard shift in order to become caregiver to her great granddaughter, had taken on the hated night shift once before in her life—so that she could raise her own children.

## EMPLOYMENT, CAREGIVING, AND HEALTH

As noted in Chapter 5, the employed women in our study were significantly more likely to rate their health in positive terms than were grandmothers who were not in the paid labor force. Fully 75% of the 25 employed caregivers rated their health as good or excellent, for example, compared to just 43% of those who were not working outside the home. Similarly, employed women were significantly more likely to rate their health as the same or better than that of other people their age (96% versus 77% of nonemployed women), with not a single working woman saying that her health was worse than that of others in her age group (compared to 13% of nonemployed women).

Because the working women in our study tended to be younger than nonemployed grandmothers, and because the working group automatically excluded women who had left the labor force due to poor health, it is not surprising that the employed caregivers reported significantly fewer problems with conditions and symptoms such as back and stomach pain, heart trouble, arthritis, and tightness in the chest. It was also not surprising that working grandmothers were more likely to report that their health "never got in the way" of doing things they wanted or needed to do (58% vs. 38%), and that far fewer reported being "very concerned" about their health (8% vs. 19%).

Although employed caregivers were in general more positive about their health status than those not in the labor force, they were also more likely to report that their health had worsened, both in the last year, and in the period since caregiving began. Fully 42% of employed caregivers said that their health was worse now than a year ago, for example, compared to just 21% of the nonemployed women. Similarly, only 12.5% of the working women reported improvement in their health status over the last year, compared to close to a third of the nonemployed women.

Roughly half of both employed and nonemployed grandmothers said that their health now was the same as before caregiving began. But among those reporting a change, employed women were again more likely to see a change for the worse (38% vs. 32%) and correspondingly less likely to say that their health had improved since their new responsibilities began (13% vs. 23%).

For several of the older working women in our sample, the combination of work and child care had perceptible health consequences, made worse by emotional exhaustion and a feeling of having "paid one's dues" many times over. As one 60-year-old grandmother put it:

> It's really hard for me. . . . I'm getting so I just hate getting up in the mornings to go to work. I'm so stiff, I'm just dragging this leg. . . . Some days I get there and I feel so stretched out I could just sit down and cry. I've been working a long time. I'm 60 years along. I had to do all the cookin' and washin' when I was young—people made children work then. And I'm tired now.

When asked to rate their emotional health, working and nonworking women in our sample had almost identical responses, with slightly more than half of both groups saying their emotional health was excellent or good, and about 45% rating it as fair or poor. The groups were also very similar in rating their emotional health now compared to before caregiving began, with approximately a third reporting no change, 29% citing improvement, and a little more than a third of each group reporting worse emotional health since caregiving began.

In comparing their emotional health now to a year ago, however, employed women were once again more likely to report a worsening of their perceived health status, with 38% reporting that their emotional health was worse than a year ago, compared to just over a quarter of the nonemployed women.

In their study of caregivers for people with Alzheimer's disease, Zarit, Todd, and Zarit (1986) found that, contrary to expectation, participants reported less stress and more success in coping emotionally with their multiple tasks after 2 years had passed. Although numerous factors may come into play in explaining these findings, some of which may be specific to coping with dementia, the overall finding is of interest. Our own findings suggest that, particularly for working grandparent caregivers, perceptions of worsening emotional health in the last year may signal a need for greater attention to the emotional stresses and needs associated with combining work and caregiving.

## ACCOMMODATING WORK AND CHILD CARE

Studies of working caregivers for the elderly have demonstrated that such individuals tend to have more frequent absences from work, and more time off during the day, than their noncaregiving colleagues (Scharlach & Boyd, 1989; Stone et al., 1987). In our study, however, contrary to expectation, although having the grandchildren often meant shift changes and sometimes also meant passing up promotions, it generally did not mean lots of extra time off work. Indeed, approximately half of the 25 working women in our study (*n* = 13) reported that they never took time off because of the grandchildren, with only 4 responding that they had to take such time at least once a week.

Several factors may help explain the relatively low rates of absenteeism due to child care for women in this study. First, although many of the children in their care did suffer from conditions such as hyperactivity and respiratory ailments, few had serious medical problems occasioning sudden health crises. Second, as will be discussed below, many of the women had arranged babysitting or child care through neighbors, adult children, or extended family members who would continue to provide coverage in the event of such problems. But third and perhaps most important, the serious financial hardships faced by many of the women in this study may help explain why the majority went to great lengths to avoid taking time off work and thus face even greater economic vulnerability.

Perhaps because of the relative lack of time taken off for child care, only three women perceived such absences as posing a serious problem with their bosses or co-workers. On the other hand, all but three of the women reported that if their regular baby-sitter fell through, no one else was available to take time off in order to care for one of the grandchildren. Husbands, adult children, siblings, and others typically were described by the grandmothers as being available only in a real emergency and sometimes not even then.

The difficulty grandmother caregivers had in identifying anyone other than themselves who could take time off to care for a sick child points to another major issue for such caregivers: the problem of affordable help with child care. Although the high cost of child care and baby-sitting was cited by almost all of the women in our study as a source of frustration and concern, it appeared particularly pronounced for grandmother caregivers working outside the home.

The employed women we interviewed had a variety of child-care arrangements. Ten of the women had either a baby-sitter or a relative stay with the children in the home while they were at work, whereas 6 took the grandkids to formal day-care centers, 3 took them to a baby-sitter's home, and 5 had a combination of sitting and day-care arrangements. Significantly, not a single grandmother reported that she left her grandchildren at home alone while she was at work—a finding consistent with other studies showing that African American parents of all income groups are less likely than whites to leave children at home unattended while on the job (Gibbs, 1990; Presser, 1989).

The heavier reliance on family and extended family members for help with baby-sitting in African American communities often is suggested as enabling the above mentioned child-care coverage (Gibbs, 1990). And indeed, for several of the women in our study, child care consisted of having an older teenage child or grandchild watch the young ones during the day or evening, with the grandmother not infrequently rushing home during her lunch or dinner break to make sure things were alright.

But such arrangements were often described as anything but ideal or long term. Women depending on their own teenage children often worried about the latter's potential resentment of their newfound child-care responsibilities. Like their counterparts in Burton's (1991a) recent study, moreover, grandparent caregivers who were relying on older teenagers for baby-sitting sometimes worried that the latter were "hanging out" on the streets in the late afternoon or early evening, exposing both themselves and the youngsters in their care to the dangers posed by drug dealers and users in the neighborhood. Grandparents also worried about the loss of time for studying, and of opportunities for socializing, participating in sports, or finding part-time jobs faced by their teen- or college-aged children who had to spend many hours a week assisting with the grandchildren. Describing the difficult transition experienced by her 17-year-old son when they had to take in the grandchildren, 49-year-old Ellie Shanas said, "He went through some changes, yes he did. And it was not easy for any of us. There are a lot of things he'd been looking forward to that he just can't do now. He's needed here."

The tenuous nature of several of the women's informal child-care arrangements also was apparent. A working grandmother who relied on her mother for after school baby-sitting was concerned, for example, that the elderly woman's own increasing frailty would soon make this arrangement unrealistic. Grandparents relying on their teenagers worried about what would happen when the older children moved away or just "got fed up with the whole situation." And a caregiver for whom a neighbor on temporarily disability provided child care while the grand-mother was at work wondered how she'd manage a few months from now when the neighbor expected to resume her own job.

For many of the women we interviewed, the government's failure to provide and/or help them afford quality child care was a source of special resentment. As one working grandmother put it:

> These aren't our kids, they're someone else's. The [government] needs to understand that we're taking on a role because there is a need to help these children. And if we have to go to work, we shouldn't have to pay out of our pockets for what we're trying to do.

## FORMAL AND INFORMAL WORKPLACE SUPPORT FOR CAREGIVING

For the great majority of working women in this study, the low-paying, blue-collar nature of jobs occupied meant that parental leave policies were nonexistent. If child-care responsibilities did mean leaving work, consequently, approximately two-thirds stated that they would take sick leave or time without pay, with the remainder taking vacation days or some other form of unpaid absence. Although the women carefully avoided having to leave work often for the grandchildren, many made clear where their priorities would lie in the event of a family crisis. When asked who she'd call upon if she was at work and couldn't get away during an emergency at home, one grandmother summed up the attitude of many when she responded: "What do you mean, 'If I can't get away?' There isn't any can't. If there's an emergency and the grandkids need me, I'm gone!"

For the majority of women in our study, the fact of having a "second shift" (Hochschild & Machung, 1989) at home composed of full-time caregiving for grandchildren was not hidden from people at work. Eighty percent of the 25 working women ($n = 20$) reported that their boss knew of their other life, more than two-thirds said that some or all of their co-workers knew, and only 2, both in relatively new jobs, stated that no one at work knew.

In general, moreover, knowledge of the grandmothers' caregiving responsibilities was combined with high perceived levels of support at the workplace. Forty percent of the employed women ($n = 10$) reported that their boss was "very supportive" of their caregiving, asking about the grandchildren, allowing the women to leave early when necessary or "looking the other way" when they came in a little late. For 4 of the grandmothers, however, bosses who were felt to be very unsupportive added greatly to their stress levels. Forty-five-year-old Sandra Morris, raising her 5-year-old granddaughter Danylle while working 40 hours a week as a licensed vocational nurse, provides a case in point. Danylle is frequently sick with respiratory problems, and as her grandmother notes:

> When she's sick I have to take sick leave. But now I can't do that as much 'cause my boss gets on me about it. . . . I told my supervisor what is going on and all the things I'm dealing with, but she just said, "Sandra—that is your problem." And I said, "I know that and I'm dealing with it the best I can," and she just said back, "We all got problems." So now I'm in a real bad situation because my supervisor thinks that Danylle is messing everything up and that I'm unreliable or something. And even though I have it coming to me, she won't grant my vacation and she won't approve my sick leave.

Several studies of employed caregivers for the elderly have demonstrated that support from co-workers can be an important potential buffer against caregiver strain (Brody, Kleban, Johnsen, Hoffman, & Schoonover, 1987; Giele et al., 1987; Rivers, Barnett, & Baruch, 1979). For close to 90% of the working women in our study ($n = 22$), co-workers were perceived as being supportive, and usually very supportive, of the grandmothers' caregiving roles. Co-workers demonstrated this support in a variety of ways, such as bringing presents or hand-me-downs for the children, or "covering" for the grandmother when needed. For most of the women, however, by far the most important show of support lay in having co-workers regularly remember to ask about the grandchildren and show an interest in how they were doing.

Although the women in our study greatly appreciated the informal support they received from their bosses and co-workers, most had neither access to nor the inclination to seek more formal forms of assistance on the job. Employee Assistance Programs (EAP) were available to less than a third of the women, and of those whose places of work did offer such programs, only one had ever taken advantage of them. Although this individual found the counseling very useful as she grappled with her new role as caregiver, most of the women remained skeptical. A hospital employee echoed the sentiments of many when she said:

> I would never use the service, even though it's there, because even a big hospital is a small place and everybody knows everybody's business.

"I was afraid of the gossip," "I didn't want my boss to know I couldn't handle things," "I didn't think it would be relevant to my situation," and "I'm used to managing on my own; I have a hard time asking for help," were among the varied reasons given by women for their nonparticipation in EAP programs.

## WHEN CAREGIVING MEANS SACRIFICING WORK

A few of the women in our study had received promotions or experienced other positive job changes since taking on their grandchildren. More often, however, the new caregiving responsibilities meant passing up a promotion or requesting a less demanding job in order to better accommodate family needs. Mildred Stenson, a 59-year-old food server raising her two grandkids, aged 2 and 3, reflected, "I was trying for a job with retirement benefits when the kids came along. Life is at a standstill now. . . . When a good job comes up, I feel frustrated that I can't apply." Although Mrs. Stenson remains adamant in her conviction that she did the right thing in taking in the grandkids, she knows that her own prospects for a financially secure retirement have dimmed considerably as a result.

Several of the women in this study were on short-term disability or layoffs from work when they took in the grandchildren on what most had hoped would be a temporary basis. Forty-two-year-old Ellen Strickland had injured her back working as a storeroom manager, but had every intention of returning to her job until two of her grandchildren and a grandnephew, all under age 3, came into her care. Although she still gets $180 each month from her former place of work, her disability payments have run out and "it's really tight now" financially. Mrs. Strickland's back problem has improved greatly, but returning to work is no longer a possibility because of her caregiving responsibilities. The classes she had been taking in adult literacy and word processing also have come to an end, and with them, at least for the foreseeable future, her hopes of improved job skills. "I put my life on hold since I got the children," she says wistfully.

Fifty-nine-year-old Lucy Thomas had been laid off of her job as an accounts clerk 2 years ago when she became an instant caregiver for four of her grandchildren, all under age 10. When it became clear that her "temporary" caregiving had become permanent, Mrs. Thomas reluctantly gave up any remaining thoughts about returning to work. She cashed in her retirement benefits, and with them her hopes for an adequate income in old age.

Most of this chapter has focused on those women who have managed to combine raising their grandchildren with continuing to work outside the home. As noted earlier, however, a significant proportion of the women we interviewed had found such combining of roles impossible to maintain. Indeed, close to a third of the nonworking women had to give up their jobs in order to become full-time caregivers, making caregiving second only to poor health as a reason for leaving work prematurely.

In their study of caregivers for frail elderly mothers, Brody and her colleagues (1987) demonstrated that caregivers most likely to have to terminate their employment included those with the least paid assistance, the least education, the lowest family incomes, and the greatest degree of family dependence on their earnings.

In our own study, the high proportion of women forced to quit work in order to fulfill their caregiving responsibilities may well reflect in part the economically disadvantaged position of most of our sample members. Indeed, for the great majority of those who quit their jobs in order to care, or who never resumed work following a disability leave or layoff because of the grandchildren, the economic costs of being without work while acquiring "more mouths to feed" made for a precarious financial situation.

For several of the women we interviewed, however, an even greater loss seemed to involve the sense of dignity and pride involved in earning one's own living and not being on welfare. Fifty-six-year-old Mrs. Brynes's statement that she "didn't feel like a whole person anymore" after giving up the job and the income that had afforded her independence and a sense of self-worth was echoed in different words by other women for whom caregiving meant the end of one's work life, at least for the near future. For these women, as for so many others in our study, the assumption of caregiving, although deeply valued as "the right thing to do," and "the only thing I could do," wreaked havoc with their former life plans and hopes for the future.

* * *

The dramatic influx of women into the paid labor force has been called "the basic social revolution of our time" (Hochschild & Machung, 1989, p. 239). Yet for African American women, the line between the public world of work and the private world of child care and other responsibilities at home has always been blurred (Collins, 1990).

For the employed women in our study, combining work outside the home with the raising of young children was usually not, in itself, a new experience. Most had worked while raising their own children, and many continued to assist with child care, helping a daughter, niece, or neighbor as they in turn attempted to juggle competing role demands. But the assumption of full-time caregiving for one's grandchildren, and doing so under the circumstances of the crack cocaine epidemic, was, for many of these women, a far more difficult experience.

Women who were just beginning to get ahead financially reported seeing their savings eaten up by the high costs of child care, whereas other women spoke of passing up an opportunity for a job advancement because of their conflicting responsibilities at home. For the majority of women, employment in jobs characterized by low wages and few fringe benefits contributed to the difficulties that the new caregiving posed. And although co-workers and supervisors were often informally supportive of the grandmother's role, few of these caregivers had access to the formal supports that could help ease the burdens posed by their dual shift reality.

The fact that the employed women in our study were significantly more likely than nonemployed women to report a worsening of their health status over the last year, and in the period since caregiving began, may be indicative of the special stresses faced by this group. Yet in the face of such realities, and of the fact that a third of the nonemployed women we interviewed had been forced to quit their jobs in order to provide full-time caregiving, respite and child-care options for working women remain woefully inadequate (Abel, 1991). As discussed in Chapter 13, recent employer surveys suggest that employee child-care benefits may become less, rather than more available in the 1990s (Litvan, 1991). And government sponsorship of high quality, free, or low-cost respite care for family caregivers remains a pipe dream in the United States, despite dramatic evidence of the need for policy change in this area (Sidel, 1992a).

# 10

---

# The Continuity of Caregiving

A recent *Newsweek* magazine cover featured a middle-aged woman looking lovingly at the disabled elderly mother whose gnarled hand rested in her own. Below the picture, a caption read, "The average American woman spends 17 years raising children and 18 years helping aging parents" (Beck, 1990).

Although a salient fact of life for women of all ethnic groups, the continuity of caregiving captured in the *Newsweek* cover story may be particularly pronounced in the African American community. A recent large-scale longitudinal study revealed, for example, that 60% of the middle-aged African American women surveyed had been members of extended families during at least part of the preceding decade and a half, most often as a consequence of having their grandchildren live with them (Beck & Beck, 1989).

As noted earlier, the relatively high proportion of black children living with their grandparents reflects, in part, a continuing pattern of coresidence and shared caregiving within the African American community that has enabled it to adapt to diverse external forces (Angel & Tienda, 1982; Billingsley, 1968; Hill, 1971; Jackson, 1991; Stack, 1974). In the late 1970s, for instance, before cocaine was a widespread problem, two thirds of African American families headed by women aged 65 and above included at least one child under 18 (U.S. Bureau of the Census, 1979). Although these children most often were the women's own grandchildren or great grandchildren, the strength of the extended family, including strong bonds with fictive kin, meant that her household also frequently included other young relatives and non-kin as well (Jones, 1973).

At the other end of the life span, caregiving for elderly parents is an increasingly common responsibility of mid-life and older black women.

Such caregiving reflects not only the strong sense of filial responsibility in the African American community (Watson, 1990; Young & Kahana, 1991) but also the demographic and health profile of older black Americans. Not only are the African American elderly growing at a faster rate than the overall population aged 65 and above, for example, but a "mortality crossover" occurs at around age 80-85. Blacks who live to this age thus have a longer remaining life expectancy than whites, and black women 85+ are one of the longest lived subgroups in the nation (National Center for Health Statistics [NCHS], 1989).

Despite the longevity of the "oldest old," African American elders as a group have more chronic and acute conditions, more functional limitations, and $1\frac{1}{2}$ times more restricted activity days than do elderly whites (NCHS, 1990). Older blacks are therefore more likely to need help with activities of daily living than are their white counterparts, with much of the needed caregiving being provided by adult daughters who often are themselves older women (Young & Kahana, 1991).

In this chapter, we will examine the continuity of caregiving in the lives of the African American women we interviewed. We will consider first the phenomenon of eldercare, and the particular burdens and challenges it may pose for women who are simultaneously caring for their grandchildren and an elderly parent or other relative. We then will examine the additional caregiving roles that grandparent caregivers may assume—as respite providers, foster care parents, and caregivers to disabled spouses or adult children—and how these complement or conflict with their grandparent caregiving responsibilities.

We will look, too, at the experiences and reflections of those women in our study who had already raised grandchildren or other young relatives only to find themselves repeating the cycle. Finally, we will attempt to place the continuity of caregiving in a deeply personal context, by looking at the relationship that many of the women in our study had had as children with their own caregiving grandparents. As we shall see, memories of a strong grandmother caregiver and of the role she had played at a critical juncture in a woman's own young life helped many of the women we interviewed gain perspective on their own roles as caregiver to their grandchildren or great grandchildren.

## COMBINING CHILD CARE AND ELDERCARE

Dr. Elaine Brody (1985) has written poignantly about the conflicts and pressures faced by America's "women in the middle"—women who are middle aged or older and caught between the competing demands of their jobs, their spouses and college-age children, and their aging parents or in-laws. Many of these women are themselves older adults—their average age is close to 60 (Stone et al., 1987)—and hence may have health problems of their own, as well as limited energy and the financial limitations imposed by their own or their spouse's impending retirement, inflation, and the college education of their offspring.

Yet such women are the nation's primary caregivers for the old, with 80%-90% of the care provided to elders being given by family members, 70% of whom are women (Stone et al., 1987).

As noted earlier, the gender division of labor not only assigns women primary responsibility for the care of elderly family members but also extends to the types of care provided. Women caregivers thus tend to provide the most tedious and time-consuming caregiving tasks, such as assistance with bathing, feeding, and other activities of daily living, whereas men more often limit their caregiving responsibilities to things like help with home maintenance and finances (Berk, 1988).

As discussed in Chapter 5, the health consequences of eldercare are often significant, with clinical depression, increased susceptibility to physical illness, and the "hidden patient" syndrome among the problems observed (Fengler & Goodrich, 1979; Gallagher, Wrabetz, et al., 1989).

Recent research by White-Means and Thornton (1991) demonstrated that African American caregivers for the elderly contributed significantly more hours to this activity than members of the white ethnic groups studied. For eight of the women in our study, caregiving for grandchildren was complicated by the need to be simultaneously serving as primary caregiver for a frail or disabled parent or other elderly relative or neighbor. The nature of such caregiving ranged from assistance 3 days a week with shopping, cooking, housekeeping, and other instrumental activities of daily living (IADLs) to round-the-clock in-home care for an incontinent and cognitively impaired elder.

Still other women had only recently ceased having major eldercare responsibilities when the interviews took place. Fifty-seven-year-old Mary Harte, for example, was not only raising her 2- and 3-year-old grandchildren but also providing full care in her home for her mentally disabled 95-year-old father until his death a few months prior to the interview. For Ella Mae Smith, extensive caregiving responsibilities for her critically ill mother-in-law had been followed by an equally intense period as "home attendant" for an elderly aunt. It was shortly after her aunt's death that the caregiving cycle resumed, with Mrs. Smith and her husband taking in their infant grandson.

Finally, not included among the eight women currently providing eldercare were several others who were attempting to provide long-distance caregiving for a disabled elderly parent. A 56-year-old grandmother thus reported that she calls her 93-year-old father in Chicago every day, and tries to arrange long distance to get him the help he needs. Though her father, she admits, is in better health than she is, with her cancer and heart disease, she still worries about him and feels badly that she is unable to see him more often and help out in person.

For two of the women we interviewed, eldercare involved significant assistance to a elderly neighbor. In addition to caring for two preschool-aged great grandchildren, for example, 70-year-old Hedda Wilson regularly helps bathe and cook and clean house for an elderly woman down the street because "she's forgetful and needs somebody."

More often, however, eldercare meant caregiving for an aging parent, and thus engaged the women in the combination of physical assistance and "emotion work" that such caregiving entails. For several of these women, moreover, the demands of parent care, in part because of its deeply emotional character, made this role more stressful than that of grandparent caregiver. Fifty-two-year-old Millie Luce, for example, found raising her 1-year-old grandchild easier than coping with the constant demands of her disabled 85-year-old mother who "wants everything now!" And for 56-year-old Mary Byrnes, watching the deterioration of a once strong and energetic mother combines with the physical demands of caregiving to make for a difficult and often heartbreaking role. Incontinent and frequently confused, Mrs. Byrnes's mother now demands five hot meals a day and bears little resemblance to the thoughtful and caring person she once was. Mary Byrnes indeed opened our first interview with her by remarking sadly, "I have three children— a 9-month-old 'crack baby', a 17-month-old who's HIV+, and my 83-year-old mother. All three are in diapers."

Parent care is not nearly so difficult to manage for 57-year-old Frances Green, because her 94-year-old mother still lives on her own and needs help only a few times a week with things like shopping, house cleaning, and transportation. Through a careful balancing act, Mrs. Green has been able to meet the needs and demands of her two young grandchildren, her mother, and her part-time job—though not as well as she'd like. She worries, too, about the effects that a hoped for return to full-time work will have on her ability to carry out her multiple caregiving responsibilities, particularly as her mother gets older and more in need of care.

Several of the women in our study reported that the combination of parent-care and child-care responsibilities left them with the feeling that "everyone is depending on me." Raising two grandchildren and a grandnephew under age 3, and providing regular assistance to her mother and the children's paternal grandfather, 40-year-old Ellen Strickland captured this feeling:

> If it's not my grandchildren it's my nieces and nephews. If it's not them it's my mother. If it's not her it's the kids' grandfather. Everybody looks to me and I have to be there for them. . . . There's not enough hours in the day!

"Being there" in the case of her mother and the children's grandfather means bringing them meals, getting them to the doctor, and frequently stepping in to help in other ways "if I see that they're neglecting themselves. Because they're just like children too." The combination of elder-care and child care has taken a toll on Mrs. Strickland's own life. Out on disability when the kids first came, she has not been able to return to work, and as her family responsibilities mounted, she also has had to give up the classes she had been taking in adult literacy and word processing. But for Mrs. Strickland and most of the parent-care providers we interviewed, assisting elderly family members has its own rewards:

> They've got nothing. They're just like children and someone has to look out for them. And when they say, "thank you for being so concerned," that makes my day.

In the United States today, close to half of the daughters engaged in caring for elderly parents are employed outside the home in addition to their caregiving responsibilities (Stone et al., 1987). Several studies suggest, moreover, that these working caregivers devote as many hours per week to their caregiving role as do their nonemployed counterparts (Brody et al., 1987; Cantor, 1983; Soldo & Myllyluoma, 1983).

As noted in Chapter 9, researchers are divided on whether or not employed caregivers experience more strain than their nonworking counterparts. Yet the multiple ways in which caregiving for an impaired elderly impacts on both the work and the home life of employed caregivers for the old have been well documented (Brody, 1985; Giele et al., 1987; Scharlach et al., 1991).

For the women in our study who were combining child care and parent care with work outside the home, the realities of life were often far different from what had been expected at this stage. Raising two great grandchildren, providing daily assistance to her 79-year-old mother, and working the graveyard shift as a nurse's aide, Ronda Leeds provides a case in point. "I had planned to kick back and relax at this stage," she reflects. "But I enjoy what I'm doing. I came from a large family, I've always been in a family, always. . . . I wouldn't trade my family for anybody's." Despite the prospect of greater parent care as her mother grows more disabled, Mrs. Leeds remains remarkably buoyant and existential in her outlook:

> I'm kind of happy-go-lucky. I don't live in a world with my hopes down all the time. If I did I'd be in bad shape. I don't worry that I don't know what's going to happen tomorrow, because tomorrow's not promised to no one.

## CAREGIVING FOR SPOUSES AND ONE'S OWN CHILDREN

Although parent care has received more media attention in recent years, caring for a disabled spouse is in reality the most common form of caregiving in the United States today (Stone et al., 1987). Among mid-life and older black couples, high rates of widowhood (Chatters & Taylor, 1990), often preceded by the disabling illness of a spouse, give black married women a high likelihood of becoming spousal caregivers during their later years.

Although none of the married women in our study were currently involved in caregiving for a spouse, nine had been widowed, some more than once, and many of the widows had served as primary caregivers to their late husbands. In cases where the husbands had played a significant role in the sharing of grandparent caregiving responsibilities, their subsequent illness and death was often particularly difficult. Fifty-six-year-old Stella Burton thus had received considerable help from her husband of 34 years in raising their two young grandchildren. When he became ill 2 years ago, she became his primary caregiver, as well as the children's. Both the loss of her husband's help as a caregiver, and the extra emotional and physical energy that went into her role in caring for him prior to his death, took a toll on Mrs. Burton that she continues to feel acutely.

For many of the women in our study, still another dimension of caregiving involved the fact that they still had children of their own living at home at the time of the interviews. Fully 55% of the women ($n = 39$) reported that at least one children remained at home, and although in most cases these were adult children, a fifth of the women had children who ranged in age from 5 to 19. Caregiving for grandchildren, in many cases, was thus complicated by the fact that the women had not yet completed the task of rearing their own children.

The great majority of grandmothers with teenaged and younger children of their own still living at home reported that these offspring had been very supportive of the decision to take in one or more grandchildren or other young relatives. "He was happy that I could do it," and "they were proud of me for taking this on," were typical of the comments that grandmothers shared. Yet often, too, even those children who had initially supported their mother's assumption of full-time caregiving for grandchildren experienced some measure of jealousy when they found her time divided between themselves and the new young family members. Indeed, for many of the women in this situation, a particularly challenging aspect of the new role was giving the grandchildren the care and attention they needed while still making sufficient time for their own teenage and younger children.

Several of the grandmothers reported that their own teenagers were a godsend in helping them with baby-sitting and respite, especially when the grandmother worked outside the home. An 18-year-old son living at home thus enabled his mother to work the night shift while he remained in the house for the two preschool-age grandchildren. Similarly, a teenage daughter arranged her college classes in a way that enabled her to be home during those times when the grandmother needed to be away.

Many women spoke appreciatively of the ways in which their older children looked out for them and helped out, even without being asked. Jacqueline Peters beamed as she told us about her 13-year-old son Calvin and the way in which he helps her with her three granddaughters:

> Sometimes when I'm getting all nervous, Calvin will give me my coat and bag and push me out the door, saying, "Bye, Mama" because he just knows that I need that time. I love that time to myself but, even so, I only stay out a couple of hours 'cause they're always on my mind.

Yet even in the case of helpful and supportive children like these, grandmothers often expressed concern about not wanting to "rely too much" on their children, lest they inadvertently create resentment of the grandchildren (see Chapter 9 this volume).

As noted earlier, a particularly tragic finding of this study was that a fourth of the women who participated had recently lost children to violence and/or drug related deaths. For still others, sickle cell anemia, heart disease, and other conditions had made an untimely claim on a child's life, sometimes preceded by a prolonged period of maternal caregiving.

For 79-year-old Lena Johnson, who has outlived three of her children and is now raising her 9-month-old great grandson, the hardest thing she has had to face was serving as caregiver to her terminally ill daughter and then accepting the woman's death. In retrospect, however, doing the shopping, cooking, and other caregiving for several months before her daughter succumbed to a drug-related heart condition helped Mrs. Johnson cope with her loss. As she reflects a year later:

> I'd given her all the help I could give her and I'd done all for her children that I could do. And when she died, I went to the funeral and I didn't cry, because I'd done everything I could for her.

Forty-seven-year-old Jacqueline Ridout had also provided significant caregiving to an adult daughter, cutting back her hours as a teacher's aide when the young woman became acutely ill with sickle cell anemia. Mrs. Ridout's previous caregiving roles had been extensive, and included raising her sister's children and 23 foster children. Yet none of these roles, nor her current responsibilities in raising two hyperactive grandchildren aged 2 and 7, was as difficult emotionally as being caregiver to a daughter who was dying.

## ADDITIONAL CHILD-CARE RESPONSIBILITIES

In her classic work, *All Our Kin,* Carol Stack (1974) explored the survival strategies that characterized everyday life in a low-income black community in the late 1960s. Key among these strategies was the fostering of a sense of mutual caring and responsibility for children through which neighbors look out for each other's offspring, and nephews, nieces, and fictive kin are kept, temporarily or indefinitely, in the homes of relatives.

Although the women in our study were all primary caregivers for at least one, and often two or more grandchildren, great grandchildren, or grandnieces or -nephews, their child-care responsibilities often didn't stop there. Fully half of the women ($n = 36$) reported that they were providing some caregiving for at least one other child, with two thirds of these caring for two or more additional children.

The extra children for whom grandmothers were providing care most often included other grandchildren, great grandchildren, or grandnieces or -nephews, but frequently also included the children of friends or neighbors. And although the nature of this additional caregiving ranged from regular baby-sitting and long-term respite to transportation and taking the children on outings, it often involved substantial daily responsibility. Twenty-two women, for example, reported having either full responsibility or regular baby-sitting for children in addition to those they were raising.

Lucy Thomas begins each weekday by picking her two grandnieces up at 6 o'clock and bringing them to the crowded two-bedroom house she shares with her four grandchildren, aged 3 to 12. Mrs. Thomas's niece recently got off crack and found a job, and so her 59-year-old aunt is "doing everything I can" to support and encourage her. Similarly, 57-year-old Gayle Street, who quit her job as a domestic worker to take in her two young grandchildren, baby-sits a third grandchild every weekday from 9 to 5 while their mother is at work. Although two of Mrs. Street's other daughters provide occasional respite nights and weekends, no assistance is available during the weekdays when she needs it most.

Several of the women we interviewed were serving as foster care parents to children they were unrelated to, in addition to raising young kin of their own. Fifty-two-year-old Millie Luce thus recently took in two "fragile babies" ("only temporarily," she hopes), and is raising them along with her 17-month-old grandchild. Living in a comfortable, modern apartment in North Oakland, Mrs. Luce had not actively sought foster care children but gave in easily when she was "recruited" because it seemed like the right thing to do. And Carolyn Moss had just opened a state licensed home for infants of crack addicted mothers when she had, quite suddenly, to assume responsibility for her drug exposed 3-year-old grandniece. A single woman in her late forties, Ms. Moss is thrilled to be launching the home that has been her dream for many years. But she also is stretched to the limit meeting the needs of the six babies in her care while getting to know and understand the needs of her grandniece.

Other grandmothers provide care for additional children through less formal means. For Jacqueline Ridout, frequent unpaid baby-sitting for the neighbors' children is a routine and expected part of the day. Describing her modest two-bedroom home as "a real neighborhood center," she remarks that baby-sitting comes easily after a lifetime of foster care parenting. In addition to providing short-term respite for the neighbors, Mrs. Ridout takes three more grandkids into her home each summer. Money is very tight—she manages on an income well below the poverty line and recently couldn't even afford meat to give the kids a holiday barbecue. But raising children, and helping neighbors and family with their children, remains the most central part of her life.

In all too many cases, the effects of the crack epidemic are also seen in these extended networks. In the words of Jacqueline Peters:

> I have a lot of children. Not just the seven of my own but lots of other children. Here in the neighborhood where I raised my kids, there were kids all over calling me Mama. I would bake cakes from scratch and they would be on my doorstep in a flash, asking "Mama, can we have a piece of cake?" And what hurts me so now is that so many of them are on crack, or dead.

## "PARENTING" THE THIRD TIME AROUND

For nine of the women in our study, "second time around parenting" was really taking place the third time around. Having raised their own children and then others as well, they now find themselves in the midst of a third round of child-care activities. In most cases, this involved taking in the children, nieces, or nephews of another adult child or relative as a consequence of the crack epidemic. Forty-seven-year-old Myra Lewis thus took in the 4-year-old son of one of her daughters several years after she had raised another child's daughter. Although the latter's physical threats and other abusive behavior made it necessary for Mrs. Lewis to end the former relationship, she was undeterred by this bad experience from taking in another grandchild several years later. Thinking aloud about her attitude toward the caregiving that has consumed much of her life, Mrs. Lewis remarked:

I took care of my own child and now my daughter's. I have no life of my own. I'm a caregiver. But then I realize, hey, this IS a life. I *give care,* and that's something!

For four of the women in our study, surrogate parenting the third time around meant raising their grandchildren, only to find themselves a generation later raising their great grandchildren as well. Seventy-nine-year-old Elvia Goode thus raised her grandson and granddaughter all their lives and has had the latter's two children, now 4 and 16, almost since birth. The children's mother is now seriously ill with AIDS, and Mrs. Goode has had to accept both her daughter's impending death and the fact that she herself will probably remain a caregiver until her own life comes to an end:

Sometimes I feel I'm sick of it. Why me? I didn't do that to my mother! But I make out all right. It's a "must," I gotta do it.

For 61-year-old Sally Fairlane, the injustice and sad irony involved in raising a grandchild, and later that grandchild's children, is particularly poignant because she had gone to such great lengths to give her granddaughter "the right kind of upbringing." Reflecting now on the sacrifices she had made to put the girl through private school, only to have her turn to crack, she says:

To see what I had to go through raising her, and to see how she is today, it's such a waste. . . . That stuff has got her like an animal. It's made an animal out of her.

Eventual acceptance of her granddaughter's condition, however, has enabled Mrs. Fairlane to move on and focus on the next round of caregiving as she raises her 3- and 5-year-old great grandsons:

It took me a long time to accept that that's the way she was. But I had to either accept it or go down *with* her. I just had to cut her loose. I still think about it, feel bad about it, I still cry about it a lot. But there's nothing I can do. So I try to go on and do for these kids.

Interestingly, most of Mrs. Fairlane's anger these days is not directed at her drug involved granddaughter but rather at the woman's mother, Mrs. Fairlane's daughter, who is neglecting her role as grandparent caregiver. "The younger grandmothers *should* do for them, but they don't," Mrs. Fairlane exclaims. Instead, great grandmothers like herself, who ought to be "on the sidelines," are thrust into center stage as full-time caregivers. "I feel like I'm filling a vacancy, just filling a vacancy" she says—a vacancy created by the children's mother and made worse by the absence of their grandmother.

## THE SPECIAL LEGACY
## OF GRANDMOTHER CAREGIVING

As suggested in Chapter 2, grandmother caregiving must be viewed in part within the broader context of women's caring and caregiving over the life course. Within the African American community, the vital and continuing role of the black grandmother as kinkeeper and caregiver across generations forms a critical part of this context (Jones, 1973; Wilson, 1989).

For many of the women in our study, the historic role of black grandmothers had a deeply personal analogue in the form of the relationships they had had as children with their own caregiving grandmothers. It is this special legacy of grandparent caregiving that provides a critical added context for better understanding the attitudes and experience of women raising their children's children as a consequence of the crack epidemic.

Close to two thirds of the women ($n = 44$) had had living grandparents when they were young, and in most cases, the grandparents had either lived with the women or close enough by that they were seen on a daily basis.

Fully 75% ($n = 33$) of the women who had had living grandparents as children reported that they had lived with these grandparents for periods ranging from 3 months to more than a decade. Although for 12 of the women this meant living, along with one or both of their parents, in a grandparent's home, for the majority it meant leaving one's parents and staying with a grandmother during at least a small part of one's early years.

For six of the women who had been taken in to live with grandparents, a mother's physical or emotional problems, or the fact that she was herself a teenager inadequate to the task of child rearing, was cited as the reason for this transition. A 48-year-old grandmother raising five of her grandchildren thus told how she had been raised by her grandmother from birth to age 8 or 9 because her mother had been "young and wild" and "didn't want to be bothered." Another study participant had lived with her grandparents for 3 years due to her mother's illness, and at a later point moved in with an older aunt who "wanted to keep me because she didn't have kids of her own." For 47-year-old Mary Ellison, living with a grandmother from age 7 on was the consequence of a bitter divorce, during which her mother was declared unfit and her father was "too shell shocked" to manage.

Other times, however, a summer or longer spent living away from home with one's grandmother represented not a response to problems at home but a valued tradition affording the opportunity for cultural enrichment.

For some of the women we interviewed, a grandmother became mother and is fondly remembered as "the only parent I had." Sixty-two-year-old Carol Innis, who lived with her grandmother from age 3 to age 8 or 9, relates that:

> My mother ran off with the oldest one, but didn't want to take care of me and the baby. When my knee was scraped, Big Mama was the one who'd say, "come here, honey, let me put something on it." Big Mama was the one who'd comb my hair and wash my snotty nose and everything. She was there for me. And it's all I can relate to now. She was there when Momma should have been. She was more like a mother because when I went to school, she was the one I came home to.

In such cases, grandmothers played a nurturing, caregiving role not unlike the one their granddaughters now saw themselves playing. As 49-year-old Betty Driscoll put it, "She was like my mother. She was very special. I want that same feeling for Sandra." And as another grand-mother remarked, thinking of her grandmother: "Here I am going through the same things she did raising these babies. I look back now. . ."

For several of the women in our study, the early years spent in a grandmother's care were the beginning of a lifetime of reciprocal caring and concern. Fifty-three-year-old Dolly Jefferson, who had grown up in the care of a grandmother who died recently at age 90, stated:

> I grew up and got married and I sent for her. She came down to Louisiana and lived with us. And when me and my husband broke up, she decided to carry two of my children back with her so I could get a job. We still kept in contact. I'd still send her money every Christmas and still call her. It was a great loss to me when she died and I still feel some effects from her death.

For 48-year-old Glenn Eaker, who spent the first decade of life in her grandmother's care, what goes around really does come around. In addition to raising her own 16-year-old daughter and five of her grandchildren, and providing assistance to her mother with transportation, shopping, and other chores, Mrs. Eaker is primary caregiver for her grandmother and "does everything for her—cooking, cleaning, bathing, shopping." For Mrs. Eaker, however, grandparent care is something she very much wants to do, both because of her grandmother's vital role in raising her, and because "I'm not ready to lose her yet." Mrs. Eaker reveals with pride that "My grandma says, 'when you were young I used to wonder what I'd do with you. Now I wonder what I'd do without you.' "

* * *

Holloway and Demetrakopoulos (1986) have argued that the role of older black women as "keepers of the clan" is extended through the responsibility to nurture and care for all who come under their roof (Ovrebo & Minkler, 1992). For the women in our study, the role of primary caregiver for grandchildren was often but one of many caregiving roles they have held, often simultaneously, over the years. Eldercare, care for disabled or dying adult children, and care for the young, whether grandchildren, great grandchildren, nieces and nephews, or foster care children, thus was understood as a normal part of the life cycle.

As noted earlier, many of the women we interviewed felt cheated by the circumstances surrounding the most recent addition to their caregiving tasks—the need to take full responsibility for the children of their drug involved kin. They further felt anger and resentment toward a government that expected them to take on this major new responsibility, but refused to provide adequate support in terms of financial aid, access to child care, and other needed benefits.

In the face of all this, however, the overriding concern of the grandmothers remained one of "keeping the family together." Like their African foremothers, for whom "survival of the tribe" took precedence over the desires of the individual family member (Holloway & Demetrakopoulos, 1986), the grandmothers in our study—and their grandmothers before them—put family, and thus caregiving across the generations, at the top of their list of priorities.

# 11

## Raising Children of the Crack Cocaine Epidemic: Special Considerations

Whether they became surrogate parents as a consequence of a child's alcohol or drug abuse, a teenage pregnancy, or the death or incapacitating injury of an adult child, grandparents and other relatives who are raising children the second time around face many challenges in common.

Each has experienced disruptions in plans and expectations for mid- or late life, giving up or cutting back on jobs or leisure time activities in order to become primary caregivers. For many, preexisting caregiving responsibilities, for their own youngest children or their elderly relatives, now compete with the new role for their time and energy.

The costs of grandparent caregiving in terms of physical and economic health may be substantial, and for almost all who inherit this role, there are significant emotional issues to be dealt with around the death or incapacitation of an adult child, niece, or nephew, or around his or her inability or unwillingness to provide care. Finally, grandparent caregivers in common face the need to navigate a complex, bewildering, and often new and very frustrating set of bureaucracies, whether these be part of the courts, child protective service or foster care systems, or of the welfare establishment.

For grandparents and other relatives who are raising children as a consequence of the crack cocaine epidemic, the above mentioned difficulties and challenges are compounded by another set of problems specific to this epidemic. In this chapter, we will explore some of the special aspects of second-time-around parenting that may be, in part at least, unique to caregiving in the crack crisis. We will look in particular at the difficulties involved in raising children who have been prenatally exposed to cocaine, and/or who have been abused or neglected as a result of a parent's crack involvement.

In addition, we will consider the problem of conflicting loyalties to one's own children and one's grandchildren, and the special difficulties involved in trying to raise children in the "drug war zones" that many inner-city neighborhoods, hard hit by the crack epidemic, have become. Although we will focus on the challenges faced by women who are parenting infant and preschool-aged children, we will look ahead, as they do, to the additional problems that may be in store for children entering school with learning deficits or behavioral problems connected to early abuse and neglect and/or drug exposure. We will consider, too, the anger caregivers often feel at the societal labeling of "crack kids," which may doom them to failure before they begin.

If raising the children of the current drug epidemic poses difficult challenges, however, it also may offer special rewards. We conclude this chapter with a look at some of the satisfactions and rewards experienced by grandparents who have taken on this critical role.

## RAISING CHILDREN PRENATALLY EXPOSED TO CRACK COCAINE

As noted in Chapter 1, approximately 11% of children born in the United States today may be prenatally exposed to drugs, including, most often, cocaine (Chasnoff, 1988).

Prenatal exposure to this drug often results in intrauterine growth deficiencies due to oxygen deprivation, and in elevated rates of distress during the birth process (Chouteau et al., 1988; Petitti & Coleman, 1990).

Infants exposed to cocaine in utero often show signs of irritability, frequent tremors and startles, poor eating and sleeping patterns, and poor muscle tone. Abnormal development patterns in motor, behavioral, cognitive, and social interactional skills may continue throughout infancy, although researchers remain unclear on whether this is a result of prenatal cocaine exposure on the central nervous system or of drug withdrawal (Chasnoff, Griffith, MacGregor, Dirkes, & Burns, 1989; Howard et al., 1989).

As also noted in Chapter 1, the debate rages on the longer term consequences of prenatal cocaine exposure. On one side of the debate, teachers, counselors, and others working with preschool- and kindergarten-age children have reported short attention spans, inconsistent behaviors and abilities, poor motor coordination, uncontrollable mood swings, language delay, and other problems in children prenatally exposed to cocaine (Norris, 1991). Yet as noted earlier, a recent 2-year follow-up study of cocaine exposed infants led Chasnoff and his colleagues (1992) to conclude that the average developmental functioning of these children was no different from that of other children their age.

Regardless of the professional debate, it is clear that the caregivers of infants and young children who have been prenatally exposed to cocaine often face a difficult caregiving challenge. As infants, their charges "are often difficult to comfort, cry excessively or have medical problems which require monitoring and frequent doctor or hospital visits" (California Senate Office on Research, 1990). As toddlers and kindergarten-aged children, they may be hyperactive and exhibit a variety of other social and behavioral problems, whether as a consequence of the drug exposure per se, or of any of a number of other factors frequently associated with birth into crack involved households (Howard et al., 1989).

More than 70% of the women in our study ($n = 51$) reported that they believed one or more of the children in their care had been prenatally exposed to cocaine. In addition, half reported that they were caring for children who had been born premature and had remained in the hospital after birth due to low birth weight or other complications.

A new baby's medical problems made the initial assumption of caregiving particularly difficult. A 57-year-old grandmother who eventually had to quit her job, recalls that she and her two granddaughters, ages 2 and 3, were in and out of the doctor's office at least once a week for the first 2 years:

> They had infections, every disease, one's breasts even began to mature too early. For the first 2 years, I had a permanent place in the waiting room.

Even older children may suffer frequent health problems due to prenatal drug exposure. Helene Wheaton saw the effects of the physical and emotional trauma combined when she took in her 5-year-old grandson Gerald:

> He was sick all the time. He had problems with his stomach because of the drugs his mama smoked when she was pregnant. And he caught every cold or bug that came around. Seemed like we were going back and forth to Children's [Hospital] 2, 3 times a week. His health was shot, his nerves were shot, and his little heart was broken.

Most caregivers said that they felt lucky that the state-funded Medi-Cal program covered most of the children's health care needs. But even so, Mrs. Wheaton ran into difficulties:

> I'm grateful for it, but it's not enough. Things get delayed, they make you wait, they run out, and lots of times you still have to pay and sometimes I just don't have the money. So I have to borrow or beg or he has to go without eye drops, or cough medicine. I hate to make him wait. These are fragile little kids—they've been through enough. They shouldn't have to wait for eye drops.

More than 50% of the women volunteered that at least one of the children in their care was severely hyperactive ($n = 40$). Although this reflects the women's perceptions, rather than medically assessed diagnoses, it is nevertheless an indication of a potentially important dimension of the burden felt by grandmother caregivers.

For many of the grandmothers in our study, the severe hyperactivity, often requiring medication so that the child could sleep at night, was a source of significant concern. Describing the two grandchildren in her care, one of whom recently started kindergarten, Shirley Russell remarked:

> Mark really has a problem. He talks so fast you can't understand half the things he says. He's doing poorly in school because his attention span's so short he notices every fly on the wall. And the little one's so hyped up he can't sit still.

A 44-year-old grandmother similarly describes her worries about her hyperactive 4½-year-old cocaine exposed granddaughter saying, "I really don't think the stuff is out of her. She's just a little motor. If she stays that way, she'll be a motor as a teenager."

Several of the grandmothers spoke about having to take their hyperactive children into a darkened room and hold them for long periods in order to quiet them. As one woman remarked, "Sometimes I have to turn off all the lights and rock him to calm him down. He's on the ceiling. What do I do when he starts school with behavioral problems?"

For many women, cuddling and the other techniques they would normally use to comfort a child proved ineffective with the drug exposed infants and youngsters in their care. Fifty-two-year-old Doris Watson describes her 3-year-old granddaughter, Diana, noting that, "When she first came she used to wake up at night crying and I'd try to embrace her, and she didn't like it. . . . She doesn't relate to cuddling. So I'd shake her and she'd go back to sleep."

## THE LONG LASTING EFFECTS
## OF A CRACK INVOLVED HOUSEHOLD

As noted in Chapter 1, it is often impossible to separate out the effects of prenatal cocaine exposure per se from those of exposure to other substances, maternal malnutrition, and a whole host of other prenatal contributors to an infant's subsequent health problems (Coles, 1991; Zuckerman, 1991). Teasing apart the effects of prenatal drug exposure and those of postnatal abuse and neglect may be equally problematic. That the latter may in fact have more lasting and severe consequences for children born into crack involved households has been suggested by several experts, however (Chasnoff et al., 1992; Coles, 1991). Indeed, Chasnoff has commented that "as I study the problem more and more, I think the placenta does a better job of protecting the child than we do as a society" (quoted in Goodman, 1992).

Many of the grandparent caregivers we interviewed supported this view, attributing their grandchildren's sleeping and eating abnormalities, and a host of behavioral problems, not to prenatal drug exposure per se, but rather to the abuse and neglect that the children had experienced prior to coming to the grandmother's home.

Several grandmothers described the unusual eating habits of formerly neglected and underfed children in their care, with comments like, "he used to eat like someone in prison—afraid they'd take the food away," "she eats to the point of throwing up," and "they think a bowl of cereal is an appetizer!" Others reported their grandchildren's unusual difficulties with food. Describing Gerald when he arrived in her care, Mrs. Wheaton told us he was "3 years old and hardly weighed a thing. Never had a vegetable, never had beans, or even a piece of meat."

Many grandmothers were shocked at the hygiene and personal habits of their grandchildren when they first brought them home. One recalled the 5-year-old twins arguing over whether or not their mother ever bathed, with one remembering "that one time after the fire in the kitchen." Other grandmothers talked about "rescuing" their grandchildren from mattresses soaked with urine in crack houses, 4-year-olds who didn't use toilet paper, and about grandchildren who thought nothing of stealing from the grocery store because they had done that for years in order to survive.

Even simple things like eating together were traumatic at first. Grandmothers described their initial shock and horror on watching a 4-year-old "dig his hands into cakes," a 3-year-old unable to use silverware, another who had never eaten at a table, and other grandchildren giving repeated evidence of having never been taught even the most rudimentary table manners.

Most grandmothers felt, as did Jewell Champion, that these problems required special attention from them. "I've got to watch them *very* carefully—make sure they get the diet they need, the rest, the sunshine, the learning. These children can't take any other strikes against them."

Others spoke of being perhaps overly attentive to every mood or symptom, particularly when they first began caring for a drug exposed baby:

> I used to write everything down. I mean every little thing because I didn't know what was important and what wasn't. I have boxes full of all the papers I wrote! And I would take all that mess into the doctor's office and ask him what it all meant and what I should do and the doctors don't know! They just say, "love them, that's all you can do." And I'd be insulted 'cause, of course, I love them. That's a given! I don't need no doctor to tell me to love my grandchildren!

The physician's lack of knowledge about the long-term effects of prenatal crack exposure often seemed particularly hard to take, given the myriad other "unknowns" the grandmothers dealt with. The frustration and fear are evident in the words of a 65-year-old grandmother:

> We need to know what to expect, what else might hit us down the line. We've been hit with a lot already—I just want to know what else is coming. We can take it. If there's going to be problems, don't put off the news. Let's just get it out in the open. I don't want this thing hitting me in the face—again.

The grandmothers also spoke with great concern about the unusual stress they saw in their grandchildren, and about the impossibility of sorting out the effects of prenatal crack exposure from those of the environments in which the children had lived the early parts of their young lives. As one grandmother remarked, describing her 3-year-old grandson:

He used to just scream. Every time I'd start getting dressed he'd think I was going to leave him. He'd say, "Don't leave me!" . . . He'd stand in the door till I got back when I went to the washroom.

In a similar vein, a 62-year-old grandmother of two explained:

They feel like they don't trust you. They have their eyes on you at all times, the minute they hear you walk. . . . I guess they lived in fear so long . . . I guess this is what they had to live with, with all the drug people in the house. They didn't know what to expect. It is this fear, fear. But they seem to be coming out of it.

Other caregivers talked of children who were bad sleepers because "his father used to keep him up all night," or "his Mom took him to those crack houses at all hours."

Some children continue to have problems sleeping. Three years later, Mrs. Wheaton's grandson "still cries out at night. I hear him sobbing but he's sound asleep." Several said that their grandchildren refused to sleep alone. For years, a 5-year-old had to be in his grandparents' bed: "I don't know if he was hurt or molested where he was, or just left alone too much, but he was scared to death to sleep alone." And still other grandmothers spoke of preschoolers who "used sex talk" and imitated sexual behaviors that they had witnessed, or in some cases, been subject to as victims of molestations.

## WHEN PARENTS COME AND GO

In most cases, at least one of the grandchildren's parents was still in contact, albeit infrequent and unpredictable, with the child and the caregiver. These visits often had profound effects on the children, especially, it seems, those still battling the effects of crack in their young lives.

A number of the grandmothers described in despair how the grandchildren in their care would "hide in the closet" or "begin acting out" when their parents came to visit, having tantrums or nightmares, refusing to eat, or behaving aggressively. In cases where the parent was allowed to take the child away from the grandmother's home, for a visit, such acting out was often particularly apparent. As one grandmother commented, "I noticed when he comes back he acts differently. He'll

beat up on his cousin. Lately I really notice it, all the mood swings."
Others found their grandchildren repeatedly reverting to earlier patterns
of distress. Helene Wheaton spoke with tears of the effect of his parents'
surprise visits on 5-year-old Gerald:

> His stomach just closes up on him again. He loves them so much that when
> they're back in his life he gets all full of them and doesn't have room for
> food or anything else. Then they're gone—leaving him with nothing but
> empty promises. When that happens, he can go for days, not talking, not
> eating, just all closed up in his private world.

Many of the grandmothers who willingly maintained contact with
their drug involved children worked hard to teach the grandchildren that
their parent's drug problem was not something for which they should be
blamed or hated. Forty-nine-year-old Jean Wettle, who had been abandoned by her own mother as an infant, talks openly with the three
grandchildren in her care about their mother's drug problem and the
"illness" that crack cocaine causes: " 'Love your mother,' I say, 'because at the moment, your mother is sick.' "

For other grandmothers, however, a fine and often difficult line exists
between attempting to foster a maternal-child bond and putting the child
at risk, again. Fifty-eight-year-old Lois Mills learned this lesson the
hard way, when she returned her grandchild to the child's mother, only
to have to take the toddler back a few months later when the mother's drug
use once again was out of control:

> To be a grandmother, you can't push that mother out of the way. You've
> got to let the mother feel a bond with the child. But when the abuse starts,
> you've got to step in.

In cases like the above, a grandmother's desire to keep the door open
to a child involved with crack sometimes ran head on into her desire to
do what was right for the grandchildren in her care, necessitating
painful decisions and choices.

## WHEN LOYALTIES COLLIDE

Accounts of the traditional role of the black grandmother promi-
nently include her responsibilities in helping family members develop

a sense family and keeping the lines of communication open between them. As Martin and Martin (1978) note:

> Fostering a sense of family involves encouraging family members to feel some obligation to their relatives. It involves helping all members to feel that they are not alone in the world, that their relatives care for them, that they have roots, and that no matter what their condition or situation is, they are always welcome at home. (p. 18)

Many of the women we interviewed were making valiant attempts to keep the lines of communication open with their drug involved children. For some, like 62-year-old Carol Innis, this means allowing her 26-year-old daughter to live at home between her long, drug induced "disappearing acts," in the knowledge that she'd always be welcome. It means, too, that Mrs. Innis constantly reminds her granddaughter "not to call me 'Mama'—that she has a real Mama," even if that "real Mama" is often living on the streets and unable to provide care.

Many women spoke of walking another fine line, this one between fostering a sense of permanence and security for their grandchildren while leaving open the possibility of family unification at a later point. Jacqueline Peters struggles with this as she raises her three granddaughters and her daughter cycles through treatment programs and the still inevitable return to the streets:

> I know how these babies feel. They were taken from their mother at a young age and when they get older, they're going to question her "Why? Why didn't you raise me?" The older one [5 years old] already does. Later on through the years, all three are going to be asking her why and she's going to have to tell them something.

Although she has become their legal guardian, Mrs. Peters feels that she must actively prepare both herself and her granddaughters for the day when they may return to their mother:

> I tell them every night to pray for their Mama. And I tell the older two "you guys gonna go live with your Mama when she gets well" and they look at me and say "yeah, but we gonna be back."

Other grandmothers let their drug involved children know that they're still part of the family and welcome to live at home but "only if they live by the rules—no crack, no friends in the house." Describing her own 34-year-old daughter, 57-year-old Louise White, who is caregiver for two toddlers, remarked, "she'll be all right for a while, then go off again" and onto crack, at which time Mrs. White tells her firmly to leave the house until she's "straightened out."

## DEALING WITH THE CHILDREN'S PARENTS

Although women like Carol Innis, Jacqueline Peters, and Louise White are still in frequent contact with their crack involved children and give them as many chances as they need to "start over," many of the women we interviewed dread visits by their crack addicted children. Not infrequently, as noted above, the adult child's visit may cause acting out on the part of the grandchildren who are confused or frightened by their parents' sudden appearance. "Mood changes," trouble sleeping or eating, and aggressive behavior after a parent's visit were noted by many of the women, with some attempting to minimize contact to prevent such occurrences. As one grandmother put it, "I have very little to say to her. Like I told her yesterday, I'm not going to let you confuse [your daughter]. You gotta get your life together."

In the words of Jewell Champion:

> When they go visit their mama, they're crazy when they get back. At her place, everybody's high all the time and they tell the baby that she's so cute, and they give her candy and any kind of junk she wants and then she comes home thinking that she's something special, which she is, but not special the way they think!

Mrs. Champion adds that her two grandchildren come back to her, hyper from all the sugar, exhausted from no rest, wound up from all the attention, and insecure about where they belong. "It usually takes me 2 or 3 days to get them to come down."

For some grandmothers, the children's periodic visits to their parents seem sadly ironic. Says Margot Carlson of her granddaughter's visits to her mother's apartment:

> While the baby's there, she [the mother] does all the pampering. She's doing what I should be doing—she's spoiling her and acting like a grandmother who can come and go as she pleases. Then they come home to me and the real world. It's all turned around.

The grandmothers know that their grandchildren are facing a complicated situation that may only become more complicated with time. Some volunteered that counseling would be of tremendous help to both them and their grandchildren:

> My granddaughter gets so sad after her mother comes around and she can't tell anyone what she's feeling. But she has got to open up to someone, and so do I! Otherwise, I'm afraid, we're all going down in a sea of sorrow.

A crack involved son or daughter's visit may also anger grandparent caregivers and confuse the grandchildren in their care who suddenly find two people in command. As a 48-year-old grandmother of three toddlers pointed out, when her daughter comes over "she wants to take over, as if I'm nothing. When she calls and tells me she's coming over, it upsets my whole day."

For other grandmothers, fear of victimization by their crack involved children, or by the people they are "hanging out" with, leads to a strong desire to have the children keep their distance. A disabled 78-year-old great grandmother described how her crack involved granddaughter, although pleased that her son had a safe place to live, nevertheless would come over, high on the drug, and cause trouble:

> She knew the baby was safe with [me]. But the overpowering thing was that she needed the [AFDC] money and that's when the conflict would come. With my handicap I can't fight her. She'd come at 12:00 at night and take the baby and if I'm alone I wouldn't challenge her because I didn't want her jumping on me.

A 72-year-old similarly expressed her fears saying, "We're the easiest prey. They don't go out there and steal from strangers. They come in and steal from us." Jewell Champion considers herself lucky: "I haven't had to put locks on my doors. But I know some grandmothers have put triple locks on their bedroom doors cause their kids will steal their jewelry, their watch, their clothes, and then their bed!" And a 59-year-old raising five of her grandchildren, talked of her worry about the six of them being trapped in the house if her daughter, or one of the woman's unsavory companions, should come by and make trouble:

> I really prefer her not to come around because I don't know what she's doing out there in the streets and who she's messin' with, ya know? It's

better for her to stay away because I feel safer with her away from me than coming to me.

Many of the women in our study had reached a point of no return where their drug involved children were concerned. They had given the latter numerous chances, tried without success to help them get over their drug habit, and finally decided that no contact was in the best interests of the rest of the household. For such women, the traditional role of keeping the family together, and helping members know they are welcome "whatever their condition," had collided head on with the need to protect the grandchildren in their care and to create a safe and loving atmosphere for them.

Several of the grandmothers described at length the difficult decision process that had led to their "letting go" of an adult child. A 61-year-old great grandmother who had raised her granddaughter and was now raising that granddaughter's two children because of their mother's crack addiction, reported:

It took me a long time to accept that that's the way she is. But I had to either accept it or go down *with* her. I just had to cut her loose. I still think about it a lot, feel bad about it. I still cry a lot. But there's nothing I can do. So I try to go on and do for these kids.

Another grandmother described how she used to go to great lengths to maintain contact with her daughter, even if it meant taking her young granddaughter with her to search the streets. The child's mother was often homeless and using prostitution to support her drug habit, and the grandmother finally ended her futile efforts at maintaining a relationship:

My [granddaughter] and I used to walk the streets looking for her mother. And when we'd find her [she'd say] "what are you running around looking for me for?" It won't happen anymore, I'm sorry.

For some of the grandmothers, cutting the ties with a drug involved child or grandchild came only after a long period of denying there was a problem, or hoping that things could still be turned around.

Claire Potts, a single grandmother raising two drug exposed children aged 1 and 2, was one of these. In her words:

I put my daughter on a pedestal. You couldn't tell me *my* kid was on drugs—not my kid! . . . I had her walk in and steal right in front of me and I'd say, "this is not my child." Denial. I was blaming me. I was thinking, "I sure did something wrong." Then one day it registered. . . . It wasn't me. . . . And I came to grips with me—I came to grips with myself and I just brushed her off. It wasn't easy. It was not easy. . . . But I had to get my head together. I had two babies to think about.

For women like Miss Potts, "keeping the family together" meant, ironically, letting one of its members go, at least until such time as he or she had truly broken the crack cocaine habit. And although some of the women expressed optimism that their children would eventually conquer the drug and be able to resume their parental responsibilities, many were not so optimistic. As one grandmother remarked, reflecting back on her 22-year-old daughter who had abandoned her young children, "She's not living for them, she's living for herself. But she's not really living for herself. As far as I'm concerned, she's a walking dead person."

## RAISING CHILDREN
## IN "DRUG WAR" NEIGHBORHOODS

*It takes a whole village to raise a child.*

African Proverb

Dr. Dorian Miller (1990), an African American physician practicing at San Francisco General Hospital, is fond of relating that when she was a child growing up in Chicago, neighbors, without her knowledge, would watch out their windows along her route to make sure she and her brother got to and from school safely. When young Dorian once took a detour in order to play on the way home, the neighborhood network sprang into action. Her parents were notified, and Dorian quickly learned that the watchful gaze of her Mom and Dad in fact extended throughout the neighborhood through this informal but highly effective network.

Several of the women we interviewed talked about neighbors looking out for each other, and for each other's grandchildren, in the Oakland communities where they lived. Yet more often, "the neighborhood" was synonymous with drugs, speeding cars, and violent crime. No longer a friend of young children, the neighborhood had become, on the contrary, one of the grandparents' greatest sources of concern and stress in raising their grandchildren and great grandchildren.

A 58-year-old grandmother in a crowded and noisy low-income housing complex compared her own environment as a child with that of the two grandchildren she is raising. "When I was comin' up," she said wistfully, "you didn't have to lock your door. We weren't afraid. You walked to church, nobody followed you. Now you're closin' your windows cause somebody's peakin' through or you might get shot. . . . So much danger! It's like a war out there."

For grandmothers who had raised their own children in the same neighborhood where they now are raising their grandchildren, the dramatic increase in drugs and violence was especially hard to take. As one such grandmother remarked, "My kids used to sleep outside. Now we don't even open that door." Jewell Champion went to check out the neighborhood park prior to taking her grandchildren there: "It shocked me and I didn't think anything could shock me anymore! But no way can I let my babies go down there and play among drug dealers and pimps and Lord knows what else!"

Liz Russell, a 62-year-old grandmother, is particularly upset by the violence in her East Oakland neighborhood because two of the four grandchildren she is raising are older boys—7 and 9—who clamor to be allowed to play outside. The neighborhood's not safe, Mrs. Russell says, because:

> A whole lot of shootin' goes on in the next block, and a bullet doesn't care who it hits. I try to keep 'em close to home but it's hard, especially with the two boys, because they want to play ball, get on their bikes.

Mrs. Russell usually insists that the children play behind a locked fence in the backyard; she gives in to the older boys some of the time, however, and then worries until they're safely back home.

Although Mrs. Russell could take comfort in the fact that, most of the time, at least, her grandchildren were safely behind a high backyard fence, other grandmothers lack even this degree of comfort. Sixty-year-old Henrietta Stillman looks out the window of her project apartment at two of her young grandchildren and sighs:

> I sit here and I am totally and completely sorry for them. The children play in the backyard and there's no protection. There's lots of drugs and things

in a place like this. And you put your kids out there, afraid they might get shot down.

Not surprisingly, Mrs. Stillman's greatest wish is that the government would provide caregivers like herself better housing in which to raise the grandchildren safely. "It's not a lot to ask," she adds.

Despite their vigilance, many of the grandmothers we interviewed felt powerless to keep negative environmental messages from reaching the children in their care. As one grandmother of a little girl put it, "Kids around here have no outlet. They see too much and know too much. So I put Jackie in the (car) and take her to the zoo, the rides. But I can't shield her from everything."

The 48-year-old grandmother of a 9-year-old boy expressed a similar concern: "By the time he was 6 he knew all the crack language. I didn't know what he was talking about, but he'd been around it so much." Another grandmother was "blown away" when her 3-year-old grandson asked her " 'Grandma, do you do cocaine?' And I knew he knew what he was asking!"

Several grandmothers commented that though they weren't worried about their grandkids getting into drug use, the easy money and nice possessions made possible by drug sales might well prove harder for kids in poor neighborhoods to resist. Fifty-six-year-old Sylvie Hayes voiced this concern about 4-year-old Rickey. On the one hand, she's not worried that the boy will get into drugs because "he knows drugs destroyed his family." But on the other hand, she says, "I'm concerned about him being exposed to the glamour, the materialism" associated with drug selling and the easy money it can bring. Many grandmothers told of neighborhood children, 7 or 8 years old, selling crack and showing off the new designer clothes and shoes purchased with the proceeds.

Although many of the grandmothers reserved their deepest anger for a government that didn't seem to take the drug problem nearly seriously enough, others lashed out at a closer and more immediate target—the young men in the neighborhood who recruit young children either to use drugs or to serve as needed lookouts in drug sales. Forty-seven-year-old Lila Dutton, a grandmother raising two children, aged 3 and 7, expressed her rage in this regard saying, "Young black men nowadays, they don't have any respect for life. It's just what they can get. Instead of teachin' the young ones, they teach 'em how to sell drugs." As our interview with Mrs. Dutton concluded, 7-year-old Jimmy Dutton came into the house. Ironically, visible beneath his jacket was the type of beeper often used by young lookouts for drug pushers in neighborhoods like this one where drug trading is a lucrative business.

In point of fact, the crime rate among young black males has grown dramatically in recent years, particularly in inner-city neighborhoods like Mrs. Dutton's. Criminal justice data suggest that 7 in 10 young adult black males in California are arrested at least once, compared to 3 in 10 young white males (Tillman, 1986).

Yet as Duster (1987a) and others (Gibbs et al., 1988; Viscusi, 1986) have pointed out, such crime statistics present only part of the picture and ignore the strong correlation between law breaking and unemployment. In inner-city areas like those in which many of the women we interviewed lived, the unemployment rate for black youths stands at 50% (Gibbs et al., 1988). Severe cutbacks in both public and private sector jobs during the 1980s, and continuing discrimination against black males in fields such as retail sales (Culp & Dunson, 1984) have further eroded job prospects for young African American males. In the process, such trends have increased the likelihood that such men will turn to crime including, importantly, the selling of crack cocaine (see Chapter 13 this volume). As they do, the safety of black inner-city neighborhoods is further compromised, and with it, the grandmothers' ability to raise their grandchildren safely.

## "CRACK BABIES:"
## THE ADDED BURDENS OF SOCIETAL
## STEREOTYPING AND LABELING

As noted earlier, not all children born to cocaine abusing mothers were prenatally exposed to the drug. Similarly, of course, not all children from crack involved households exhibit medical, behavioral, or other problems as a result of either drug exposure in utero or early abuse and neglect (Villarreal et al., 1992).

For many of the mass media and key opinion leaders, however, children whose parents are involved with cocaine are homogenized and labeled "crack babies," and images are conjured up of a frenzied, out-of-control generation of "crack kids" descending on the nation's public schools and threatening to wreak havoc on society.

Newspaper columnist Paul Harvey (1991) has labeled cocaine exposed children civilization's "broken dolls," and has lamented the plight of public schools left to confront these children's "crippling problems with learning and/or behavior." A local San Francisco TV station did a sensitive five-part story on the experience of these children in kindergarten but heavily promoted the program with the title "Cracks in the System." And in an even more stinging indictment, Dr. Edith Fifer, director of early childhood special education for the Chicago public schools, expressed in the *Chicago Tribune* her fear that drug exposed children "may mature as a new biological underclass, incapable of learning or living normal lives" (quoted in Harvey, 1991).

Dr. Claire Coles (1991) of the Department of Psychiatry at Emory University School of Medicine has pointed out that such media reports and related accounts have had profound and disturbing consequences. With little or no scientific evidence to back them,

> theories of brain chemistry have been put forth. New neurological syndromes have been invented; Children have been discovered who are "addicted at birth" or who "lack the ability to love." Classrooms have been prepared to receive children who, contrary to the experience of all other organisms on the planet, are "unable to learn" through reinforcement. And once again, the cause of attention deficit disorder has been discovered. (pp. 5-6)

Dr. Coles (1991) goes on to note that based on such inferences, "public policy decisions are being made . . . teachers are deciding that all children with certain behavior patterns are 'crack babies;' . . . Children are learning that they are damaged for life and most look forward to a life of failure and predetermined drug addiction" (p.6).

Although researchers have already begun to examine the long-range consequences of early cocaine exposure (Chasnoff et al., 1992), little attention is being paid to the potential deleterious effects of children being labeled and treated as a dangerous and troubled generation of "crack kids." Yet research in the field of social psychology has long suggested that such labeling may adversely effect the opportunities afforded students and others whose treatment by professionals is wittingly or unwittingly influenced by the labels assigned (Rosenthal & Jacobsen, 1989).

For many of the grandmothers in our study, the labeling, and marking of their grandchildren as "crack babies" and hence as potential troublemakers and problem children, as they prepare to enter the public schools, adds another layer of problems to an already difficult situation.

Ironically, as some of the women pointed out, even efforts by the media to demonstrate and publicize the successes of prenatally drug exposed children have a tendency to backfire. A great grandmother expressed her outrage when a local paper printed a picture of a 4-year-old making her debut as a ballerina, but captioned the print with the phrase "crack baby" next to the girl's name. "Why should a beautiful, talented child's performance be marred with those two words?" the great grandmother asked, pointing out that because of them, the child will probably never be able to show that picture without embarrassment.

As Goodman (1992) has suggested, perhaps the most deleterious consequence of media and societal distortions surrounding crack cocaine "is the sense of hopelessness dispensed with the title, 'crack kid.'" Whether on the part of teachers, parents and caregivers, or the children themselves, such hopelessness penalizes those who are so labelled, and further draws attention away from "our growing population of children in deep trouble," whether or not they were prenatally exposed to drugs. "If you need a label," Goodman (1992) concludes, "call them kids who need help."

## THE OTHER SIDE OF RAISING CHILDREN OF THE CRACK EPIDEMIC: SPECIAL REWARDS

The bulk of this chapter has focused on problematic aspects of grandparent caregiving in the crack epidemic. Yet as with other forms of caregiving, raising one's grandchildren, even under the often traumatic circumstances described, is not without its rewards.

Studies of family caregivers for the elderly have found that many report satisfactions and rewards in the new role including feeling that one grew as a result of the caregiving experience, general satisfaction at having helped someone in need, and discovering new personal strengths and capacities as a result of caregiving (Hinrichsen & Hernandez, 1991). In addition, as Dressel and Clark (1990, p. 776) have demonstrated, what appears at first to be expressive, other-directed behaviors among family caregivers, such as hugging or telephoning, "may instead be instrumental ones undertaken in the service of having one's own needs met." For grandparent caregivers as well, such rewards provide an important, albeit only partial counter to the often overwhelming stresses and problems that come with raising children in the crack cocaine epidemic.

Many of the women in our study described with pride how they had taken in an infant who was near death, or young children who were emotionally disturbed or severely behind in their learning, and managed to "turn things around" through patience, love, and hard work. A great grandmother in her sixties described having saved her great grandson from almost certain death had he remained with his mother:

> He was 5 months old and weighed 11 pounds. He was almost in the fetal stage, and the doctor told me not to let him lay in one position too long. He couldn't sit up, he couldn't do anything. He had this bloated look about him. If she'd kept him another week, he would have been dead.

A grandmother who took in four of her grandchildren similarly talked about the major changes she had been able to make in their lives. When they first came, she said, the children were hungry: "They had no clothes, no nothing. The boys' pants were all torn. They had no shoes . . . their hair wasn't cut. They were just on the streets asking everybody [for food]." One of the two older children had lit several fires, burning the house, a mattress, and a garage on separate occasions. But once with their grandparents, they began to settle down and became "much happier," with many of the older boy's problem behaviors seeming to disappear.

As noted in Chapter 5, almost all of the women in our study reported feeling that they were appreciated (89%) and that they were fulfilling their duties (96%), with many talking about the rewards inherent in taking in the children, "doing the Lord's work" and "doing the right thing." "It gives me a sense of worth to be able to care for him," a 54-year-old grandmother said, looking at the hyperactive 4-year-old in her care. "He's as good for me as I am for him."

Some women said that taking in a drug exposed grandchild was finally something positive that they could do for their drug addicted child, and that this brought them a satisfying peace. Speaking of her troubled daughter, and her granddaughter Maria, Patricia Sloan said:

> She knows that this is a safe place for her baby. She knows that my home is gentle. She remembers that she felt love in this house, that we touch a lot, that we carry on our little traditions. She's beyond help now but it's

not too late for the baby. Maria is going to need a lot of help and my daughter knows she can't give it to her. I guess I can.

Other women remarked on the special strengths they had found within themselves when faced with the challenge of raising youngsters who were suffering the effects of prenatal drug exposure, or of parental abuse and neglect because of crack.

And for still others, raising a child who was suffering the consequences of prenatal drug exposure gave new meaning and purpose to life. Forty-three-year-old June Sparrow, whose granddaughter came to her unable to swallow and with a host of other medical and behavioral problems related to crack, put it this way: "Before I never wanted to commit suicide, but if I didn't live until tomorrow it didn't matter. Now I have to live to tomorrow. It's better this way."

* * *

As women like Mrs. Sparrow make clear, grandmothers raising the children of the crack cocaine epidemic *do* experience some special rewards. Such rewards may take the form of the relief that comes with knowing that a grandchild is finally safe and cared for, pride and satisfaction in doing an important job well, or a heightened sense of self-worth and purpose.

Yet as this chapter has attempted to demonstrate, raising the children of the epidemic is also fraught with difficulties. Grandmother caregivers must deal with the immediate physical and emotional needs of children whose parents are unwilling or unable to care for them—children who may be suffering the consequences of prenatal drug exposure or of early abuse and neglect and related problems. At the same time, the grandmothers must confront and deal with having adult children involved with crack in a country that speaks of a "war on drugs" but puts few resources into drug prevention and treatment programs (see Chapter 13 this volume).

The grandmothers must face, too, the realities of raising young children in neighborhoods that often have become unsafe—neighborhoods where poverty and high unemployment among young black males go hand in hand with crack dealing and violence in the streets. And the grandmothers also must confront the wall of prejudice and misunderstanding that their grandchildren may face, particularly as they reach school age, as a consequence of media-created images of inhuman "crack babies" descending on society.

Finally, within the context of these broader problems and issues, the grandmothers additionally often find themselves thwarted, rather than helped, by a government that regards grandparent caregivers as "second class citizens." Frequently blocked in their attempts to get the bureaucracy to take seriously their concerns about the safety and well-being of grandchildren in crack involved households, they may eventually gain custody of the children, only to be denied adequate support and assistance for raising them (see Chapters 6 and 13). Not surprisingly, in the face of these problems and obstacles, many grandmothers have turned to other grandparents for emotional support, and increasingly for the development of political muscle to help bring about change. It is to these and related efforts to assist grandparent caregivers that we now turn.

# 12

---

## Community Interventions to Support Grandparent Caregivers

Four years ago, when the death of her sister left her parents to care for their 8-year-old granddaughter, Sylvie de Toledo witnessed firsthand the problems and challenges faced by grandparent caregivers. A licensed clinical social worker at the Psychiatric Clinic for Youth in Long Beach, California, de Toledo began Grandparents as Parents (GAP), a support and therapy group to assist people like her own parents who suddenly find themselves raising their grandchildren (Larsen, 1990).

Three thousand miles away in Media, Pennsylvania, grandparent caregiver Diane Werner found herself getting increasingly angry that all of the money and the media attention directed at the "war on drugs" seemed to bypass entirely the needs of the children of drug abusing parents, and of people like herself—the grandparents raising those children. Werner approached Michelle Daly, a social worker with the county's family and community service agency, and together they formed a support group called Second Time Around Parents (Larsen, 1990).

In Colleyville, Texas, Barbara Kirkland and her husband Gerald became caregivers for the only child of their divorced son, who died in an industrial accident. Although friends encouraged them to attend parenting classes, the Kirklands realized that their needs and concerns were very different from those of the young, first-time-around parents at whom such programs are directed. Barbara Kirkland began her own support and advocacy group, Grandparents Raising Grandchildren, and with it an impressive career as an activist and advocate for grandparent caregivers throughout the nation (Larsen, 1990).

Although accurate figures are hard to come by, there are an estimated 250 support groups for grandparent caregivers in the United States today

(D. Werner, personal communication, April 1992). Respite programs for grandparent caregivers, community coalitions, hot lines, and peer training programs are among the other developments that have come into being in the last few years to support grandparent caregivers in their often daunting new role.

In this chapter, we will highlight a number of these supportive interventions, as well as efforts on the state and national levels to promote and coordinate such activities. Although support groups and other community-level interventions cannot take the place of needed policy changes that would provide legal recognition and instrumental support to such caregivers, the former also have an important role to play. Moreover, as we shall see, many local support groups and programs for grandparent caregivers are using their "people power," access to the media, and other resources to help fight for needed social changes that would improve the quality of life for grandparents and the children in their care.

## SUPPORT GROUPS
## FOR GRANDPARENT CAREGIVERS

As noted above, the late 1980s and early 1990s saw the birth of some 250 support groups for, and often by, grandparent caregivers. With names such as ROCK (Raising Our Children's Kids), GAIN (Grandparents Are Indeed Needed) and GOLD (Grandparents Offering Love and Direction), the groups operate out of senior centers and churches, public schools, private homes, and health and social service agencies. Attendance at the weekly or monthly support group meetings ranges from a handful to 75 or more, and may include great-aunts and -uncles, as well as grandparents and great grandparents.

Although most grandparent caregiver support groups are independent entities, others have spawned a whole network of "chapters" or loosely affiliated groups sharing common goals and approaches. The Texas-based organization, Grandparents Raising Grandchildren, for example, had helped give birth to approximately 40 chapters by 1991 and has been incorporated as a private nonprofit organization (Brookdale, 1992a). The founder of GAP Long Beach similarly has helped to start some 130 support groups around the nation, a number of which have adopted the GAP name (S. de Toledo, personal communication, November 1991).

As noted in Chapter 7, although the women in our study who had joined support groups at first did so primarily for the emotional and informational support they provided, the often significant instrumental assistance they received frequently became at least as important as the less tangible forms of support experienced. Such instrumental aid often included help provided by group facilitators in linking the women with needed services for themselves or their grandchildren, or in providing treats and "extras" around the holidays, or access to needed respite care.

Given the often considerable needs of grandparent caregivers for assistance that goes beyond emotional and informational aid, it is not surprising that a number of support groups around the country have broadened their original missions to include more tangible assistance. In addition to providing emotional and informational support, for example, some support groups now provide emergency financial aid, or food and housing assistance on a case-by-case basis. Support groups that are run in conjunction with local public and private hospitals or health and social service agencies similarly often arrange for individual counseling and medical or psychological testing for the grandchildren of group members. And many support groups now offer counseling on child protective services and legal guardianship, as well as information on the ins and outs of accessing needed programs and services in a whole range of areas.

As support groups and their facilitators become increasingly concerned with the need to foster support for grandparent caregivers on the broader legislative and policy levels, these groups also have frequently expanded their focus to include advocacy efforts. In Pennsylvania, Second Time Around founders Werner and Daly make it part of the business of the support group to sensitize and educate judges, attorneys, and policymakers to the needs of grandparent caregivers. Their effective advocacy efforts so impressed the vice chairman of the Senate Aging and Youth Policy Committee that he asked the group's input on a proposed child custody bill (Grobman, 1991). In San Francisco, the hospital-based Grandparents Who Care program includes in its mission statement channeling the feelings of isolation, anger, and despair expressed in its six support groups "into positive instruments of change . . . to affect state and federal system and policy changes" (*Grandparents Who Care,* 1991).

Toward this end, the support group served as a cosponsor of the city's successful "Children's Bill," a 1991 ballot measure that required that one half of one percent of the City's budget go to programs for children and youth (D. Miller, 1991).

Texas's Grandparents Raising Grandchildren organization also describes securing the passage of legislation supporting the rights of children and their grandparent caregivers as critical to its mission of providing both emotional support and "political muscle" to caregivers (Kirkland, 1988). The advocacy of group members further has been given part of the credit for the passage of recent legislation making it possible for group insurance companies to cover grandchildren in the care of their grandparents (see Chapter 13 this volume).

Later in this chapter we will examine some recent efforts by leaders of grandparent caregiver support groups in different parts of the country to coordinate their efforts in fighting for broader system change. In the meantime, however, we will turn our attention to several other promising community-level interventions that have been developed for, and often by, grandparent caregivers.

## BEYOND SUPPORT GROUPS

### Hot Lines, Warm Lines

Early in 1989, Alameda County, California, Supervisor Don Perata discovered that a growing number of calls to his office were from distraught grandparents who had suddenly found themselves the full-time caregivers for their grandchildren. Staff member Celestine Greene, who handled many of the calls, saw the need for "a warm line,—not a hotline for crisis intervention, but a warm line that would give grandparents emotional support, and a feeling that someone out there is putting their arms around them and really cares" (Brookdale, 1992b).

Appropriately titled GASP, or Grandparents as Second Parents, the warm line relies upon the assistance of volunteer grandparent caregivers who, following a brief training course, serve as peer counselors for those who call in on a toll free number. Public service announcements on a local television station and coverage in the city's major newspaper, combined with word of mouth to result in 1,000 calls within the first 6 months of operation from all over northern California (Brookdale, 1992b; Ness, 1991).

The public service announcements had a welcome unanticipated side effect as well: In addition to calls from grandparent caregivers, concerned individuals, businesses, social clubs, and other organizations called to offer donations of baby furniture, diapers, infant formula, and other forms of direct assistance. Donors of baby furniture and other large items were linked, where possible, with interested individual grandparent caregivers, whereas contributed cases of baby formula and other smaller items were stored at the project office for grandparents to access on an as-needed basis.

An estimated 750 of the warm line's first 1,000 callers received direct assistance with information and referral, emotional support, and sometimes tangible material aid. In addition, three support groups grew out of the project, to help meet some of the ongoing needs of callers for emotional and informational support (Brookdale, 1992b).

The early success of GASP led to its being sponsored, beginning in 1992 by the East Oakland Fighting Back Project, a community-based coalition of 35 organizations that support drug abuse prevention and related efforts. With funding from the Robert Wood Johnson Foundation, GASP has also been able to expand in several new directions: A resource directory for grandparent caregivers has been developed, as has a newsletter, which is printed and disseminated 3 times annually (Brookdale, 1992b).

Although relative caregivers calling in on the warm line are its primary beneficiaries, grandparents who staff the program also report benefiting from their involvement. A great grandmother in her seventies, who staffs the warm line several afternoons a week, remarked, "It really gives you a good feeling to know you've been there and now you're helping others deal with it. I talk to them, show them I understand—little things mean so much! And it makes me feel good to know I've been able to reach out and help somebody else" (Molo, 1991).

Oakland's GASP warm line is one of several efforts around the country to provide information, referral, and emotional support to relative caregivers by means of a dedicated telephone line. And the need they meet appears to be substantial: Southern California's GOLD hot line reported receiving some 3,000 calls in 1991 alone! (M. Davis, personal communication, January 1992). So successful are these hot lines, moreover, that leaders of the grandparent caregiver movement nationwide hope to see a toll free number established in the near future that would enable grandparent caregivers throughout the country to have access to this vital service (Brookdale, 1992a).

## Peer Training

The growing popularity of support groups for and by grandparent caregivers underscores the fact that many individuals in this situation seek contact with others who may be going through a similar experience. As the Grandparent Caregiver Study has demonstrated, moreover, participants in support groups often get as much out of sharing their insights and advice with others as they do from learning how others are coping with and managing the new role.

Building on this realization, and recognizing that grandparent caregivers are in a unique position to assist others as they assume the new caregiver role, several promising efforts have been made to provide peer training for grandparent caregivers.

Perhaps the most ambitious of these efforts to date is the peer training program for grandparents and the children in their care provided as part of the intergenerational project, Families United Against Crack Cocaine, in Oakland, California. Initiated in October 1990 under the auspices of the city's Office on Aging, and funded through a $73,000 grant from the Administration on Aging in Washington, DC, Families United saw the training and use of peer counselors as a core component of its multisystems approach to meeting the needs of grandparent caregivers and the children impacted by the crack epidemic (Gross, 1991; Nathan, 1990). Through such training, according to former Project Director Zakiya Somburu, it was hoped that both grandparents and youth would be enabled "to better negotiate their environment and better advocate for themselves at the family, community and legislative levels" (Brookdale, 1992a).

By December 1991, 30 grandparent caregivers and 30 young people aged 12 and under had been trained through a multidisciplinary curriculum that included sessions on addiction as a family disease, communication, child development, nutrition, expressive arts, and peer counseling skills. Graduates of the program are now helping to staff the earlier mentioned warm line, facilitating support groups, writing and disseminating an intergenerational newsletter, speaking to schools, and in other ways working to assist families and the larger community in the fight against crack cocaine (Brookdale, 1992a).

Peer training has also become a key component of the Grandparents Who Care program at San Francisco General Hospital. With the help of a small neighborhood empowerment grant from the Mayor's Office, an intensive 2-day program was established, through which 18 grandparent caregivers were helped to develop skills in group facilitation. A follow-up practicum then was offered, consisting of four morning sessions on topics such as working effectively with social workers and other pro-viders, crisis management, codependency, and empowerment. As part of the practicum, participants also were able to observe and critique support group facilitation, and to practice the skills learned in their own groups.

Several of the grandparents who completed the peer training program are now serving as support group cofacilitators, with one serving as an office assistant and ombudsperson to the project (S. Trupin, personal communication, April 1992).

Through programs like these, grandparent caregivers are being helped to move from the role of change target to that of change agent, working with their peers to make positive changes in their individual and col-lective well-being.

## Respite Services

As noted earlier, one of the two greatest needs expressed by partici-pants in the Grandparent Caregiver Study was for respite care that would allow them even a short break from the daily demands of second time around parenting. Responding to this need, a number of support groups now provide free on-site baby-sitting for attendees, with some offering additional respite a set number of hours per month as a benefit for group members.

Limited respite services also are offered as part of several of the more comprehensive programs for grandparent caregivers around the country.

The Intergenerational Project of Aid to Imprisoned Mothers in Atlanta, Georgia, provides a variety of group and individualized pro-grams for the children of prisoners, in part as a means of offering respite to the grandparents serving as their primary caregivers (Barnhill & Chambers, 1992). Limited respite services also are provided in Boston, Massachusetts, through Aid to Incarcerated Mothers, in recognition of the fact that relief from constant child care is critical to the emotional health and wellbeing of grandparent caregivers.

In Deerfield Beach, Florida, a local senior center began a respite/intergenerational child-care program in 1987 when staff realized that seniors with extensive child-care responsibilities were unable to attend center functions (Fischer, 1991). Although not restricted to grandparents with full-time caregiving responsibilities, the program offers an important model for other senior centers where grandparent caregiving is prevalent.

Respite care programs for grandparent caregivers also are being planned in conjunction with churches and other community agencies. In Oakland, California, seed money from the congregation's Community Health Project and a local community fund-raiser enabled the Bethlehem Lutheran Church to begin work on the development of the Loving Hands, Loving Hearts respite program (Saunders, 1992). Working in conjunction with other local churches, Loving Hands, Loving Hearts is designed to provide center-based respite to relative caregivers of children from crack involved households. Trained volunteers will provide the respite care, which will include field trips and other activities to enhance the social development of children while giving their caregivers needed time to themselves (Saunders, 1992).

## PROGRAMS AND SERVICES
## FOR SPECIAL POPULATIONS

The programs and services described thus far have in common the goal of supporting grandparents who assumed caregiving for their grandchildren under a variety of conditions. The support groups, peer training, and respite programs described, for example, typically include grandparents raising grandchildren because of the drug or alcohol involvement of the children's parents, others whose adult children are young teenage parents, and still others who inherited their grandchildren because of the death, incarceration, or incapacitation of an adult child.

Another set of programs and services, however, have emerged in response to the needs of specific subpopulations of grandparent caregivers and the children in their care.

In Cupertino, California, Elder Link Consultants has identified grandparents raising juvenile offenders as an often neglected group of caregivers who may have special support needs. Trainings therefore are conducted for probation officers working with juvenile offenders in the care of grandparents, covering such topics as family systems and multigenerational families, child abuse, and elder abuse. The training also provides enrollees with information so that they can refer grandparents to support groups and other relevant programs and services. By affording probation officers a better understanding of grandparent caregiver issues, the training project hopes to create a cadre of officers better able to assist both grandparents and the juveniles in their care (J. Barton & V. Daugherty, personal communication, November 1991).

Grandparents raising drug exposed children also have been targets of special services and programs, with support groups, educational programs, and manuals and directories developed in different parts of the country specifically to meet the needs of this group. In Los Angeles, California, the National Association of African American Grandmothers (NAAAG) was established in 1991 with the specific objective of providing supportive services to African American grandmothers who are primary caregivers to drug exposed children (Walters, 1991).

A private nonprofit organization cosponsored by the Los Angeles County Department of Health Services, the program includes a 20-week educational course for grandparent caregivers, and an informal support group for those participating in the educational sessions. An emphasis is placed on family interaction, and on providing education and consultation using a training model that is tailored to the African American culture and heritage of participants (Walters, 1991).

Among the most comprehensive programs for special populations are those targeting grandparent caregivers for the children of women who are in prison. The earlier mentioned Intergenerational Project of Aid to Imprisoned Mothers (AIM) in Atlanta, Georgia, is exemplary in this regard.

Established first on a pilot basis in 1990, the Intergenerational Project was designed to round out the agency's family systems philosophy and approach by extending counseling and support services to grandmothers who provide the bulk of primary caregiving to the children of incarcerated mothers in the state. The caregivers receive biweekly individualized counseling at the AIM office, where the agency's two part-time therapists provide emotional support and help them develop skills in crisis management (Barnhill & Chambers, 1992).

Grandmothers also participate in a monthly support group, and work on an individual basis with AIM's full-time family advocate, who helps the women gain access to programs such as Medicaid and food stamps, and, if needed, to emergency food and clothing for their families (Brookdale, 1992b).

For grandmothers raising preschool-aged children, transportation in the AIM van is available to make it possible for them to take the children to visit their incarcerated mothers. The importance of the latter service is underscored when it is realized that Georgia's main prison for women is a 5-hour drive from Atlanta, and that few of the grandparents own reliable cars (Dressel & Barnhill, 1991).

As Project Director Sandra Barnhill points out, the Intergenerational Project also supports grandparent caregivers through the educational, social, and counseling programs it has developed for the grandchildren in their care. "Both by helping such children deal with their feelings about a parent's incarceration, and by providing regular periods of respite for grandmothers while their grandchildren attend AIM activities, the Intergenerational Project seeks to alleviate some of the stress experienced by grandparent caregivers" (Brookdale, 1992b).

The phenomenon of grandparent caregiving is most prevalent in urban areas, and the great majority of supportive programs to date serve these populations. Yet the growth and "rediscovery" of grandparent caregiving in rural areas has led to several recent efforts to support relatives raising young children in these less populated regions.

One such effort, in upstate New York, has involved the use of rural extension agents. When the Cornell Cooperative Extension Center of Ontario County discovered that an increasing number of grandparents in that area were raising grandchildren, they developed and implemented a four-session educational course covering topics such as custody issues, financial assistance for family caregivers, and child behavior. Fifteen grandparent caregivers from a wide geographic radius attended the class, which in turn led to the formation of a bimonthly support group and individual-level counseling and referral services. Based on the success of this effort, extension agents in nearby areas are considering the development of similar activities (I. Jensen, personal communication, March 1992).

## COALITION BUILDING

The needs and concerns of grandparent caregivers cross many professional and disciplinary boundaries. Social service agencies, the judicial system, health care providers, educators, policymakers, and grandparent caregivers themselves all have a part to play in helping the latter as they seek to fulfill this challenging new role.

In several regions of the country, coalitions are developing to help concerned individuals, community groups, and agencies as they pursue the common goal of supporting and assisting grandparent caregivers.

Some of these coalitions are made up primarily of professionals, and have specific and time limited objectives. An interagency consortium representing 10-12 organizations in Pinellas County, Florida, for example, was formed in 1991 with the specific goal of developing a directory of services and information for relative caregivers raising drug exposed children (C. Boardman, personal communication, November 1991).

Other coalitions are broader in scope, such as the community coalition on grandparent caregiving developed by Washington, DC's Kincare Program and funded through a $20,000 grant from the Administration on Aging. Cosponsored by the DC Commission for Women and the DC Office on Aging, the coalition is comprised of grandparent caregivers, church leaders, educators, and representatives of the business and voluntary sectors.

The idea for such a coalition grew, in part, out of its founders' desire to help grandparent caregivers become more involved in the schools their grandchildren attend. Although estimates vary, grandparents are believed to be the sole or primary caregivers for many of the children living in the nation's capitol—a fact that underscores the need for such involvement (C. Lowe, personal communication, January 1992).

Through focus groups and other needs assessment techniques, founders of the coalition were able to identify a number of unmet needs faced by grandparent caregivers in their area and including transportation, respite, tutoring for the children in their care, counseling on legal and custody issues, and help in accessing needed programs and services. Based on the findings of these initial efforts, a resource fair for grandparent caregivers, and a variety of other action strategies and activities are being explored (Brookdale, 1992b).

Coalition building on the local level is also under way in the State of California. In the Bay Area region, the Coalition for Grandparents Parenting Grandchildren meets monthly at a local senior center and consists of approximately 40 concerned professionals, legislative aides, community activists, and grandparent caregivers. Housed in the office of the Berkeley/Oakland Gray Panthers, this regional coalition is dedicated to educating policymakers and the general public, and to advocating for policy changes in both the public and private sectors that would support grandparent caregivers.

Coalition building is also taking place on the state level. Approximately 60 grandparent caregivers, support group leaders, and concerned activists and professionals met in Los Angeles in February 1992 and began laying the groundwork for the founding of a statewide organization.

At follow-up meetings in Oakland and San Diego the newly formed California Coalition for Grandparents And Caregivers established its goals and objectives, developed a mission statement, and agreed upon the membership of a statewide steering committee for the coalition.

Initial efforts toward statewide organizing also have begun in the state of Washington, which hopes eventually to include both Oregon and Idaho in a regional coalition (T. Sher, personal communication, March 1992).

Finally, an important step toward nationwide organizing took place in October 1991, with the first "Washington Summit" on grandparent caregiving. Representing diverse regions of the United States, 10 leaders of the grandparent caregiver movement descended on the nation's capital to meet with each other and with policymakers and key groups and organizations about the needs of relative caregivers raising children in "skipped generation" families (Brookdale, 1992a).

Summit attendees spoke with their Washington hosts about the critical next steps they'd like to see for increasing the visibility and political support of grandparent caregivers. The formation of a national coalition, which would preserve the autonomy of individual support groups and other organizations while providing a unifying structure for advocacy and action, was key among the suggestions made, and the groundwork was laid for the establishment of such an organization (Brookdale, 1992a).

## ASSESSING THE STATE OF THE ART OF SUPPORTIVE INTERVENTIONS FOR GRANDPARENT CAREGIVERS

As suggested above, an increasing number and variety of efforts currently are under way to help meet the needs of grandparent caregivers. To better understand the scope and magnitude of these efforts, uncover unmet needs, and facilitate the sharing of innovative ideas and approaches nationwide, the Brookdale Grandparent Caregiver Information Project was established in the fall of 1991 (Brookdale, 1992a).

Funded through a grant from the Brookdale Foundation Group to the Western Consortium for Public Health in Berkeley, California, the Project is conducting a state-of-the-art survey of community interventions and service programs for grandparent caregivers. In cooperation with the Foundation's "Age Base" service, a computerized data base of programs and services for the elderly nationwide, a data base of programs targeted at grandparent caregivers also is being developed. The latter will enable professionals, community groups, and others to receive up-to-date information on supportive interventions in their geographic area. Relevant research and policy developments on the state and national levels also are being followed (Brookdale, 1992a).

Through the publication and wide distribution of a newsletter on grandparent caregiving 3 times annually, the Project further seeks to facilitate the dissemination and sharing of program ideas, research findings, and policy developments, while increasing the visibility of the concerns and issues of grandparent caregivers.

*    *    *

The programs and activities highlighted in this chapter are suggestive of a broad range of supportive interventions for, and often by, grandparent caregivers. Developments like these may make an important difference in the lives of many caregivers, particularly in helping them feel less isolated as they cope with the demands and challenges of the new caregiving role.

Yet all too often, supportive community-level programs and services for grandparent caregivers are unfunded or underfunded, and lack the institutional support that could help them survive through economically tough times.

In part because of their lack of funds and informal nature, few programs serving grandparent caregivers have built in evaluative components to help determine their effectiveness. The resultant lack of outcome data may in turn hamper such programs' chances for subsequent funding and/or institutional support.

The national review of supportive interventions currently being undertaken by the authors in conjunction with the Brookdale Grandparent Caregiver Information Project suggests that all but a tiny handful of the programs are without funding or other operational support. When health or social service professionals are involved in such programs, moreover, they typically appear to be squeezing that involvement into an already overcrowded schedule of job assignments and pressures.

The heavy reliance of many community programs and services for grandparent caregivers on the caregivers themselves, although positive and empowering on one level, also may have a serious down side. Our interviews with Oakland grandparent caregivers who were volunteering as support group facilitators, peer counselors, newsletter contributors, and warm line operators revealed, for example, that even though many enjoyed these new roles, they also not infrequently felt stretched to the limit. For several, the demands of caregiving for young children while attempting to fulfill numerous preexisting roles and obligations, left them with little reserve of either physical or emotional energy. Under such conditions, their new volunteer roles, although willingly embraced, sometimes acted as additional stressors and put the women at high risk for burnout.

Finally, overemphasizing self-help and other community/mutual aid approaches as "solutions" to problems of the magnitude faced by many grandparent caregivers runs the risk of deflecting attention from the need for larger, structural change. As Pilisuk and Minkler (1985) have noted:

> Self help is neither selfless nor cheap. Family and community effectiveness in the provision of social support is heavily dependent upon the broader economic and social environment. Where this larger environment misallocates resources, where it creates and tolerates . . . poverty and injustice, social ties on the individual and community levels will suffer. (p. 11)

Effective community-level support for grandparent caregivers and the children in their care is, in the last analysis, heavily dependent on the provision of programs, services, and policies on a broader societal level, which can help meet basic human needs (Pilisuk & Minkler, 1985).

As noted earlier, several of the community groups and interventions described in this chapter have aimed, in part, at changing policies on the state and national levels so that they do better meet the needs of grandparent caregivers and their families. Yet much remains to be done. In the final chapter of this book, we turn to these policy issues, focusing special attention on the areas that were of greatest importance to the grandmother caregivers who shared with us their insights and concerns.

# 13

## Implications for Policy

Physician and public health leader Victor Sidel is fond of saying that "statistics are people with the tears washed off." In this book, we have tried to get behind the statistics to help bring alive the experiences of grandmothers who are raising their grandchildren as a direct consequence of the crack cocaine epidemic. At the same time, we have tried to move from the "personal troubles" of grandparent caregivers to the "public issues" (Mills, 1959) that so intimately help shape and determine their reality.

In this final chapter, we bring together a host of societal policy issues, along with their underlying values and assumptions, as these influence the experiences of grandparents raising grandchildren. Many of these themes and issues have been introduced earlier in the book and woven throughout several of its chapters. In bringing them together here, however, we attempt to underscore again the critical need for moving beyond the private pain and the personal stories of caring and courageous women, to focus on needed social change.

A long tradition in U.S. health and social welfare policy has involved carefully differentiating between "deserving" and "undeserving" subgroups in the population and developing different programs and policies for people on the basis of whether they are seen as fitting within one or the other of these categories (Abramowitz, 1988; Estes, 1979; Katz, 1986, 1989; Margolis, 1990). Like the British before us, Americans have had a preoccupation with worthiness that has often made it a primary consideration in policy deliberations over resource allocation and related issues.

By the early 1920s, for example, 40 states had passed "mother's pension" laws to aid poor mothers and children without removing the latter from their homes (Costin & Rapp, 1984). Yet the intense concern of local authorities with separating the "worthy and deserving,"—predominantly white widows—from those deemed less worthy of assistance resulted in a profound skewing of aid distribution (Costin & Rapp, 1984). As Sidel (1992b) has noted:

> Widows . . . were thought to be the most legitimate recipients of funds, and other groups—such as women who were deserted by their husbands or divorced or separated, those whose husbands were imprisoned or disabled, or, most suspect of all, unmarried mothers—were eliminated whenever possible. (p. 83)

As Sidel (1992b, p. 83) went on to point out, investigations into the character of a prospective recipient, to see if the mother was "physically, mentally, and morally fit to raise her children" (Costin & Rapp, 1984) resulted in the "weeding out of almost everyone except white widows."

Such preoccupations continued, both in the punitive and restrictive rules governing receipt of AFDC, and in the differential treatment accorded widows raising children and low-income mothers who are either single or separated or divorced. By placing most African American women in the undeserving category and denying them aid, moreover, the new legislation was able to ensure a continuing supply of low paid domestic and casual workers for the marketplace (Abramowitz, 1988).

The phenomenon of grandparents raising grandchildren raises a number of policy issues, but at the base of these lies the fact that in most states, the great majority of grandparent caregivers are treated via policies predicated in part on the notion of "undeservingness."

As noted in Chapter 6, for example, participants in the Grandparent Caregiver Study who were receiving government financial assistance in raising their grandchildren were enrolled in either AFDC or AFDC-Foster Care, rather than the more generous and nonstigmatizing Foster Care program. A program like AFDC is described by Margolis (1990, p. 15) as having a low "compassion index"; it "carefully screens applicants and vigilantly regulates its beneficiaries." The application process itself discourages women from applying, and as a consequence the program misses some of the neediest qualifiers.

The earlier mentioned "family ethic" (Abramowitz, 1988), which also underlies many of our social welfare policies, assumes that grandparents have "a duty to care" for grandchildren, and therefore don't deserve more than minimum compensation for what should be a labor of love (see Chapter 2 this volume). In the case of grandparents raising grandchildren because of the drug involvement of their own adult children, an additional question of worthiness or deservingness frequently is raised in the often unspoken assumption that such grandparents couldn't have been very good parents themselves or they wouldn't be in this situation today.

Whatever the spoken or unspoken underlying rationale, however, grandparent caregivers, particularly if they have only informal custody of their grandchildren, often find themselves treated as second-class citizens vis-à-vis both public and private programs and services.

In this chapter, we begin by reviewing the differential treatment that government accords grandparent caregivers depending upon whether they are AFDC or AFDC-Foster Care recipients. We will look, too, at the much larger treatment differences between grandparent caregivers as a group in states like California that lack "kinship care" programs, and "real" foster care parents who are unrelated to the children in their care. Other policies in both the public and private sectors that may work against the best interests of grandparents and the children they are raising also will be explored.

We then will examine several other policy areas frequently discussed by participants in the Grandparent Caregiver Study, including government policy around removal of children from the home of a substance abusing parent, and the policies and realities surrounding drug treatment and assistance (or lack of assistance) for the parents of children who are in their grandparents' care. Once again, we will draw on the observations and experiences of grandparents themselves to add a personal dimension to the facts and figures presented, and to help direct our thinking toward needed policy change.

Finally, we will consider both promising policy developments and setbacks in the policy arena that are likely to impact on grandparent caregiving in the years ahead.

## GRANDPARENT CAREGIVERS:
## SECOND-CLASS CITIZENS?

The great majority of grandparent caregivers in the United States have grandchildren in their care either by default (e.g., because a child is absent due usually to incarceration or substance abuse), or through an informal arrangement with the grandchild's parents (Barry, 1991).

As noted in Chapter 6, although such grandparent caregivers often qualify for AFDC payments, in no state is the amount of support received enough to bring low-income caregivers above the poverty line (Sidel, 1992b).

Moreover, recent and often substantial cuts in AFDC in many states in order to reduce costs and "discourage welfare dependency" have had the effect of penalizing still further grandparents raising their grandchildren. In California, the cuts in welfare enacted in 1991 and planned for 1992, along with a 5-year freeze on benefits, are projected to amount to a 45% reduction when inflation is taken into account (Kerschner, 1991).

Despite policymakers' frequent declarations of the need to cut "costly" welfare programs, however, AFDC remains a low-cost alternative to foster care in terms of the state's pocketbook. The national average of the cost to a state of placing an additional child with his or her grandparent, for example, was just $109 per month in 1991, compared to $371 per month if that same child were placed in foster care (Creighton, 1991; Jost, 1991). Given such cost differentials, it is not surprising that the worsening fiscal crisis facing many states, coupled with a continuing rise in the number of children requiring placement, has had the effect of encouraging relative placement, rather than costlier foster care arrangements for dependent children (Jost, 1991).

In point of fact, of course, nonrelative placement of children has also been on the rise over the last several years (Wells & Biegel, 1991). Recent and dramatic increases in the number of prenatally drug exposed children has been cited as the major factor responsible for the rapid growth in the number of children in foster care (Barth, 1991a; Feig, 1990). Barring major policy changes, the number of children in out-of-home placements overall is expected to rise close to 75% by the mid-1990s (U.S. House of Representatives, Select Committee on Children, Youth and Families, 1990). Yet placement with relatives has undergone the most dramatic increase, and is now the fastest growing component of the foster care system (Jost, 1991).

In New York, for example, the number of children placed with grandparents and other relatives rose from 1,000 in 1986 to about 20,000 in 1990, and over this same period, Illinois experienced a 121% increase, from 3,700 to 8,200 (Jost, 1991). The escalation was most pronounced in urban inner cities, a fact many observers have attributed to the crack cocaine epidemic, which peaked during this period, hitting disproportionately low-income African American families with a strong cultural tradition of "taking care of our own" (Jost, 1991).

In several states including New York and Illinois, however, the dramatic rise in relative caregiving can also be attributed to the recent development and rapid expansion of "kinship care" programs. Designed specifically to encourage the official placement of children with their grandparents and other relatives as a form of foster care, kinship care programs provide enrollees with the same amounts of support as foster care parents who are unrelated to the children in their care. But to be eligible for kinship care, grandparents must give formal custody of their grandchildren to the state—a step most are unwilling to take (Creighton, 1991).

In California, kinship care is not an option, and as discussed in Chapter 6, the vast majority of grandparent caregivers not only receive lower rates of payment than foster care parents, but also are far less likely to receive such special services for the children in their care as physiological workups, physical and speech therapy, and clothing allowances, or to receive respite care for themselves, or family counseling (Barry, 1991). Since many physicians refuse to accept Medicaid (Health Access Foundation, 1988), low-income grandparents who receive AFDC but are not eligible for AFDC-Foster Care with its attendant health benefits, sometimes find it difficult to obtain quality medical care for their grandchildren.

Finally, above and beyond the often substantial difference between AFDC and foster care benefits in terms of levels of payment and support service entitlements, is the stigma attached to being in one of these programs rather than the other (see Chapter 6 this volume). As Pennsylvania grandmother and support group founder Diane Werner has pointed out, "Just the difference between saying you're a foster parent and saying you're on welfare is phenomenal in terms of your self-esteem" (Personal communication, November 1991).

As noted earlier, many grandparent caregivers, of course, *do* manage to become AFDC-Foster Care parents, but the specific requirements that must be met before grandparents can qualify tend to put this option out of reach for many of the neediest caregivers. Foster care (Title IV-E) benefits, for example, currently are only available in instances where children have been removed from the home of their parent or another relative by court order and placed with the grandparent. For the many grandparents whose grandchildren are already living with them when the court makes a determination of dependency, foster care benefits are not available (Barry, 1991).

## "IT'S NOT JUST THE MONEY"

Although inequities in state-level financial and other supportive services for grandparent caregivers are the primary factors responsible for their feelings of "second-class citizenship," they are far from being the only factors. Many insurance companies, for example, won't allow a grandparent to carry a grandchild as a dependent (Rosenfeld, 1991). Although Texas recently challenged this practice with a law saying that such grandchildren "may" be covered under group health insurance policies, the wording of the new law was intentionally mild, and many companies have been reluctant to comply (Rosenfeld, 1991).

Grandparents raising drug exposed children often find themselves particularly jeopardized in terms of insurance coverage. Since many of these children were premature at birth and/or had other health problems believed to be connected to their prenatal drug exposure, insurance companies frequently deny coverage on the grounds that the children had "preexisting conditions" (D. Aroner, personal communication, March 1992)

In some parts of the country, too, grandparents are finding that schools may not admit the grandchildren in their care if the children's parents live in another school district. Finally, although the stepchild of a deceased or disabled stepfather can receive social security survivors' benefits whether or not the child was formally adopted, a grandchild totally dependent on his or her grandparents is not entitled to survivors/ disability social security benefits, except in rare instances, even if the deceased grandparent had legal guardianship (Kirkland, 1988).

The whole matter of grandparent treatment by the courts in decisions concerning the granting of legal custody or adoption was one of concern to caregivers, who sometimes felt they were second-class citizens in this respect as well. On the one hand, the family reunification concept in the Federal Adoption Assistance and Child Welfare Act of 1980 states that when a child is placed in dependency, relatives should be considered for placement before nonrelatives. On the other hand, however, many grandparents are unaware that they may be effectively "locked out" of the custody process unless they intervene early (E. Barry, personal communication, June 1992).

Finally, as Barry notes, "there is great variation in the way the courts and social service agencies treat relatives seeking custody." Grandparents not infrequently are told that they are "too old" to be raising children; that they are physically not up to the task; or that they were not good parents to their own children. Racial and cultural biases also have operated to preclude the consideration of certain family members in decisions regarding custody or adoption (E. Barry, personal communication, June 1992).

For the many grandparent caregivers without legal custody and/or formal adoption of their grandchildren, additional instances of perceived second-class citizenship status can be cited. Physicians, for example, can refuse to treat a child, except in life threatening situations, unless the child has been formally adopted by his or her grandparents. And without legal custody, grandchildren being raised by military retirees are not covered under CHAMPUS, the military's health insurance plan (Kirkland, 1988).

Ironically, although grandparent caregivers who do not have legal custody often feel like second-class citizens because of rules and policies like the above, several of the grandparents we interviewed reported that the help they received from county social workers diminished substantially when they did get custody. In the words of one grandmother, "Now that [my grandson] is in permanent placement, the social worker says, 'I have a big caseload.' " For women like this one, there was a cruel irony in being treated as if their needs for help and support had ended with the awarding of custody, when in fact those needs had only just begun.

In reality, of course, grandparents' perceptions that social workers had less time for them once they had formal custody of their grandchildren may reflect, in part, another phenomenon: the huge increase in welfare workers' case loads over the last few years. The general assistance (welfare) caseload for singe adults in Alameda County, California, for example, jumped 260% between 1985 and 1990 (Ronningen, 1991). And between 1986 and 1990, California counties combined had a 167% increase in referrals of drug exposed babies to Child Protective Services (California Senate Office on Research, 1990). Although a number of the grandmothers we interviewed were understanding of the impossible workload of county caseworkers, many of the women still felt themselves to be "at the bottom of the totem pole" in terms of the social workers' priority clients. In the words of one grandmother, "I call them [the county social workers] with emotional problems, but there's no help for me. If I was a *real* foster mother, they'd help."

Of particular concern, moreover, was the feeling expressed by many that social workers and "the system" failed to respond to grandparents' reports of the serious abuse and neglect that their grandchildren were experiencing at the hands of the children's parents. It is to this area, and policy issues surrounding child protective services, that we now turn.

## CHILD WELFARE?

Like the nation's courts, county social service agencies' child protective services departments operate on the principle that parents have a right to their children (Haas, 1991). This normally accepted principle, however, becomes problematic for grandparents who see their grandchildren abused or neglected at the hands of the children's parents, and who discover that as grandparents without legal custody, they are sometimes hard pressed to get the authorities to intervene.

Many of the grandparents in our study had taken in their grandchildren after discovering that they were being badly neglected or mistreated by their drug involved parents. Yet for many, such a discovery was only the beginning of a nightmare that got worse as they took the often painful step of contacting a child protective services department that was reluctant to intervene (see Chapter 4 this volume).

As discussed in Chapter 4, a number of grandparents described their shock and anger on learning that a malnourished child, or an infant or toddler "dragged from crack house to crack house," was permitted to stay with the parents if a box of crackers was found in the home (evidence that food was available), or if a homeless woman who had used her rent money for drugs lied to the authorities and said that she and the children had a place to stay.

Even once the children were safely living with their grandparents, however, those without legal guardianship often discovered how tenuous their "safe havens" really were. Natural parents who have had no contact with their children for months or even years can appear on a grandparent's doorstep and demand a parent's "fundamental right" to raise his or her offspring regardless of whether this is in the best interest of the child (Kirkland, 1988).

More typically, a parent on drugs can appear after a far shorter interval demanding, and at least temporarily often getting, the child that he or she had abandoned or given to the grandparent days or weeks before.

Even those grandparents who take the drastic step of temporarily turning grandchildren in their care over to Child Protective Services to protect them from being taken by a drug involved parent often learn the hard way the extent to which the system tends to "look the other way."

Seventy-six-year-old Lena Johnson recounted with anger and disgust how she had given her 9-month-old great grandson to Child Protective Services when the child's mother had come over, abusive and high on crack and alcohol, and tried to take the infant. To Mrs. Johnson's horror, CPS returned the baby to its mother the next day, and it was close to 2 weeks before Mrs. Johnson got the child back again.

For many grandmothers, negative and sometimes traumatic experiences with the child protection system led to a lashing out, in the interview, against social workers and other CPS personnel. Yet hampered as they are by huge caseloads and the regulations governing the removal of children from their natural parents, social workers cannot justifiably be blamed for the great majority of problems faced. Rather, changes on multiple levels would need to occur if experiences like those recounted by the grandmothers in our study are to be prevented.

Changes in the legislation regarding child protection are widely seen as being critical in this regard. Indeed, following her look at grandparent caregiving nationally for *U.S. News and World Report,* Linda Creighton (1991, p. 89) concluded that, "If grandparents could wave a magic wand, at the top of their wish list would be liberalization of the laws regulating child custody." Many of the Oakland grandmother caregivers we interviewed appeared to agree with this assessment, as do many leaders of grandparent support groups across the country with whom we have spoken.

## LEGISLATING CHANGE

Effective and comprehensive legislation clearly is needed if we are to strengthen the legal status of the grandparent caregiver relationship and provide for equity in the allocation of financial and other supportive services for relative caregivers. Although movement in this direction has been slow, there are occasional glimmers of hope.

On the federal level, two provisions of the Family Preservation Act, introduced by Representative Thomas Downey (D-NY) in 1992, could, if enacted, make an important difference. By removing the AFDC linkage currently required to receive foster care benefits, and by suggesting that children do not have to have been removed from their homes by the courts in order for grandparents to qualify for foster care benefits, the proposed legislation could make a significant contribution to the fight for equitable benefits (S. Hughes, personal communication, April 1992).

On the state level, an important step forward took place in 1989 when the ninth circuit court in Oregon decided, in *Lipscomb v. Simmons* (1990) that the state's policy of denying foster care benefits to children in the care of relatives was unconstitutional. Although a rehearing, requested by the state, resulted in the earlier "unconstitutional" verdict being overturned, the case may go all the way to the U.S. Supreme Court. Should that happen, and a decision favorable to relatives be reached, it could benefit grandparent caregivers in states like California, where earlier court decisions (e.g., California's *King v. McMahon,* 1986) have held that children placed with relatives are not entitled to foster care benefits (Barry, 1991).

Until such a time, however, the likelihood of movement in this direction in states like California appears slim indeed. Representing the county where our study took place, Assemblyman Tom Bates (D-Alameda County) has been key among lawmakers around the country in introducing legislation to seek equitable benefits and treatment under the law for relative caregivers. Yet the bills he has introduced in this regard have repeatedly been vetoed by the governor, whose fiscal analysts report that the cost of implementation would run from $50 million to $170 million (D. Aroner, personal communication, March 1992).

As noted earlier, the initiation in several states of kinship care programs is viewed by many as a major breakthrough in the quest for equity for grandparent caregivers (Jost, 1991). Yet as Takas (1992) has noted, there are significant practical and legal consequences of the shift from informal to formal placement with relatives, and whether these are, on balance, for the better or for the worse is open to debate. The lack of permanency planning, adequate services for caregivers, prescreening, and postplacement supervision thus are among the risks to children of informal placements that are not subject to federal and state protective legislation.

On the other hand, as Takas (1992) points out:

> Relatives designated as foster care providers may face regulations and policies far more suitable to non-relative providers than to relatives, such as square footage requirements for their homes, training designed for professional foster parents, and even income or marital status requirements. The state may face difficult policy choices between underprotection and over-intrusion, as well as challenges in allocating resources between parents and kinship caregivers. (p. 3)

Underlying the above dilemma is the fact that current policy options providing for child out-of-home placements were never designed with relative caregivers in mind. Guardianship thus provides "a less than full guarantee of legally protected permanency," whereas formal adoption was designed for adoptive families who have no ties to a child's biological parents, and usually desire no such ties. In most states, formal adoption requires the total curtailment of all parental rights, and not just their custodial rights—an action that may not be in the best interests of the child (Child Welfare League of America [CWLA], 1992, p. 6).

Neither of these options really addresses the status of children whose primary caregiver is a grandparent or other relative—children "who may already call their grandmother 'Mama' and think of their birth mother much as they might an aunt or older sister" (Takas, 1992, p. 8). Yet in the 30 states whose record keeping enables the separate identification of kinship placement, close to a third of all children in legal custody are in the care of relatives (Kusserow, 1991).

In light of such figures, the need for developing a separate option specifically tailored to relative caregiving is underscored. One such alternative, proposed by Marianne Takas of the American Bar Association's Center on Children and the Law, is kinship adoption. Although this option would permanently end a parent's custodial rights to his or her children, it would leave intact such other rights as appropriate visitation and access to school records. The grandparent or other "kinship adopter" would thus become the child's legal parent, but the biological parent would remain "a valued relative with a legally defined role" (Takas, 1992, p. 8).

Kinship adoption is among the options currently being explored by the Child Welfare League of America's North American Kinship Care Policy and Practice Committee. Established in January of 1992, the 50-member committee is attempting to develop guidelines and policy recommendations that would define a role for kinship care in child protective services and in other ways provide "new thinking" about how to formalize the kinship caregiving relationship (CWLA, 1992). Until such policy directions are implemented, however, both the welfare of children in the care of grandparents, and the rights of their caregivers, are likely to remain in jeopardy.

## TREATMENT FOR
## SUBSTANCE ABUSING PARENTS

On September 22, 1990, newspapers across the nation carried the story of a Bronx, New York, teenager whose parents had chained her to a radiator in a desperate effort to keep her off drugs. Perhaps more revealing than the incident itself, however, was the fact that neighbors in this low-income community told reporters that they could understand how and why the parents had resorted to this act of desperation.

A number of the grandmothers we interviewed offered their own harsh prescriptions for dealing with the crack involved young people whose drug use had harmed both themselves and the children they had brought into the world. "Tie their tubes" and "throw them in jail and throw away the key!" were typical of the comments made in this regard.

Yet more often, the grandmothers we interviewed held a ray of hope that their crack involved children and others like them could be helped, if help were available. For these women, anger over the lack of adequate treatment programs, and over a "war on drugs" more concerned with penalizing users than with preventing and treating drug problems, were among the themes most often articulated.

A 53-year-old grandmother remarked, for example, that if she could give one piece of advice to the government it would be, "when these drug addicted kids call out for help, don't put them on long lists. Don't have the programs so crowded that they can't get in and have to go on a long list." A grandmother in her forties similarly expressed her anger and despair that her own crack involved daughter had finally agreed to get help, only to be told that their would be "a 2 week wait" before she could enter a treatment program. The young woman was going through painful drug withdrawal, and the grandmother was very worried that her daughter's resolve would melt before she made it through the waiting period.

Grandmothers whose daughters were pregnant again at the time of the study were among those most adamant about the importance of expanding treatment availability, since both their adult daughters and the children they carried had a vital stake in such assistance. Yet the prospects for having these women get into treatment programs were often particularly dim. There are only 45 residential treatment beds for pregnant drug users in the whole of Alameda County, for example, despite hundreds of requests for new placements each month (Mathiessen, 1992).

Across the nation, only 11% of pregnant users of crack and other illicit drugs are in treatment, and many programs admit that they deny enrollment to expectant mothers (Telsch, 1990). A recent survey in Washington, DC, revealed that less than 20% of drug treatment centers admit pregnant women, regardless of their income or health insurance status (Norris, 1991), and a similar survey in New York City found that more than half of the 78 treatment programs studied refused to enroll pregnant users (National Institute on Drug Abuse [NIDA], 1990). Nationwide, according to the National Association of State Alcohol and Drug Addiction Directors, "Pregnant substance abusers have the least access to treatment" (Norris, 1991). Citing as their reasons for nonadmission inadequate staffing or insurance to cover special needs or complications posed by pregnancy, both public and private treatment centers have made pregnant women "the pariahs of drug treatment" (Norris, 1991). As suggested above, changing such shortsighted policies, and expanding treatment options for substance abusing women, particularly if they are pregnant, was a major policy priority of the grandmothers we interviewed.

Some important inroads are being made in this direction with the establishment of NIDA research and demonstration grants to develop and identify effective treatment approaches for pregnant users, postpartum women and women of childbearing age. The 20 programs, funded for 5 years each, offer a range of medical and social services in addition to drug abuse treatment, and together they should assist an estimated 6,000 women nationwide (NIDA, 1990). The effectiveness of such comprehensive approaches has already been demonstrated. A recent General Accounting Office (GAO) report, for example, noted a drop in the incidence of low birth weight babies from 50% to just 18% when pregnant drug addicted women received a combination of drug treatment and prenatal care (USGAO, 1991). Yet such encouraging efforts remain in their infancy. When it is recalled that some 375,000 babies born each year may be prenatally exposed to cocaine and other drugs (USGAO, 1990), the need for far greater resources in the areas of prevention and treatment is underscored.

## TREATMENT AND EDUCATIONAL ASSISTANCE
## FOR CHILDREN OF SUBSTANCE ABUSING PARENTS

At least as high on the priority list of grandparent caregivers as treatment for their substance abusing offspring was access to treatment and special assistance for the youngsters in their care. Grandmothers raising drug exposed children were often particularly outspoken in this regard. A number mentioned that the children's doctors didn't seem to know what to do for them, and as a consequence, television talk shows such as *Geraldo* and *Oprah Winfrey* were among the grandmothers' greatest sources of information. From programs like these, the grandmothers reported learning about breakthroughs being made with intensive intervention programs. But learning about such developments and being able to access help for one's own grandchildren were often two different things.

Finally, even being able to get a learning delayed grandchild into a needed Head Start program could be difficult to achieve. Sixty-two-year-old Carol Innis spoke of her anger on learning that her 4-year-old granddaughter was being denied admission to Head Start for the second year in a row, since priority was being given to Cambodians in the neighborhood. Other grandmothers similarly shared their frustration that overcrowded programs were keeping out some of the very children who needed such help the most.

In Oakland and the rest of the San Francisco Bay Area today, the criteria for admission into early childhood intervention programs are so restrictive that many children with minimal learning deficits fail to qualify (Mathiessen, 1992). Yet such deficits, which frequently manifest among prenatally drug exposed children, can lead to greater difficulties later on if early help is unavailable.

Across the nation, 80% of children eligible for Head Start are not enrolled (Miller, 1992), despite dramatic evidence of the long-term differences this program can make in rates of high school graduation and employment, teen pregnancy, juvenile delinquency, and other indicators of health and social functioning (Weikart, 1989). And although Congress increased funding for Head Start in 1992, it would have to triple the program's funding in order to serve all those in need, including many of the children of the crack cocaine epidemic. Further, it would have to mandate that Head Start programs address the special needs of children who may have been prenatally drug exposed. Indeed, at this writing, only one Head Start program in the nation (in Compton, California) focuses specifically on intervention for drug exposed children (Mathiessen, 1992).

Although children from drug involved families should have access to Head Start and other programs of early childhood education and intervention, many experts now agree that, once in school, such children should not be singled out for special treatment (Le Draoulec, 1992; Goodman, 1992). As noted in Chapter 11, such singling out all too often leads to the children's being labeled and branded as a "biological underclass" of "crack kids." As Barth (1991b, p. 130) has pointed out, "labels can create powerful expectations," whereas "mislabeling can compromise appropriate educational efforts on behalf of these children." Leading educators, social workers, and medical authorities indeed have argued that once they reach the classroom, drug exposed children and/ or children from crack involved households should be considered "children at risk" or "children who need help," like so many others, but not treated as a separate group (Barth, 1991b; Le Draoulec, 1992; Goodman, 1992).

## RESPITE AND CHILD CARE

As noted earlier, the need for relief from constant child care, or from an unbroken cycle of work and child care, was second only to adequate financial assistance as the greatest expressed need of the grandparent caregivers we interviewed. As one 64-year-old grandmother put it, "It's not that you don't love the children, but you just need a break. Everybody needs a break from *anything* for a while."

The comment of a younger grandmother that "I just need 20 minutes a day to myself" was characteristic of the way in which many of the women interviewed described their feelings concerning the need for respite. For the most part, they did not talk about needing 2 weeks off for a vacation, but rather of just having enough time to get to the store, do the ironing, go to a church meeting, or occasionally have one's hair done, without having the children constantly underfoot.

The few women who regularly received 4 hours' respite each month as a benefit of their support group participation talked about the difference even this small amount of relief could make for grandparent caregivers. Research is not yet available on the impact of respite programs for such individuals, and indeed, the effectiveness of respite services in reducing caregiver burden and strain among family members caring for the disabled elderly remains subject to debate. Several studies (Eskew, Sexton, Tars, & Wilcox, 1983; Gallagher, Lovett, & Zeiss, 1989) have demonstrated the positive role respite services can play, suggesting that such interventions have the effect of increasing caregiver quality of life. On the other hand, a recent controlled study of respite services for caregivers of persons with Alzheimer's Disease found the intervention ineffective in relieving caregiver burden or improving mental health (Lawton, Brody, & Saperstein, 1989).

Whatever the objective effectiveness of respite care, however, it has emerged in several studies as the "top priority unmet need" expressed by family caregivers (Lawton et al., 1989).

Although respite programs are widely available in Western Europe, they remain few and far between in the United States (Abel, 1991; Stone, 1985). The development of such programs, however, could benefit not only caregivers for the elderly, but also, as we have seen, the growing number of grandparents who are caregivers for their grandchildren.

Among grandmother caregivers we interviewed who were working outside the home, the need for adequate and affordable child care was also a top priority. When it is recalled, moreover, that a third of the women in the Grandparent Caregiver Study had been forced to quit their jobs in order to become full-time caregivers, the particular need for improved child care access and availability is highlighted.

Child-care and eldercare programs and incentives for employees have both been recognized as among the most prized employee benefits of the 1990s (Scharlach, Lowe, & Schneider, 1990). Yet even though a small number of corporations and other workplace settings have begun offering such incentives, they remain rare exceptions, and some employer surveys even suggest that such programs may become less, rather than more, available over the next few years (Litvan, 1991). In a 1987 survey, for example, 57% of employers reported that they were prepared to spend more on child-care programs for their employees. In 1991, however, only 28%, of the 300 companies surveyed said they had plans to expand child care, whereas 40% reported that they had decided against it (Litvan, 1991).

The notion of employer sponsored child care options, of course, assumes employment in companies and other agencies that provide benefits for their workers. Yet for the great majority of women in our study, the nature of the jobs held, with low wages and few if any fringe benefits, makes the notion of employer-based child care foreign indeed. For many of these women, government sponsorship of high quality, free, or low-cost child care for grandparent caregivers, though admittedly seen as a pipe dream, was nevertheless often mentioned as something grandparents deserve, and as "not too much to ask" from a government that expects so much of them and provides so little.

## THE BIGGER PICTURE

The needs of grandparents raising the children of the crack cocaine epidemic are significant, and range from more equitable and generous financial and other benefits, to respite programs, to a continuum of caring programs and services, both for the youngsters in their care and for their adult children who are on crack. These needs are pressing and vital, and they must be addressed.

Yet on a broader level, far more fundamental and deep-seated problems must be confronted and attended to if we are to prevent such symptomatic problems as abused and neglected children whose grandparents must take the place of parents.

By 1990, one in four American preschoolers, and one in two black preschoolers, were living in poverty (National Center for Children in Poverty, 1990). Indeed, close to 40% of the nation's poor were children, and more than half of these lived in female headed households (Children's Defense Fund, 1991). Almost three quarters of all poor African American families were headed by single women (U.S. Bureau of the Census, 1990) —a fact highly correlated with the continued erosion of the job market for young black males, whose low marriage rates reflect their poor economic prospects (Easterlin, 1987; Gibbs, 1990; Gibbs et al., 1988).

Not only did 1991 see a worsening of poverty, but the most dramatic erosions occured, as well, in the nation's already fragile "safety net" in fully a decade (Shapiro et al., 1991). Nine states cut AFDC benefits, and 31 others froze them at current rates, effectively cutting aid, since the benefits did not keep pace with inflation. In the state of Michigan, general assistance was eliminated completely as of December 1, and 14 other states reduced these benefits, affecting a total of half a million people (Shapiro et al., 1991)

At the same time that the safety net was being pulled out from under some of society's most vulnerable members, the gap between rich and poor was reaching record heights. By 1990, the top fifth of American earners were taking home more money than the other four fifths combined—the greatest portion since World War II (Reich, 1991).

Given these realities, and the increasing sense of hopelessness and alienation they helped to engender among the nation's dispossessed, the stage was set for the rioting that followed the Rodney King verdict in Los Angeles, California, in late April of 1992. The violent beating of King, a 35-year-old black man, by four white police officers had been videotaped and seen around the world. And the "not guilty" verdict submitted by a suburban, all white jury was, as a consequence, met with shocked disbelief as well as intense feelings of anger and rage. The riots that followed left 41 dead, 2,000 injured, and some 6,000 arrested in Los Angeles alone, with the violence quickly spreading to other cities including San Francisco and Seattle, Atlanta and Detroit (Brown, 1992).

Although President Bush declared the looting and rioting a case of "mob behavior, pure and simple," they were in fact far more than that. For as Martin Luther King, Jr., once remarked, "a riot is the language of the unheard" (Brown, 1992). The riots that began in Los Angeles and spread across the land were, indeed, expressions of a rage and despair with roots far deeper than "mob behavior" or than an isolated trial verdict, however shocking and incomprehensible it may have been.

History may look back on the riots of spring, 1992, as a deafening reminder of just how wide the gap between haves and have nots in America has become. Alternately, however, they may be regarded as simply another indication of the need for change on the individual, rather than the broader societal, level. Indeed, although the social and economic conditions giving rise to the riots were building inexorably during the 1980s and early 1990s, social science research on poverty was continuing to reflect what M. Katz (1989, pp. 237-238) has referred to as "the peculiarly American tendency to transform poverty from a product of politics and economics into a matter of individual behavior." Terms like *the underclass* (Auletta, 1982) and *welfare dependency* had achieved wide currency, and increasingly were used as moral, rather than sociological, categories (Katz, 1989).

Similarly, America's drug problem, although heavily connected to U.S. foreign policy and to the economics of poverty and exclusion at home (Scott & Marshall, 1992; Waters, 1989) has been reduced to a behavioral problem, and specifically a problem of African Americans.

The report of Senator John Kerry's U.S. Senate Subcommittee on Narcotics, Terrorism and International Operations (1990) spelled out in detail the role of the Reagan-Bush Administration in having foreign policy interests in Nicaragua and elsewhere get in the way of the conduct of any meaningful and effective "war on drugs." In Kerry's words:

> The flow of drugs from Central and Latin America [is] a different kind of threat from anything we have yet defined it as. The administration frequently allowed other foreign policy interests . . . to interfere with the prosecution of the war on drugs, and even to interfere with the normal and natural application of the law . . . particularly in Florida.

Just as the government's role in encouraging drug problems has been largely neglected (Waters, 1989), so has the phenomenon of cocaine sales and use in white America. Although federal surveys show that well over two thirds of cocaine users are white, and although whites sell most of the nation's cocaine, blacks and other people of color fill up the nation's courtrooms and prisons because "in a political climate that demands that something be done, they are the easiest people to arrest" (Harris, 1991). President Bush's much touted "war on drugs" became, in effect, "a war on black people." Indeed, fully 74% of the drug war's $9.2 billion budget was targeted not at prevention and treatment, nor at ending high-level international complicity in drug sales and distribution, but rather at law enforcement, disproportionately concentrated in black communities (Harris, 1991).

Ironically, law enforcement officials themselves are increasingly coming forward to decry the shortsightedness of this approach and to argue instead for a greater emphasis on education and treatment, and on job training in poor communities to provide economic alternatives to the lucrative drug trade (Harris, 1991). Yet with half of all new jobs created paying below minimum wage, and with a continuing decline in the real wages of young males, and particularly if they are black (Easterlin, 1989), the prospects for significant economic incentives that might counter drug use and sales appear slim indeed.

*     *     *

Intervening in a systemic way truly to "declare war" on drugs, to reduce poverty and unemployment, and to counter the growing inequities between rich and poor in American society will not, of course, eliminate the need for grandparent caregiving. Current health planning estimates, for example, suggest that in New York City alone, at least 20,000 children will have been orphaned due to HIV/AIDS by the mid-1990s (Lambert, 1989). And in the majority of these cases, grandparents are expected to come forward, as they have in years past, to fill the breach.

Yet as Graham (1987, p. 223) has pointed out, "Poverty and caring are, for many women, two sides of the same coin. Caring is what they do;

poverty describes the economic circumstances in which they do it." If we are to address the needs of low-income caregivers and their families, a coherent, comprehensive, and humane family policy is needed. Such a policy, moreover, must not consist solely, or even principally, of programs targeted at low-income families, because such programs are both stigmatizing and politically risky (Katz, 1989; Ryan, 1981; Sidel, 1992b).

Instead, as Sidel (1992b, p. 219) has noted, "A family policy with benefits for all, regardless of income, maximizes the likelihood of passage of relevant legislation and minimizes both the cutback of benefits and the stigma of recipients." Within a coherent family policy, universal programs, such as a comprehensive national health program, family leave policies, affordable child and eldercare, and a higher minimum wage, could then be combined with "targeted programs for poor families" to provide a true safety net for society's most vulnerable members (Sidel, 1992b). "Above all," as Sidel (1992b, p. 220) notes, "we must recognize that life is too complex for families to go it alone." Serious efforts to assist grandparent caregivers must, in the last analysis, address the economic injustices that characterize not only their own situations as caregivers, but the broader community context within which much of this caregiving is provided. Humane public policies truly committed to building a just and caring society for all, must provide the context within which we can better help to address the needs of America's "forgotten caregivers" and the children in their care.

# Appendix:
# Interview Summary

The interviews with individual grandmother caregivers used a detailed interview schedule designed specifically for this purpose. As described in detail in Chapter 3, the interviews combined standardized, scaled questions with original open-ended questions to explore as fully as possible the experience of caregiving within the context of the crack cocaine epidemic.

The interviewers attempted to establish as warm and conversational a tone as possible, allowing the respondent to tell her own story at her own pace and in her own order. However, this flexibility was balanced by the interviewers' knowledge of the interview schedule. Eventually, all of the relevant questions were asked of each grandmother caregiver, most often in the order indicated below.

## Interview #1

The first interview was conducted by one of the Research Directors and a Research Assistant. The questions covered a wide range of topics and were designed to obtain all of the essential information about the respondent's caregiving circumstances and needs. Because of the depth of questioning and the need to establish rapport and trust in this first meeting, Interview #1 often lasted several hours. Below are the areas covered in the first interview.

*Demographics,* including:

> Age, marital status, education, occupation, religion
>
> Number of children, grandchildren, great grandchildren
>
> Number of people in household
>
> Number of children in Bay Area, amount of contact with them
>
> Age, health, location of parents or other older relatives, amount and nature of contact with them

*Background on the grandchildren she is raising,* including:
  Number of grandchildren in her care, ages of each

  Age of children when primary caregiving began

  Location and circumstances of children's parents, amount of contact

  Additional assistance with caregiving, additional caregiving responsibilities

*Physical and emotional health status,* including:
  Self-ratings of physical health, emotional health, comparisons to a year ago, comparisons to before caregiving began, comparisons to others her age

  Specific physical and emotional health concerns

  Use of health care services

*Typical day,* including:
  Detail on yesterday

  Coping styles, including the most difficult situation she has faced lately

  Changes in a typical day since caregiving began

*Marriage* (if appropriate), including:
  Husband's physical and emotional health

  Changes in relationship since caregiving began

*Work* (if appropriate), including:
  Typical workday

  Child-care arrangements while at work

  Effect of caregiving on hours, schedule, work arrangements

  Co-workers' awareness of, and response to, caregiving demands

  Leave policy of the workplace

  Changes in feelings about work since caregiving began

*Grandchildren,* including:
  Descriptions of each child for which she is primary caregiver

  Eating, sleeping habits

  Effects of parent visits on child's behavior and emotions

*Events that triggered caregiving,* including
  Realization that she would have to take on primary responsibility

  Physical and emotional condition of the children when she took them in

  Changes in the child since caregiving began

*Child care,* including:

      Morning, afternoon, and evening routines

      Favorite time of the day, hardest time

      Physical effects of lifting, carrying, and so forth

      Sources of assistance with any of the specifics of child care, such as clothes, outings, reading, toys/equipment, health care appointments

      Needs for assistance or support

      Comparison to raising their own children

      Play space, neighborhood environment, safety

*Grandchildren's health,* including:

      Physical and emotional health status

      Medical problems at birth, drug exposure, risk factors

      Use/accessibility of health care services, including physician, dentist, psychologist

*Finances,* including:

      Self-reported financial status prior to caregiving

      Changes in financial status since caregiving began

      Sources and amount of financial support for the grandchildren

      Sources and amount of financial support for the household

      Expenses of caregiving

*Adult child's situation,* including:

      Grandchildren's relationships with parents

      Current circumstances of the grandchildren's parents

      Changes in grandchildren's relationships with parents since caregiving began

      History and circumstances of adult child's drug involvement

      Grandmother's relationship with her adult child

*Other children,* including:

      Circumstances and experiences of the grandmother's other children

      Effects of caregiving on her relationships with her other adult children

      Concerns or worries about any of her other children

      Relationship of adult children to the grandchildren she is caring for and their parents

*Personal concerns,* including:

      What she expected this time in her life to be like

Comparison to the experiences of other women her age

Degree to which she shares her experience with others

Presence of a confidante

What would happen to the grandchildren if she could not continue caring for them

How she has changed since caregiving began

Her hopes for her grandchildren

*Support group membership* (if applicable), including:

Participation in support group

Benefits, costs, satisfaction, importance of support group

*Advice,* including:

What she would tell health care workers, church leaders, social workers, government officials, local politicians, national figures

What she would tell grandmothers about to assume responsibility for their grandchildren

## Interview #2

Interview #2 was usually conducted one week after the first. In most cases, the Research Assistant met with the woman alone for this second interview. The purpose of the second meeting was to probe additional areas, check for the reliability of certain responses, provide an opportunity for the respondent to elaborate on areas she had thought about since the first meeting, and to provide another point of contact between grandmother caregivers and the research team. The second interview, often considerably shorter than the first, covered the areas listed below.

*Physical health,* including:

Repeat of self-ratings and comparisons (as a check for reliability)

More detailed questions on specific health concerns, illnesses, and conditions

More detailed questions on use of health care services

Changes in weight, diet, exercise, smoking, alcohol use since caregiving began and since the previous year

*Emotional health,* including:

More detailed questions on specific emotional health concerns

*Daily routine,* including:

Sleep patterns (of grandmother and grandchildren)

Meals

Time for personal activities, housecleaning, other chores, relaxation

Changes in all of the above since caregiving began and over the past year

*Typical day,* including:

Repeat of typical day questions from Interview #1

Church attendance

Social activities, personal appointments

*Work* (if applicable), including:

Repeat of work questions from Interview #1

*Social support,* including:

Membership or participation in social groups or organizations

Relationships with friends and relatives

Contact with friends and relatives

Changes in contact or relationships with friends, relatives, confidantes since caregiving began and over the past year

Relationships with other grandchildren

Additional caregiving responsibilities, particularly for any older relatives, neighbors or friends

Support in an emergency

*Grandmother's relationship with her own grandmother,* including:

Any periods of time in which grandmother lived with her own grandmother or other relative

Relationship with her own grandmother as she was growing up

Relationship with any other special relatives (or fictive kin) during her childhood

*Experience of her own children with their grandmothers,* including:

Any periods when her own children lived with their grandmother or other relatives

Circumstances and effects of the above (if applicable)

*Concerns for her grandchildren,* including:

Her perception of the hardest things facing young African American children today

Her worries about drugs, school, work, environment

Her comparison of the environment in which children grow up now compared to when she was growing up and when she was raising her own children

*Final thoughts,* including:

        Anything else we should have asked

        Anything she had thought of since the first interview

# References

Abel, E. K. (1987). *Love is not enough: Family care of the frail elderly.* Washington, DC: American Public Health Association.

Abel, E. K. (1991). *Who cares for the elderly?: Public policy and the experiences of adult daughters.* Philadelphia: Temple University Press.

Abramovitz, M. (1988). *Regulating the lives of women: Social welfare policy from colonial times to the present.* Boston: South End Press.

Allen, W. R. (1978). The search for applicable theories of black family life. *Journal of Marriage and the Family, 40,* 117-129.

Andersen, R. M., Mullner, M., & Cornelius, L. J. (1987). Black-white differences in health status: Methods or substance? *The Milbank Quarterly, 65,* 72-99.

Angel, R., & Tienda, M. (1982). Headship and household composition among blacks, Hispanics, and other whites. *Social Forces, 61,* 508-531.

Antonucci, T. C. (1985). Personal characteristics, social networks and behavior. In R. H. Binstock & E. Shanas (Eds.), *Handbook of aging and the social sciences* (pp. 94-128). New York: Van Nostrand Reinhold.

Archbold, P. G. (1983). An impact of parent-caring on women. *Family Relations, 32*(January), 39-45.

Arling, G. A. (1987). Strain, support and stress in old age. *Journal of Gerontology, 42*(1), 107-113.

Aschenbrenner, J. (1978). Continuities and variations in black family structure. In D. B. Shimkin, E. M. Shimkin, & D. A. Frate (Eds.), *The extended family in black societies* (pp. 181-200). Chicago: Aldine.

Auletta, K. (1982). *The underclass.* New York: Random House.

Baines, C., Evans, P., & Neysmith, S. (Eds.). (1991). *Women's caring: Feminist perspective on social welfare.* Toronto: McClelland & Stewart.

Ball, R. E., & Robbins, L. (1986). Marital status and life satisfaction among black Americans. *Journal of Marriage and the Family, 48,* 389-394.

Barnhill, S., & Chambers, A. (1992). *Intergenerational project of Aid to Imprisoned Mothers.* Unpublished grant proposal. Atlanta, GA: AIM.

Barry, E. M. (1991, September). Grandparent caregivers: The need for services and support. *State Bar Association of California Newsletter,* pp. 5-6.

Barth, R. (1991a). Adoption of drug-exposed children. *Children and Youth Services Review, 13,* 323-342.

Barth, R. (1991b). Educational implications of prenatally drug-exposed children. *Social Work in Education, 13,* 130-136.

218

Bates, T. (1989, October). *Remarks. Hearing on drug exposed infants: The role of grand-mothers as caretakers.* Assembly Human Services Committee, State of California. Sacramento: Joint Publications Office, State Capitol.

Beattie, M. (1987). *Codependent no more.* New York: Harper & Row.

Beck, M. (1990, July 16). Trading places: More and more women are on the daughter track: Working, raising kids and helping aging parents. *Newsweek,* pp. 48-55.

Beck, R. W., & Beck, S. H. (1989). The incidence of extended households among middle-aged black and white women: Estimates from a 5-year panel study. *Journal of Family Issues, 10,* 147-168.

Bellah, R. N., Madsen, R., Sullivan, W. M., Swidler, A., & Tipton, S. M. (1985). *Habits of the heart: Individualism and commitment in American life.* Berkeley: University of California Press.

Belle, D. (Ed.). (1982). *Lives in stress: Women and depression.* Beverly Hills, CA: Sage.

Belle, D. (1987). Gender differences in the social moderators of stress. In R. C. Barnett, L. Biener, & G. K. Baruch (Eds.), *Gender and stress* (pp. 257-277). New York: Free Press.

Bengtson, V. L., & Robertson, J. (Ed.). (1985). *Grandparenthood: Research and policy perspectives.* Beverly Hills, CA: Sage.

Berk, S. F. (1988). Women's unpaid labor: Home and community. In A. H. Stromberg & S. Harkess (Eds.), *Women working.* Mountain View, CA: Mayfield.

Berkman, L. F. (1985). The relationship of social networks and social support to morbidity and mortality. In S. Cohen & S. L. Syme (Eds.), *Social support and health* (pp. 241-262). New York: Academic Press.

Berkman, L. F., & Syme, S. L. (1979). Social networks, host resistance, and mortality. A nine year follow-up study of Alameda County residents. *American Journal of Epidemiology, 109,* 186-204.

Biegel, D. E., & Blum, A. (Eds.). (1990). *Aging and caregiving: Theory, research and policy.* Newbury Park, CA: Sage.

Biegel, D. E., Sales, E., & Schulz, R. (1991). *Family caregiving and chronic illness.* Newbury Park, CA: Sage.

Biegel, D. E., Shore, B., & Gordon, E. (1984). *Building support networks for the elderly: Theory and application.* Beverly Hills, CA: Sage.

Billingsley, A. (1968). *Black families in white America.* Englewood Cliffs, NJ: Prentice-Hall.

Blood, R. O., & Wolfe, D. M. (1960). *Husbands and wives.* Glencoe, IL: Free Press.

Brewer, J., & Hunter, A. (1989). *Multimethod research: A synthesis of styles.* Newbury Park, CA: Sage.

Brody, E. M. (1981). Women in the middle and family help to older people. *The Gerontologist, 21*(5), 471-480.

Brody, E. M. (1985). Parent care as a normative family stress. *The Gerontologist, 25*(1), 19-28.

Brody, E. M., Kleban, M. H., Johnsen, P. T., Hoffman, C., & Schoonover, C. B. (1987). Work status and parent care: A comparison of four groups of women. *The Gerontologist, 27,* 201-208.

Brookdale Grandparent Caregiver Information Project (Brookdale). (1992a, January). *Brookdale Grandparent Caregiver Information Project Newsletter, 1*(1), pp. 1-6.

Brookdale Grandparent Caregiver Information Project (Brookdale). (1992b, June). *Brookdale Grandparent Caregiver Information Project Newsletter, 1*(2), pp. 1-6.

Brooks-Gunn, J., & Chase Lansdale, P. L. (1991). Children having children: Effects on the family system. *Pediatric Annals, 20*((9), 467, 470-481.

Brouard, A., & Joslin, D. (1991, March). *Grandparents as parents of last resort: A survey of three Department of Health child health clinics*. New York: The City of New York, Department of Health and Department for the Aging.

Brown, S. (1969). *The Negro in American fiction* (2nd ed.). New York: Atheneum.

Brown, W. L. (1992, May 3). Rodney King case: Riots echo decades old anguish of dispossessed. *San Francisco Examiner*, p. A13.

Burnette, D. (1991). *The management of chronic illness by older persons living alone: A multi-method investigation*. Unpublished doctoral dissertation, School of Social Welfare, University of California, Berkeley.

Burton, L., & Bengtson, V. L. (1982). Research in elderly minority communities: Problems and potentials. In R. C. Manuel (Ed.), *Minority aging: Sociological and social psychological issues* (pp. 215-222). Westport, CT: Greenwood Press.

Burton, L., & Bengtson, V. L. (1985). Black grandmothers: Issues of timing and continuity of roles. In V. L. Bengtson & J. F. Robertson (Eds.), *Grandparenthood* (pp. 61-77). Beverly Hills, CA: Sage.

Burton, L. M. (1985). *Early and on time grandmotherhood in multigenerational black families*. Unpublished doctoral dissertation, University of Southern California.

Burton, L. M. (1991a, May/June). Caring for children. *The American Enterprise*, pp. 34-37.

Burton, L. M. (1991b, October 18). *Intergenerational perspectives on teenage pregnancy: A program of research*. Paper presented at the School of Public Health, University of California, Berkeley.

Burton, L. M., & Dilworth-Anderson, P. (1991). The intergenerational roles of aged black Americans. *Marriage and Family Review, 16*(3/4), 311-330.

California Senate Office on Research. (1990). *California's drug-exposed babies: Undiscovered, unreported, underserved*. Sacramento: California Senate Office on Research.

Campbell, A., Converse, P., & Rodgers, W. (1986). *The quality of American life*. New York: Russell Sage.

Cantor, M. (1983). Strain among caregivers. *The Gerontologist, 23*(6), 597-604.

Cantor, M. H., & Little, V. (1985). Aging and social care. In R. H. Binstock & E. Shanas (Eds.), *Handbook of aging and the social sciences* (pp. 745-781). New York: Van Nostrand Reinhold.

Carlaw, R. W., Mittlemark, M., Bracht, N., & Luepker, R. (1984). Organization for a community cardiovascular health program: Experiences from the Minnesota Heart Health Program. *Health Education Quarterly, 11*, 243-252.

Cassel, J. (1976). The contribution of the social environment to host resistance. *American Journal of Epidemiology, 104*, 107-122.

Chasnoff, I. J. (1988). *A first: National hospital incidence study*. Chicago: National Association for Perinatal Addiction Research.

Chasnoff, I. J., Griffith, D. R., Freier, C., & Murray, J. (1992). Cocaine: Poly drug use in pregnancy: Two year follow-up. *Pediatrics, 89*(2), 284-289.

Chasnoff, I. J., Griffith, D. R., MacGregor, S., Dirkes, K., & Burns, K. A. (1989). Temporal patterns of cocaine use in pregnancy: Perinatal outcome. *Journal of the American Medical Association, 261*, 1741-1744.

Chasnoff, I. J., Landress, H., & Barett, M. (1990). The prevalence of illicit drug or alcohol use during pregnancy and discrepancies in mandatory reporting in Pinellas County, Florida. *New England Journal of Medicine, 332*(17), 1202-1206.

Chatters, L. M., & Taylor, R. J. (1989). Life problems and coping strategies of older black adults. *Social Work, 34*(4), 313-319.

Chatters, L. M., & Taylor, R. J. (1990). Social integration. In Z. Harel, E. A. McKinney, & M. Williams (Eds.), *Black aged: Understanding diversity and service needs* (pp. 82-99). Newbury Park, CA: Sage.

Cherlin, A. J., & Furstenberg, F. F., Jr. (1986). *The new American grandparent.* New York: Basic Books.

Child Welfare League of America (CWLA). (1992). Kinship care: A new look at an old idea. *Children's Voice, 1*(3), 6.

Children's Defense Fund. (1991). *The state of America's children 1991.* Washington, DC: Author.

Chodorow, N. (1978). *The reproduction of mothering: Psychoanalysis and the sociology of gender.* Berkeley: University of California Press.

Chouteau, M., Manerou, P., & Leppert, P. (1988). The effects of cocaine abuse on birthweight and gestational age. *Obstetrics and Gynecology, 72,* 147-151.

Christian, B. (1985). *Black feminist criticism: Perspectives on black women writers.* Elmsford, NY: Pergamon.

Chychula, N. M., & Okore, C. (1990). The cocaine epidemic: A comprehensive review of use, abuse and dependence. *Nurse Practitioner, 15*(7), 31-39.

Clark, N. M., & Rakowski, W. (1983). Family caregivers of older adults: Improving coping skills. *The Gerontologist, 23,* 637-645.

Cobb, S. (1976). Social support as a moderator of life stress. *Psychosomatic Medicine, 38,* 300-314.

Cohen, M. (1984). The ethnomedicine of Garfina (black Caribs) of Rio Tinto, Honduras. *Anthropological Quarterly, 57,* 16-27.

Cohen, S., & Syme, S. L. (Eds.). (1985). *Social support and health.* New York: Academic Press.

Coles, C. D. (1991, May 15). *Substance abuse in pregnancy: The infant's risk: How great?* Paper presented at the American Psychiatric Association Annual Meeting, New Orleans, LA.

Coles, C. D., & Finnegan, L. P. (1991). *Substance abuse in pregnancy.*

Collins, P. H. (1986). Learning from the outsider within: The sociological significance of black feminist thought. *Social Problems, 33*(6), 14-32.

Collins, P. H. (1990). *Black feminist thought: Knowledge, consciousness, and the politics of empowerment.* London: Harper Collins Academic.

Costin, L. B., & Rapp, C. A. (1984). *Child welfare: Policies and practice.* New York: McGraw-Hill.

County of Los Angeles, Department of Children's Services. (1991). *Information sheet about foster care payments for relative caregivers (Youakim).* Los Angeles: Author.

Creedon, M. A. (1988). *The corporate response to the working caregiver.* Washington, DC: Government Printing Office.

Creighton, L. (1991, December 16). Grandparents: The silent saviors. *U.S. News and World Report,* pp. 80-89.

Culp, J., & Dunson, B. H. (1986). Brothers of a different color: A preliminary look at employer treatment of white and black youth. In R. B. Freeman & H. J. Holzer (Eds.), *The black youth unemployment crisis* (pp. 233-260). Chicago: University of Chicago Press.

Dance, D. (1979). Black Eve or Madonna? A study of the antithetical views of the mother in black American literature. In R. Bell, B. Parker, & B. Guy-Sheftall (Eds.), *Sturdy black bridges: Visions of black women in literature* (pp. 123-132). Garden City, NY: Anchor.

delVecchio, R. (1991, June 3). Bay Area crack baby epidemic declines—Oakland shows steepest drop among newborns. *San Francisco Chronicle*, p. A13.

Denzin, N. K. (1970). *The research act: A theoretical introduction to sociological methods.* Chicago: Aldine.

Devault, M. L. (1990). Talking and listening from women's standpoint: Feminist strategies for interviewing and analysis. *Social Problems, 37*(1), 96-116.

Dilworth-Anderson, P., Johnson, L. B., & Burton, L. M. (in press). Reframing theories for understanding race, ethnicity, and families. In P. G. Boss, W. Doherty, R. La Rossa, W. Schumm, & S. Steinmetz (Eds.), *Sourcebook of family theories and methods: A contextual approach.* New York: Plenum.

Dodson, J. (1988). Conceptualizations of black families. In H. P. McAdoo (Ed.), *Black families* (pp. 77-90). Newbury Park, CA: Sage.

Dressel, P. L., & Barnhill, S. K. (1991, November). *Three generations at economic risk: Imprisoned African-American women and their families.* Paper presented at the Annual Meeting of the Gerontological Society of America, San Francisco.

Dressel, P. L., & Clark, A. (1990). A critical look at family care. *Journal of Marriage and the Family, 52,* 769-782.

Du Bois, B. (1983). Passionate scholarship: Notes on values, knowing and method in feminist social science. In G. Bowles & R. D. Klein (Eds.), *Theories of women's studies* (pp. 105-116). London: Routledge & Kegan Paul.

Duster, T. (1987a). Purpose and bias. *Society, 24*(2), 8-12.

Duster, T. (1987b). Youth unemployment and the black urban underclass. *Crime and Delinquency, 300,* 310-312.

Duster, T. (1992). Genetics, race and crime: Recurring seduction to a false precision. In P. R. Billings (Ed.), *DNA and crime: Applications of molecular biology in forensics* (pp. 129-140). Cold Spring Harbor, NY: Cold Spring Harbor Laboratory Press.

Easterlin, R. (1987). The new age structure of poverty in America: Permanent or transition? *Population and Development Review, 13,* 195-208.

Eng, E., Hatch, J., & Callan, A. (1985). Institutionalizing social support through the church and into the community. *Health Education Quarterly, 12*(1), 81-92.

England, S. E., Keigher, S. M., Miller, B., & Linsk, N. L. (1991). Community care policies and gender justice. In M. Minkler & C. L. Estes (Eds.), *Critical perspective on aging: The political and moral economy of growing old* (pp. 227-244). Amityville, NY: Baywood Publishing.

Enright, R. B., & Friss, L. (1987). *Employed caregivers of brain-impaired adults.* San Francisco: Family Survival Project.

Eskew, R., Sexton, R., Tars, S., & Wilcox, F. (1983). Day treatment program evaluation. In M. Smyer & M. Gatz (Eds.), *Mental health and aging* (pp. 63-84). Beverly Hills, CA: Sage.

Estes, C. L. (1979). *The aging enterprise.* San Francisco: Jossey-Bass.

Farley, R., & Allen, W. R. (1987). *The color line and the quality of life in America.* New York: Russell Sage.

Feig, L. (1990, January 29). *Drug exposed infants and children: Service needs and policy questions.* Washington, DC: Department of Health and Human Services.

Fengler, A. P., & Goodrich, N. (1979). Wives of elderly disabled men: The hidden patients. *The Gerontologist, 19*(2), 175-183

Ferraro, K. F. (1980). Self rating of health among the old and the old old. *Journal of Health and Social Behavior, 21,* 377.

Field, T. M., Widmayer, S. M., Stringer, S., & Ignatoff, E. (1980). Teenage, lower class black mothers and their preterm infants: An intervention and developmental follow-up. *Child Development, 51,* 426-436.

Fischer, B. A. (1991, September 12). Center gives grandparents a break from child care. *Thursday Times.*

Flaherty, M. J. (1988). Seven caring functions of black grandmothers in adolescent mothering. *Maternal-Child Nursing Journal, 17*(3), 191-207.

Frazier, E. F. (1966). *The Negro family in the United States* (Rev. ed.). Chicago: University of Chicago Press.

Furstenberg, F., & Crawford, D. B. (1978). Family support: Helping teenagers to cope. *Family Planning Perspectives, 10,* 322-333.

Gallagher, D. (1985). Intervention strategies to assist caregivers of frail elders: Current research status and future directions. In M. P. Lawton & G. Maddox (Eds.), *Annual review of gerontology and geriatrics* (pp. 249-282). New York: Springer.

Gallagher, D., Lovett, S., & Zeiss, A. (1989). Intervention with caregivers of frail elderly persons. In M. Ory & K. Bond (Eds.), *Aging and health care: Social service and policy perspectives* (pp. 167-190). New York: Tavistock.

Gallagher, D. A., Wrabetz, S., Lovett, S., DelMaestro, S., & Rose, J. (1989). Depression and other negative affects in family caregivers. In E. Light & B. D. Lebowitz (Eds.), *Alzheimer's disease treatment and family stress: Directions for research* (pp. 218-244). Rockville, MD: U.S. Department of Health and Human Services, Public Health Service.

Gartner, A., & Riessman, F. (Eds.). (1984). *The self-help revolution.* New York: Human Services Press.

Generations United. (1991). *G.U. sets public policy agenda for 2nd session of 102nd Congress.* Washington, DC: Newsline.

Genovese, E. D. (1976). *Roll, Jordan, roll: The world the slaves made.* New York: Random House.

George, L., & Gwyther, L. (1986). Caregiver well-being: A multi-dimensional examination of family caregivers of demented adults. *The Gerontologist, 26*(6), 253-259.

Gibbs, J. T. (1990). Developing intervention models for black families: Linking theory and research. In H. E. Cheatham & J. B. Stewart (Eds.), *Black families: Interdisciplinary perspectives* (pp. 325-352). New Brunswick, NJ: Transaction Books.

Gibbs, J. T., Brunswick, A. F., Connor, A. F., Dembo, R., Larson, T. E., Reed, R. J., & Solomon, B. (Eds.). (1988). *Young, black, and male in America: An endangered species.* Dover, MA: Auburn House.

Gibson, R. C. (1982). Blacks at middle and late life: Resources and coping. *Annals of the Americans Academy of Political and Social Science, 464,* 79-90.

Gibson, R. C. (1986). Outlook for the black family. In A. Pifer & D. L. Bronte (Eds.), *Our aging society: Paradox and promise* (pp. 181-197). New York: Norton.

Gibson, R. C. (1991). Race and self-reported health of elderly persons. *The Journals of Gerontology, 46*(5), S235-S242.

Giddings, P. (1984). *When and where I enter: The impact of black women on race and sex in America.* New York: Morrow.

Giele, J. Z., Muschler, P. H., & Orodenker, S. Z. (1987). *Stress and burdens of caregiving for the frail elderly* (Working Paper No. 36). Waltham, MA: Brandeis University.

Gilligan, C. (1982). *In a different voice: Psychological theory and women's development.* Cambridge, MA: Harvard University Press.

Glaser, B. G., & Strauss, A. L. (1967). *The discovery of grounded theory: Strategies for qualitative research.* San Francisco, CA: Sociology Press.

Goodman, E. (1992, January 14). "Crack babies" may be damaged but they are not doomed. *Boston Globe.*

Gore, S. (1985). Social support and styles of coping with stress. In S. Cohen & S. L. Syme (Eds.), *Social support and health* (pp. 263-287). New York: Academic Press.

Graham, H. (1984). Women's poverty and caring. In C. Glendinning & J. Millar (Eds.), *Women and poverty in Britain.* Brighton, Sussex, UK: Wheatsheaf Books.

Grambs, J. D. (1989). *Women over forty: Visions and realities.* New York: Springer.

Grambs, J. D. (1991). *Grandparents who care.* Unpublished brochure.

Grobman, L. (1991, June). Grandparents' Day is everyday for some. *The Pennsylvania Social Worker,* p. 3.

Gross, J. (1991, April, 21). Help for grandparents caught up in the drug war. *The New York Times.*

Gross, J. (1992, March 29). Collapse of inner-city families creates America's new orphans. *The New York Times.*

Gutman, H. G. (1976). *The black family in slavery and freedom.* New York: Pantheon.

Haas, J. G. (1991, December 22). Duty's grand gesture: Many sacrifice leisure of golden years to raise children's children. *Orange County Register.*

Hagestad, G. O., & Burton, L. M. (1986). Grandparenthood, life context, and family development. *American Behavioral Scientist, 29,* 471-484.

Hall, B. (1975). Participatory research: An approach for change. *Convergence, 8*(2), 24-27.

Harris, R. (1991, April 24). Experts say the war on drugs has turned into a war on blacks. *San Francisco Chronicle,* p. A12.

Harvey, P. (1991, December 13). Cocaine babies are our civilization's broken dolls. *Cape Coral Breeze.*

Hatchett, S. J., Cochran, D. L., & Jackson, J. S. (1991). Family life. In J. S. Jackson (Ed.), *Life in black America* (pp. 46-82). Newbury Park, CA: Sage.

Hayes-Bautista, D. E. (1976). Termination of the patient-practitioner relationship: Divorce, patient style. *Journal of Health and Social Behavior, 17*(1), 12-21.

Haynes, S. G., McMichael, A. J., & Tyroler, H. A. (1977). The relationship of normal, involuntary retirement to early mortality among U.S. rubber workers. *Social Science and Medicine, 11,* 105-114.

Health Access Foundation. (1988). *The California dream, the California nightmare: 5.2 million people with no health insurance.* San Francisco: Health Access Foundation.

Hill, R. (1971). *The strength of black families.* New York: Emerson-Hall.

Hill, R. B., & Shackleford, L. (1975). The black extended family revisited. *The Urban League Review, 1*(2), 19-24.

Hinrichsen, G. A., & Hernandez, N. (1991, November). *Problems and rewards in the care of depressed older adults.* Paper presented at the annual meeting of the Gerontological Society of America, San Francisco.

Hochschild, A. R. (1983). *The managed heart: Commercialization of human feeling.* Berkeley: University of California Press.

Hochschild, A. R., & Machung, A. (1989). *The second shift: Working parents and the revolution at home.* New York: Viking.

Hogan, D. P., Hao, L., & Parish, W. L. (1990). Race, kin networks, and assistance to mother-headed families. *Social Forces, 68,* 797-812.

Holloway, K. F. C., & Demetrakopoulos, S. (1986). Remembering our foremothers: Older black women, politics of age, politics of survival as embodied in the novels of Toni Morrison. In M. J. Bell (Ed.), *Women as elders: The feminist politics of aging.* New York: Harrington Park Press.

Hooks, B. (1984). *From margin to center.* Boston: South End Press.

Hooks, B. (1989). *Talking back: Thinking feminist, thinking black.* Boston: South End Press.

Horowitz, A. (1985). Family caregiving to the frail elderly. In M. P. Lawton & G. Maddox (eds.), *Annual Review of Gerontology and Geriatrics* (pp. 194-246). New York: Springer.

Howard, J., Rodning, C., & Kropenske, V. (1989). The development of young children of substance-abusing parents: Insights from seven years of intervention and research. *Zero to Three, 9*(5), 8-12.

Issacs, S. O., Martin, P., & Willoughby, J. H. (1987). "Crack" (an extra potent form of cocaine) abuse: A problem of the eighties. *Oral Surgery, Oral Medicine, and Oral Pathology, 63,* 12-15.

Jackson, J. (1986). Black grandparents: Who needs them? In R. Staples (Ed.), *The black family: Essays and studies* (pp. 186-194). Belmont, CA: Wadsworth.

Jackson, J. S. (Ed.). (1991). *Life in black America.* Newbury Park, CA: Sage.

Jackson, S. (1990). "Crack babies" are here! Can you help them learn? *CTA Action, 29*(3), 11-13.

Jenson, J. M., & Whitaker, J. K. (1987). Parental involvement in children's residential treatment. *Children & Youth Services, 9,* 81-100.

Jones, F. C. (1973). The lofty role of the black grandmother. *Crises, 80,* 19-21.

Jordan, J. (1985). *On call.* Boston: South End Press.

Jost, K. (1991). Foster care crisis. *Congressional Quarterly Researcher, 1*(20), 705-729.

Kane, R., & Kane, R. (1981). The extent and nature of public responsibility for long term care. In J. Melker, F. Farrow, & H. Richman (Eds.), *Policy options for long term care* (pp. 78-114). Chicago: University of Chicago Press.

Kaplan, G. A., & Comacho, T. C. (1983). Perceived health and mortality: A nine year follow-up of the human population laboratory cohort. *American Journal of Epidemiology, 117,* 292-304.

Kaplan, G. A., Haan, M. N., Syme, S. L., Minkler, M., & Misynski, M. (1987). Socio-economic position and health. In R. W. Amber & H. B. Dull (Eds.), *Closing the gap: The burden of unnecessary illness* (pp. 125-129). New York: Oxford University Press.

Katz, A., & Bender, E. (1976). *The strength in us: Self-help groups in the modern world.* New York: Franklin-Watts.

Katz, M. B. (1986). *In the shadow of the poorhouse: A social history of welfare in America.* New York: Basic Books.

Katz, M. B. (1989). *The undeserving poor: From the war on poverty to the war on welfare.* New York: Pantheon.

Kennedy, D. (1991, November 18). Bearing the burden: Grandmothers hold drug addicted families together. *West County Times.*

Kershner, V. (1991, December 10). Wilson plan puts welfare in the spotlight. *San Francisco Chronicle.*

Kessler, R. C., McLeod, J. D., & Wethington, E. (1985). The cost of caring. In I. G. Sarason & B. R. Sarason (Eds.), *Social support: Theory, research and applications.* The Hague, The Netherlands: Martinus Nijhof.

Kessler, R. C., Price, R. H., & Wortman, C. B. (1985). Social factors in psychopathology: Stress, social support, and coping processes. *Annual Review of Psychology, 36,* 531-572.

Kiecolt-Glaser, J. K., Glaser, R., Schuttleworth, E. C., Dyer, C. S., Ogrocki, P., & Speicher, C. E. (1987). Chronic stress and immunity in family caregivers of Alzheimer's disease victims. *Psychosomatic Medicine, 49,* 523-535.

King v. McMahon, 186 Cal. App. 3rd 648 (Cal. App. 1 Dist., 1986).

Kirkland, B. (1988). *Grandparents raising grandchildren.* Unpublished brochure.

Kivett, V. R. (1991). Centrality of the grandfather role among older rural black and white men. *The Journals of Gerontology, 46*(5), S250-S258.

Klein, R. D. (1983). How to do what we want to do: Thoughts on feminist methodology. In G. Bowles & R. D. Klein (Eds.), *Theories of women's studies* (pp. 88-104). London: Routledge & Kegan Paul.

Koppelman, J., & Jones, J. M. (1989, Fall). Crack: It's destroying fragile low income families. *Public Welfare,* pp. 13-15.

Koren, G., Shear, K., Graham, K., & Einarson, T. (1989, December 16). Bias against the null hypothesis: The reproductive hazards of cocaine. *The Lancet,* 1440-1442.

Kornhaber, A. (1985). Grandparenthood and the "new social contract." In V. L. Bengtson & J. F. Robertson (Eds.), *Grandparenthood* (pp. 159-172). Beverly Hills, CA: Sage.

Kropotkin, P. (1972). *Mutual aid: A factor in evolution.* New York: New York University Press.

Kusserow, R. P. (1991, October). *Issues in relative foster care.* Washington, DC: Department of Health and Human Services, Office of the Inspector General.

La Rue, L. (1970, May). The black movement and women's liberation. *The Black Scholar, 1,* 36-42.

Ladner, J. (1971). *Tomorrow's tomorrow.* Garden City, NY: Anchor Books.

Ladner, J. (1986). Black women face the 21st century: Major issues and problems. *The Black Scholar, 17*(5), 12-19.

Ladner, J., & Gourdine, R. M. (1984). Intergenerational teenage motherhood: Some preliminary findings. *Sage: A Scholarly Journal on Black Women, 1*(2), 22-24.

Lambert, B. (1989, July 17). AIDS legacy: A growing generation of orphans. *The New York Times,* pp. A1, B5.

Larsen, D. (1990-1991, December-January). Unplanned parenthood. *Modern Maturity,* pp. 31-36.

Lawton, M. P., Brody, E. M., & Saperstein, A. R. (1989). A controlled study of respite services for caregivers of Alzheimer's patients. *The Gerontologist, 29*(1), 8-16.

Lazarus, L. W., Stafford, B., Cooper, K., Cohler, B., & Dysken, M. (1981). A pilot study of an Alzheimer's patient's relatives discussion group. *The Gerontologist, 21*(1), 353-358.

Le Draoulec, P. (1992, March). Early intervention after birth may help drug children face challenges. *San Diego Union/Tribune.*

Legal Services for Prisoners with Children. (1990). *Manual for grandparents and caregivers of drug-exposed infants and children* San Francisco: Legal Services for Prisoners with Children.

Lesnoff-Caravaglia, G. (1982). The black "Granny" and the Soviet "Babushka": Commonalities and contrasts. In R. C. Manuel (Ed.), *Minority aging: Sociological and social psychological issues* (pp. 103-108). Westport, CT: Greenwood Press.

Lewis, K. D., Bennett, B., & Schmeder, N. H. (1989). The care of infants menaced by cocaine abuse. *Maternal Child Nursing Journal, 14*(5), 325-328.

Light, I., & Bonacich, E. (1988). *Immigrant entrepreneurs: Koreans in Los Angeles, 1965-1982.* Berkeley: University of California Press.

Lipscomb v. Simmons, 89 Daily Journal D.A.R., 1990.

Litvan, L. (1991, May 16). Child-care policy stirs three-way debate. *The Washington Times.*

Lofland, J. (1974). Styles of reporting qualitative field research. *American Sociologist, 9,* 101-111.

London, B., & Giles, M. W. (1987). Black participation: Compensation or ethnic identification? *Journal of Black Studies, 18*(1), 20-44.

Lowenthal, M. F., & Haven, C. (1968). Interaction and adaptation: Intimacy as a critical variable. *American Sociological Review, 33,* 20-26.

Lowenthal, M. F., & Robinson, B. (1976). Social networks and isolation. In R. H. Binstock & E. Shanas (Eds.), *Handbook of aging and the social sciences* (pp. 432-456). New York: Van Nostrand Reinhold.

Lubben, J. (1988). Assessing social networks among elderly populations. *Family and Community Health, 11*(3), 42-52.

March, L. (1912). Some researches concerning the factors of mortality. *Journal of the Statistical Society, London Journal Series A, 75*(5), 505-538.

Margolis, R. J. (1990). *Risking old age in America.* San Francisco: Westview.

Marshall, P., & Rossman, G. B. (1989). *Designing qualitative research.* Newbury Park, CA: Sage.

Marti-Costa, S., & Serrano-Garcia, I. (1983). Needs assessment and community development: An ideological perspective. *Prevention in Human Services, 2*(4), 75-88.

Martin, E., & Martin, J. M. (1978). *The black extended family.* Chicago: University of Chicago Press.

Matthiessen, C. (1992, May 3). A fighting chance. *Image Magazine, San Francisco Examiner,* pp. 9-15, 34.

McAdoo, H. P. (1978). Factors related to stability in upwardly mobile black families. *Journal of Marriage and the Family, 40,* 761-776.

McAdoo, H. P. (1980). Black mothers and the extended family support network. In L. F. Rodgers-Rose (Ed.), *The black woman* (pp. 125-144). Beverly Hills, CA: Sage.

McAdoo, H. P. (1982). Stress absorbing systems in black families. *Family Relations, 31*(4), 479-488.

McAdoo, H. P. (1986). Strategies used by black single mothers against stress. In M. C. Simms & J. Malveaux (Eds.), *Slipping through the cracks: The status of black women* (pp. 153-166). New Brunswick, NJ: Transaction Books.

McAdoo, H. P. (1990). A portrait of African American families in the United States. In S. Rix (Ed.), *The American woman 1990-91: A status report* (pp. 71-93). New York: Norton.

228                                      GRANDMOTHERS AS CAREGIVERS

McLellan, A. T., O'Brien, C. P., Metzger, D., Alterman, A. L., Cornish, J., & Urschel, H. (1992). How effective is substance abuse treatment—Compared to what? In C. P. O'Brien & J. H. Jafle (Eds.), *Addictive states* (pp. 231-252). New York: Raven Press.

Mellor, M. J., Rzetelny, H., & Hudis, L. E. (1984). Self-help groups for caregivers of the aged. In A. Gartner & F. Riessman (Eds.), *The self-help revolution* (p. 265). New York: Human Services Press.

Miles, M. B., & Huberman, A. M. (1984). *Qualitative data analysis: A sourcebook of new methods.* Beverly Hills, CA: Sage.

Miller v. Youakim, 440 U.S. 125, 1979.

Miller, C. A. (1992). Wanting children [Editorial]. *American Journal of Public Health, 82*(3), 341-343.

Miller, D. (1990, April, 25-29). *The extended family.* Paper presented at Rebirth of a Race: National Conference on Crack Cocaine, San Francisco.

Miller, D. (1991, November, 24). *The "Grandparents Who Care" support project of San Francisco.* Paper presented at the Annual Meeting of the Gerontological Society of America, San Francisco.

Mills, C. W. (1959). *The sociological imagination.* New York: Oxford University Press.

Minkler, M., Roe, K. M., & Price, M. (1992). The physical and emotional health of grandmothers raising grandchildren in the crack cocaine epidemic. *The Gerontologist, 32*(6), 5752-5761..

Minkler, M., & Stone, R. (1985). The feminization of poverty and older women. *The Gerontologist, 25,* 351-258.

Molo, E. (1991, November). *Forgotten caregivers.* Paper presented at the annual meeting of the Gerontological Society of America, San Francisco.

Monson, S. (1990, September 9). The second time around. *Seattle Times,* p. K1.

Moody, F. (1990, June 20). Cocaine babies. *Seattle Weekly,* pp. 34-37.

Moriwaki, S. Y. (1974). The affective balance scale: A validity study with aged samples. *Journal of Gerontology, 29*(1), 73-78.

Morycz, R. (1985). Caregiving strain and the desire to institutionalize family members with Alzheimer's disease. *Research on Aging, 7*(3), 329-361.

Mossey, J. M., & Shapiro, E. (1982). Self-reported health: A predictor of mortality among the elderly. *American Journal of Public Health, 72,* 292.

Moynihan, D. P. (1965, March). *The Negro family: A case for national action.* Washington, DC: U.S. Department of Labor, Office of Policy, Planning and Research.

Mullen, P. A. (1985-1986). Generating grounded theory. Two case studies. *International Quarterly of Community Health Education, 6*(3), 177-214.

Myrdal, G. (1944). *An American dilemma.* New York: Harper & Brothers.

Nathan, S., (1990). *Meeting the challenges of crack cocaine through intergenerational programming.* Unpublished grant proposal. Oakland, CA: Office on Aging.

National Center for Children in Poverty. (1990). *Five million children.* New York: Columbia University School of Public Health.

National Center for Health Statistics (NCHS). (1989). *Vital statistics of the United States, 1986. Vol. 2: Mortality* (Part A). Washington, DC: Government Printing Office.

National Center for Health Statistics (NCHS). (1990, January). *The health of black and white Americans, 1985-1987* (Series 10, No. 171). Hyattsville, MD: Author.

National Institute on Drug Abuse (NIDA). (1990). NIDA seeks to identify ways to overcome treatment barriers for pregnant women. *NIDA Notes, 5*(4), 13.

National Planning Data Corporation. (1989). *Income measures by zip code.* [Unpublished data.] Ithaca, NY.

Neighbors, H. W., Jackson, J. S., Bowman, P. J., & Gurin, G. (1983). Stress, coping and black mental health: Preliminary findings from a national study. *Prevention in Human Services, 2,* 4-29.

Ness, C. (1991, February 25). Oakland hot line helps grandmothers in need. *San Francisco Examiner.*

Nobles, W. (1974). African root and American fruit. The black family. *Journal of Social and Behavioral Sciences, 20,* 52-64.

Nobles, W. (1978). Toward an empirical and theoretical framework for defining black families. *Journal of Marriage and the Family, 40,* 679-688.

Nobles, W. (1988). African-American family life: An instrument of culture. In H. P. McAdoo (Ed.), *Black families* (pp. 44-53). Newbury Park, CA: Sage.

Norris, M. (1991, July 8-14). The class of crack's innocent victims: The first wave of drug-disabled children jolts the ill-prepared schools. *The Washington Post National Weekly Edition,* p. 11.

Oakland Public Schools, Department of Research and Evaluation. (1991). *School district information summary 1990-91.* Oakland, CA: Oakland Unified School District.

O'Reilly, A. (1989, October 30). *Testimony: Assembly Human Services Committee Hearing on Drug Exposed Infants: The role of grandmothers as caregivers* (pp. 62-67). San Francisco: California State Assembly.

Ovrebo, B., & Minkler, M. (1993). The lives of older women: Perspectives from political economy and the humanities. In T. Cole, A. Achenbaum, P. Jakobi, & R. Kastenbaum (Eds.), *Voices and visions: Toward a critical gerontology* (pp. 289-308). New York: Springer.

Pearlin, L., Mullan, J. T., Semple, M. A., & Skaff, M. M. (1990). Caregiving and the stress process: An overview of concepts and their measures. *The Gerontologist, 30*(5), 583-591.

Pearlin, L. I., & Aneshensel, C. (1986). Coping and social supports: Their functions and applications. In L. H. Aiken & D. Mechanic (Eds.), *Applications of social science to clinical medicine and health.* New Brunswick, NJ: Rutgers University Press.

Petitti, D. B., & Coleman, B. (1990). Cocaine and the risk of low birth weight. *American Journal of Public Health, 80*(1), 25-28.

Phibbs, C., Bateman, D., & Schwartz, R. (1991). Neonatal costs of maternal cocaine use. *Journal of the American Medical Association, 266*(11), 1521-1526.

Phillips, K. P. (1990). *The politics of rich and poor: Wealth and the American electorate in the Reagan aftermath.* New York: Random House.

Pilisuk, M., & Minkler, M. (1985). Social support: Economic and political considerations. *Social Policy, 15*(3), 6-11.

Pilisuk, M., & Park, S. H. (1988). Caregiving: Where families need help. *Social Work, 33*(5), 436-440.

Poe, L. M. (1992). *Black grandparents as parents.* Unpublished manuscript.

Poole, T. (1990). Black families and the black church: A socio-historical perspective. In H. E. Cheatham & J. B. Stewart (Eds.), *Black families: Interdisciplinary perspectives* (pp. 33-48). New Brunswick, NJ: Transaction Books.

Portes, A., & Rumbaut, R. (1990). *Immigrant America, a portrait.* Berkeley: University of California Press.

Portes, A., & Zhou, M. (1991, September). *Gaining the upper hand: Old and new perspectives in the study of foreign-born minorities.* Paper prepared for the Conference on Poverty, Inequality and the Crisis of Public Policy, Joint Center for Political and Economic Studies, Washington, DC.

Presser, H. B. (1989). Some economic complexities of child care provided by grandmothers. *Journal of Marriage and the Family, 51,* 581-591.

Rabins, P., Mace, N., & Lucas, M. J. (1982). The impact of dementia on the family. *Journal of the American Medical Association, 248*(3), 333-335.

Rainwater, L. (1966). Crucible of identity: The lower-class Negro family. *Daedalus, 95,* 172-216.

Reed, I. (1988, May 13). Living at ground zero. *Image Magazine, San Francisco Examiner,* pp. 10-14.

Reich, R. B. (1991, January 20). Secession of the successful. *The New York Times Magazine,* Section 6, pp. 1-4.

Rheinharz, S. (1983). Experiential analysis: A contribution to feminist research. In G. Bowles & R. D. Klein (Eds.), *Theories of women's studies* (pp. 162-191). London: Routledge & Kegan Paul.

Rivers, C., Barnett, R., & Baruch, G. (1979). *Beyond sugar and spice: How women grow, learn, and thrive.* New York: G. P. Putnam.

Ronningen, J. (1991, December 4). New audit report paints picture of crisis in county welfare system. *Oakland Tribune.*

Rosenfeld, M. (1991, October 16). Grandparents rights. *The Washington Post.*

Rosenthal, R., & Jacobsen, L. (1989). *Pygmalion in the classroom: Teacher expectations and pupils' intellectual development.* New York: Irvington.

Ruben, V. (1991, March). *Oakland's economy in the 1990's: A sourcebook of planning and community development issues facing the City, its neighborhoods, and the region.* Oakland, CA: University of California, Oakland Metropolitan Forum.

Rubin, L. B. (1985). *Just friends: The role of friendship in our lives.* New York: Harper & Row.

Ryan, W. (1981). *Equality.* New York: Vintage.

Saunders, F. (1992). *Loving hands, loving hearts: A community based intervention for caregivers of crack involved children* [Unpublished grant proposal]. Oakland, CA: Bethlehem Lutheran Church.

Schaef, A. W. (1986). *Co-dependence: Misunderstood-mistreated.* New York: Harper & Row.

Scharlach, A. E. (1987). Role strain in mother-daughter relationships in later life. *The Gerontologist, 27,* 627-631.

Scharlach, A. E., & Boyd, S. (1989). Caregiving and employment. Results of an employee survey. *The Gerontologist, 29*(3), 382-387.

Scharlach, A. E., Lowe, B. F., & Schneider, E. L. (1990). *Eldercare and the work force: Blueprint for action.* Lexington, MA: Lexington Books.

Scharlach, A. E., Sobel, E. L., & Roberts, R. E. L. (1991). Employment and caregiver strain: An integrative model. *The Gerontologist, 31*(6), 778-787.

Schulz, R., & Rau, M. T. (1985). Social support through the life course. In S. Cohen & S. L. Syme (Eds.), *Social support and health* (pp. 129-149). New York: Academic Press.

Schulz, R., Visintainer, P., & Williamson, G. M. (1990). Psychiatric and physical morbidity effects of caregiving. *Journal of Gerontology, 45*(5), 181-191.

Scott, H. (1984). *Working your way to the bottom: The feminization of poverty.* Boston: Pandora Press.

Scott, P. D., & Marshall, J. (1992). *Cocaine politics.* Berkeley: University of California Press.

Sennett, R. (1970). *Families against the city: Middle class homes of industrial Chicago, 1872-1890.* Cambridge, MA: Harvard University Press.

Shanas, E. (1979). Social myth as hypothesis: The case of the family relations of old people. *The Gerontologist, 19,* 3-9.

Shapiro, I., Gold, S., Sheft, M., Strawn, J., Summer, L., & Greenstein, R. (1991). *The state of the poor: How budget decisions in 1991 affected low income people.* Washington, DC: Center on Budget Priorities and the Center for the Study of the States.

Sidel, R. (1990). *On her own: Growing up in the shadow of the American dream.* New York: Penguin.

Sidel, R. (1992a). Women and children first: Toward a U.S. family policy. *American Journal of Public Health, 82,* 664-665.

Sidel, R. (1992b). *Women and children last: The plight of poor women in affluent America* (2nd ed.). New York: Penguin.

Simms, M. C. (1986). Black women who head families: An economic struggle. In M. C. Simms & J. Malveaux (Eds.), *Slipping through the cracks: The status of black women* (pp. 141-153). New Brunswick, NJ: Transaction Books.

Simms, M. C., & Malveaux, J. (Eds.). (1986). *Slipping through the cracks: The status of black women.* New Brunswick, NJ: Transaction Books.

Slaughter, D. T., & Dilworth-Anderson, P. (1991). Sickle cell anemia, child competence, and extended family life. In H. E. Cheatham & J. B. Stewart (Eds.), *Black families: Interdisciplinary perspectives* (pp. 131-148). New Brunswick, NJ: Transaction Books.

Snyder, B. (1992, January 5). Single women head 2 out of 3 Oakland black families. *Oakland Tribune,* p. 23.

Soldo, B., & Myllyluoma, J. (1983). Caregivers who live with dependent elderly. *The Gerontologist, 23,* 607-611.

Sorensen, J., & Bernal, G. (1987). *A family like yours.* San Francisco: Harper & Row.

Specht, H. (1986). Social support, social networks, social exchange and social work practice. *Social Work Review, 60*(2), 218-240.

Spender, D. (1983). Theorising about theorising. In G. Bowles & R. D. Klein (Eds.), *Theories of women's studies* (pp. 27-31). London: Routledge & Kegan Paul.

Stack, C. (1974). *All our kin: Strategies for survival in a black community.* New York: Harper & Row.

Staples, R. (1973). *The black woman in America.* Chicago: Nelson-Hall.

Steckler, A., McLeroy, K. R., Goodman, F. M., Bird, S. T., & McCormick, L. (1992). Toward integrating qualitative and quantitative methods: An introduction. *Health Education Quarterly, 19*(1), 1-8.

Stephens, S. A., & Christianson, J. B. (1986). *Informal care of the elderly.* Lexington, MA: Lexington Books.

Stone, R., Cafferata, G. L., & Sangl, J. (1987). Caregivers of the frail elderly: A national profile. *The Gerontologist, 27*(5), 616-626.

Stone, R. I. (1985). *Recent developments in respite care services for caregivers of the impaired elderly* (Administration on Aging Grant No. 90AP9003). Washington, DC: Government Printing Office.

Strauss, A. L., & Corbin, J. M. (1990). *Basics of qualitative research: Grounded theory procedures and techniques.* Newbury Park, CA: Sage.

Sudarkasa, N. (1981). Interpreting the African heritage in Afro-American family organization. In H. P. McAdoo (Ed.), *Black families* (pp. 37-53). Beverly Hills, CA: Sage.

Syme, S. L., & Berkman, L. F. (1976). Social class, susceptibility and sickness. *American Journal of Epidemiology, 104,* 1-8.

Takas, M. (1992). *Kinship care: Developing a safe and effective framework for protective placement of children with relatives.* Washington, DC: American Bar Association Center on Children and the Law.

Taylor, R. J. (1986). Religious participation among elderly blacks. *The Gerontologist, 26,* 630-636.

Taylor, R. J., Chatter, L. M., Tucker, M. B., & Lewis E. (1990). Developments in research on black families: A decade review. *Journal of Marriage and the Family, 52,* 993-1014.

Telsch, K. (1990, March 20). In Detroit, a drug recovery center that welcomes the pregnant addict. *The New York Times.*

Tillman, R. (1986). *The prevalence and incidence of arrest among adult males in California* (Bureau of Criminal Statistics Special Report Series). Sacramento, CA: Department of Justice.

Tinsley, B. R., & Parke, R. (1984). Grandparents as support and socialization agents. In M. Lewis (Ed.), *Beyond the dyad* (pp. 161-195). New York: Plenum.

Tinsley, B. R., & Parke, R. D. (1987). Grandparents as interactive and social support agents for families with young infants. *International Journal of Aging and Human Development, 25,* 259-277.

Toseland, R. W., & Rossiter, C. M. (1989). Group intervention to support family caregivers: A review and analysis. *The Gerontologist, 29,* 438-448.

Toufexis, A. (1991, May 16). Innocent victims. *Time,* pp. 56-59.

Troester, R. R. (1984). Turbulence and tenderness: Mothers, daughters and "othermothers" in Paule Marshall's "Brown girl: Brownstones." *Sage: A Scholarly Journal on Black Women, 1*(2), 13-16.

Troll, L. E. (1985). The contingencies of grandparenting. In V. L. Bengtson & J. F. Robertson (Eds.), *Grandparenthood* (pp. 135-150). Beverly Hills, CA: Sage.

U.S. Bureau of the Census. (1979). *Marital status and living arrangements in 1978* (Series P-20, No. 340). Washington, DC: Government Printing Office.

U.S. Bureau of the Census. (1990). *Current population reports: Money income and poverty status in the United States: 1989 (Advanced data from the March 1990 Current Population Survey* (Series P-60, No. 168). Washington, DC: Government Printing Office.

U.S. Bureau of the Census. (1991a). *Current population reports: Marital status and living arrangements: March 1990.* (Series P-20 No. 450). Washington, DC: Government Printing Office.

U.S. Bureau of the Census. (1991b). *Statistical abstracts of the United States* (111th ed.). Washington, DC: Government Printing Office.

U.S. Bureau of Labor Statistics. (1990, January). *Employment and earnings* (Vol. 37, No. 1). Washington, DC: U.S. Department of the Census.

U.S. Department of Justice. (1991, March). *Women in prison: Survey of inmates in state correctional facilities.* Washington, DC: U.S. Department of Justice, Office of Justice Programs, Bureau of Justice Statistics.

U.S. General Accounting Office (USGAO). (1990, June, 28). *Drug-exposed infants—A generation at risk* (GAO/HRD-90-138). Washington, DC: Government Printing Office.

U.S. General Accounting Office, Human Resources Division. (1991). *Drug abuse: The crack cocaine epidemic: Health consequences and treatment.* Washington, DC: Government Printing Office.

U.S. House of Representatives, Select Committee on Aging. (1988, August). *Exploding the myths: Caregiving in America.* Washington, DC: Government Printing Office.

U.S. House of Representatives, Select Committee on Children, Youth and Families. (1990). *No place to call home: Children in America* (Publication No. 25-744). Washington, DC: Government Printing Office.

U.S. Senate, Subcommittee on Narcotics, Terrorism, and International Operations. (1990, February). *Drug money laundering, banks and foreign policy: A report to the Committee on Foreign Relations.* Washington, DC: Government Printing Office.

Veroff, J., Douvan, E., & Kulka, R. (1981). *The inner Americans: A self-portrait from 1957-1976.* New York: Basic Books.

Villarreal, S. F., McKinney, L., & Quackenbush, M. (1992). *Handle with care: Helping children prenatally exposed to drugs and alcohol.* Santa Cruz, CA: ETR Associates.

Viscusi, W. K. (1986). Market incentives for criminal behavior. In R. B. Freeman & H. J. Holzer (Eds.), *The black youth unemployment crisis* (pp. 301-346). Chicago: University of Chicago Press.

Walker, A. (1983). *In search of our mothers' gardens.* New York: Harcourt Brace Jovanovich.

Walters, L. (1991). *National Association of African American Grandmothers.* Unpublished program brochure. Los Angeles: NAAAG.

Waters, M. (1989, July 24/31). Drugs, democrats and priorities. *The Nation,* pp. 141-144.

Watson, L., Irwin, J., & Michalske, S. (1991). Pearls, pith, and provocation: Researcher as friend: Methods of the interviewer in a longitudinal study. *Qualitative Health Research, 1*(4), 497-514.

Watson, W. H. (1990). Family care, economics, and health. In Z. Harel, E. A. McKinney, & M. Williams (Eds.), *Black aged: Understanding diversity and service needs* (pp. 50-68). Newbury Park, CA: Sage.

Webber, P. A. (1991). *Service utilization patterns of caregivers of people with Alzheimer's disease.* Unpublished doctoral dissertation, University of California, Berkeley, School of Social Welfare.

Weems, R. (1984). Hush, Mama's gotta go bye bye: A personal narrative. *Sage: A Scholarly Journal on Black Women, 1*(2), 25-28.

Weikart, D. P. (1989). *Quality preschool programs: A long term social investment.* New York: Ford Foundation.

Weinstein, G. (1989, October). Help wanted—The crisis of elder care. *Ms.,* pp. 72-79.

Wells, K., & Biegel, D. E. (Eds.). (1991). *Family preservation services: Research and evaluation.* Newbury Park, CA: Sage.

White-Means, S. I., & Thornton, M. C. (1990). Ethnic differences in the production of informal home health care. *The Gerontologist, 30*(6), 758-768.

Whyte, W. F., Greenwood, D. J., & Lazes, P. (1991). Participatory action in research: Through practice to science and social research. In W. F. Whyte (Ed.), *Participatory action research* (pp. 19-55). Newbury Park, CA: Sage.

Wilson, M. N. (1986). The black extended family: An analytical consideration. *Developmental Psychology, 22*(2), 246-259.

Wilson, M. N. (1989). Child development in the context of the black extended family. *American Psychologist, 44*(2), 380-385.

Wilson-Ford, V. (1990). Poverty among black elderly women. *Journal of Women & Aging, 2*(4), 4-20.

Woodhouse, L., & Livingood, W. C. (1991). Exploring the versatility of qualitative design for evaluating community substance abuse prevention projects. *Qualitative Health Research, 1*(14), 434-445.

Wortman, C. B. (1984). Social support and cancer: Conceptual and methodological issues. *Cancer, 53*(10), 2339-2360.

Young, R. F., & Kahana, E. (1991, November). *Racial dimensions of caregiving.* Paper presented at the Annual Meeting of the American Public Health Association, Atlanta, GA.

Zarit, S. H. (1989). Do we need another stress and caregiving study? *The Gerontologist, 29*(2), 147-148.

Zarit, S. H., Todd, P. A., & Zarit, J. M. (1986). Subjective burden of husbands and wives as caregivers: A longitudinal study. *The Gerontologist, 26,* 260-270.

Zuckerman, B. (1991). Drug exposed infants: Understanding the medical risk. *The Future of Children, 1,* 26-32.

Zuckerman, B., Frank, D. A., Hingson, R., Amaro, H., Levenson, S. M., Kayne, H., Parker, S., Vinci, R., Aboagye, K., Fried, L. E., Cabral, H., Timperi, R., & Bauchner, H. (1989). Effects of maternal marijuana and cocaine use on fetal growth. *New England Journal of Medicine, 320,* 762-768.

# Index

# About the Authors

**Meredith Minkler,** Dr. PH, is Professor of Community Health Education at the School of Public Health, University of California, Berkeley. She was founding director of the U.C. Berkeley Center on Aging, and is a member of the Scientific Advisory Board of the Buck Center for Research on Aging. She cofounded the Tenderloin Senior Outreach Project (TSOP), a nationally recognized community organizing and empowerment program in San Francisco, and currently serves as director of the Brookdale Grandparent Caregiver Information Project. She is a Kellogg National Fellow, and has served as a consultant to numerous organizations and agencies including the U.S. Congress Office of Technology Assessment, the White House Conference on Aging, the Ford Foundation, the National Institute of Mental Health, and the Health Promotion Directorates in several Canadian provinces. Her research interests include social support and health of the elderly, the political economy of aging, and intergenerational issues. Dr. Minkler's recent publications include two coedited books, *Critical Perspectives on Aging* (1991) and *Readings in the Political Economy of Aging* (1984).

**Kathleen M. Roe,** Dr. PH, is Associate Professor of Community Health Education at San Jose State University, San Jose, California. With Meredith Minkler, she was the Co-Investigator of the Grandparent Caregiver Study and is currently Associate Director of the Brookdale Grandparent Caregiver Information Project. She is an evaluator of two innovative community programs; the Community Partnership of Santa Clara County, a 5-year community development project funded by the federal Office of Substance Abuse Prevention; and the Kaiser Center for Health Careers, a San Jose-based demonstration program funded by the Kaiser Family Foundation. She is a frequent consultant to local health departments in California and Arizona, specializing in training, advocacy, and

239

evaluation, particularly in the areas of AIDS education, women's health, and health promotion. She also serves as a consultant to national, state, and local health education programs, including, most recently, the Names Project (AIDS Memorial Quilt), the State of California Tobacco Control Program, Planetree Health Education Resource Center in San Jose, and the Peer Education Program at San Jose State University. She is a member of the Board of Directors of the Health Education and Training Center, San Jose, California; the Women's Resource Center at San Jose State University; and the Northern California Chapter of the Society for Public Health Education (SOPHE). Her research interests include the use of qualitative methodologies, contemporary women's history, and the experience of American families. Dr. Roe is an Associate Editor of the *Journal of the American College Health Association;* her publications have appeared in *Social Science and Medicine; Cancer: The Journal of the National Cancer Institute;* and *Open Hand Magazine.*